W9-AAH-444

The Intelligent Wireless Web

H. Peter Alesso
Craig F. Smith

Addison-Wesley

Boston · San Francisco · New York · Toronto · Montreal
London · Munich · Paris · Madrid
Capetown · Sydney · Tokyo · Singapore · Mexico City

Many of the designations used by manufacturers and sellers to distinguish their products are claimed as trademarks. Where those designations appear in this book, and Addison-Wesley, Inc. was aware of a trademark claim, the designations have been printed with initial capital letters or in all capitals.

The authors and publisher have taken care in the preparation of this book, but make no expressed or implied warranty of any kind and assume no responsibility for errors or omissions. No liability is assumed for incidental or consequential damages in connection with or arising out of the use of the information or programs contained herein.

The publisher offers discounts on this book when ordered in quantity for special sales. For more information, please contact:

Pearson Education Corporate Sales Division
201 W. 103rd Street
Indianapolis, IN 46290
(800) 428-5331
corpsales@pearsoned.com

Visit us on the Web at www.aw.com/cseng/

Library of Congress Cataloging-in-Publication Data

Alesso, H. P.
    The intelligent wireless Web / H. Peter Alesso, Craig F. Smith.
       p. cm.
    Includes bibliographical references and index.
    ISBN 0-201-73063-4
    1. Wireless communication systems.   2. World Wide Web.   3. Artificial intelligence
 I. Smith, C. F. (Craig Forsythe), 1950–   II. Title.

    TK5103.2 .A44 2002
    004.67'8—dc21

                    2001053299

ISBN 0-201-73063-4
Text printed on recycled paper
1 2 3 4 5 6 7 8 9 10—CRS—0504030201
First printing, November 2001

This book is dedicated to our mothers.

To Fannie Piccione
Her inquiring mind and unfailing good humor provided
the nurturing environment for the seeds of many new
and entertaining ideas.

To Veronica Forsythe Smith
Her support, love, and dedication remain
a lasting inspiration.

Contents

List of Figures. xiii

List of Tables xv

Introduction. xvii

Acknowledgments xxv

About the Authors xxvii

PART I   **Connecting People to Devices**. 1

CHAPTER 1   Developing a Framework for the Intelligent
Wireless Web 3

The Wireless Communication Process. 7

User Interface: From Click to Speech 10

Personal Space: From Wired to Wireless 14

    Project Oxygen. 15

Networks: From Wired to Integrated Wired/Wireless 16

Protocols: From IP to Mobile IP 19

Web Architecture: Dumb and Static to Intelligent and Dynamic. . . 22

    Self-Organizing Software and Adaptive Protocols 25

    Web IQ 27

Conclusion 27

CHAPTER 2   Speech Recognition and Understanding 31

Man-Machine Communications 32

    Voice Recording and Analysis. 32

    Language. 34

    Speech/Sound Recording, Compression, and Analysis 36

Speech Recognition and Understanding 39
Speech Recognition. 43
Speech Representation, Storage, Transmission, and Analysis . . .45
Speech Understanding 45
Examples of Voice Activation. 47
Future Trends. 48
Challenges and Opportunities 50
Conclusion 50

PART II   **Connecting Devices to Devices**. 53
CHAPTER 3 Wireless Personal Area Networks 55
Personal Space 55
Proliferating Personal Devices 57
Personal Area Networks for the Home .62
PAN Technologies and Standards for the Home 66
Mobile Software. 70
Bluetooth 72
Jini 74
Universal Plug and Play 78
Ubiquitous Computing Research. 79
MIT's Project Oxygen. 79
Challenges and Opportunities 85
Conclusion 87

CHAPTER 4 Merging Wired and Wireless Networks 89
Wired Networks. 90
Routers and Switches 96
Asynchronous Transfer Mode. 99
SONET Networks 100
Ethernet Networks 100
Wired Multiplexors. 101
Signals. 102
Dense Wavelength Division Multiplexing. 102
Switching 103
Wireless Networks 106
Benefits of Wireless Networking 108
Concerns 109

Crowded Airways. 109
Terrestrial Microwave 111
Wireless Local Area Network 112
Radio Based 114
Medium Access Control 114
Spread Spectrum Modulation 115
Narrowband Modulation 115
Wireless Local Bridges. 115
Infrared Light-based Wireless Local Area Networks 116
Diffuse Infrared-Based Local Area Networks 116
Wireless Point-to-Point Networks 116
IEEE 802.11 Standard 116

Wireless Wide Area Networks. 118
The State of Wireless Wide Area Networks 122
Wireless Application Service Provider. 123

Network Integration 124
Migrating Networks 126

Broadband Access. 128
Mobility and the Wireless Web. 130

MIT's Project Oxygen Network 21 132

Challenges and Opportunities 133

Conclusion 135

CHAPTER 5   Merging Wireless Devices with the Web. 137

Mobile Wireless 137
How Cellular Technology Works 138

Second-Generation Mobile Wireless Technologies. 141
Global System for Mobile Communication 142
Time Division Multiple Access. 143
Code Division Multiple Access. 143

Third-Generation Mobile Wireless Technologies 144
The General Packet Radio Service 145
Migration Strategies 147
Wireless Streaming Video Technologies 147
Technology Projections. 148
Wireless Handheld Devices. 149

The Internet 151
     Internet Transfer Protocols. 152
     Mobile Protocols 154
     Mobile IP 155

The Wireless Internet. 157
     How WAP Works. 158
     Communications Between Client and Server. 159

Wireless Markup Language. 160
     Alternatives to WML. 161

Comparing Wireless Web Services 162

Challenges and Opportunities 164

Conclusion 165

PART III   **Connecting Devices to People**. 167

CHAPTER 6   **Artificial Intelligence**. 169

Intelligence 170

Artificial Intelligence Methods 173
     Problem Solving Through Search 174
     Knowledge Representation and Inference. 176
     Expert Systems. 177
     Learning, Neural Net, and Adaptation 178
     Neural Networks 179
     Adaptive Software 180
     Data Mining. 182
     Agents. 183

Distributed Artificial Intelligence. 184

Conclusion 188

CHAPTER 7   **Merging Artificial Intelligence with the Web** 189

How Smart Are Web Applications Today? 190
     Enterprise Information Portals 190
     Extensible Markup Language Standards, Frameworks,
         and Schema. 192
     Web Services 195
     Comparing J2EE and .NET 197

What Is Web Intelligence? 200

How Does the Web Learn?. 202
    Databases and Machine Learning. 204
    Extensible Markup Language 207
    Resource Description Framework and Topic Map
        Convergence 210
    Semantic Web Road Map 213
    The Logic Layer 214
    Self-Organizing Software and Adaptive Protocols 215
    Genetic Algorithms 218
Where Does Web Intelligence Reside? 220
    Distributed Computing and Distributed Artificial
        Intelligence 220
Challenges and Opportunities 223
Conclusion 225

CHAPTER 8   Speech Synthesis and Translation 227
Text-to-Speech Generators 227
Speech Synthesis Markup Language. 230
Translation 233
Challenges and Opportunities 236
Conclusion 236

CHAPTER 9   Technological Revolution. 239
How Does Revolutionary Change Occur? 239
How Does the Information Age Save Time? 243
    Global Economic Integration. 245
    The Impact of Information Technology Spending
        on Productivity. 247
Why Intelligent Wireless Devices Improve Productivity 248
Conclusion 251

CHAPTER 10   Progress in Developing the Intelligent Wireless Web . . . 253
Future Wireless Communication Processes. 254
User Interface: From Click to Speech 258
Personal Space: From Wired to Wireless 260
Networks: From Wired to Integrated Wired/Wireless 260

Protocols: From Internet Protocol to Mobile Internet
Protocol 262
Web Architecture: Dumb and Static to Intelligent
and Dynamic. 264
Strategic Planning Guidelines. 264
Balancing Hardware and Software Innovation. 266
Balancing Proprietary and Open Standards 267
Balancing Centralized and Distributed Web Architectures. . . .268
Conclusion 269

APPENDIX A Standards Organizations 273

APPENDIX B Wireless Standards. 281

APPENDIX C Graphs and the Web 283

APPENDIX D Dynamic Languages. 287

APPENDIX E Wireless Security. 291

APPENDIX F Visual Prolog 295

APPENDIX G Knowledge Management: Case Study of
Convera's RetrievalWare 299

APPENDIX H List of Acronyms 309

APPENDIX I Glossary 315

Bibliography 331
Index 335

List of Figures

Figure 1-1   The communication process 12
Figure 1-2   Transitioning the user interface 13
Figure 1-3   Transitioning your Personal Space 17
Figure 1-4   Transitioning networks 20
Figure 1-5   Transitioning protocols 22
Figure 1-6   Transitioning Web architecture 24

Figure 2-1   User interface 36
Figure 2-2   Percentage of word accuracy by speech recognition 44

Figure 3-1   Personal Space 60
Figure 3-2   Transmeta chip 82

Figure 4-1   Networks 97
Figure 4-2   Connections from the backbone of the Internet to your home . 97
Figure 4-3   Spectrum 110
Figure 4-4   Delivering data 127
Figure 4-5   Delivering data over wired and wireless modems 131

Figure 5-1   How cellular technology works 140
Figure 5-2   Base stations and cell sites 140
Figure 5-3   Wireless software 149
Figure 5-4   ISO/OSI seven layer model 153
Figure 5-5   TCP/IP model 153
Figure 5-6   Protocols 156
Figure 5-7   Wireless application protocol architecture 159
Figure 5-8   Wireless application protocol layer 160

Figure 6-1   Expert system architecture 178
Figure 6-2   Learning algorithms 179
Figure 6-3   Artificial intelligence server architecture 186

Figure 7-1   Example of an EIP Web Service architecture 198
Figure 7-2   Simple statement graph template 212
Figure 7-3   Proof validation: A language for proof 214
Figure 7-4   AI portals 219
Figure 7-5   Web architecture 224

Figure 8-1   Text-to-speech architecture 228

Figure 9-1   Moore's law 249

Figure 10-1   Wireless communication process 256
Figure 10-2   Building the user interface 259
Figure 10-3   Building your Personal Space 261
Figure 10-4   Building integrated networks 263
Figure 10-5   Building mobile Internet protocols 263
Figure 10-6   Building AI servers with Semantic Web Architecture 265
Figure 10-7   Timeline 269

Figure G-1   RetrievalWare's text search process 301

List of Tables

Table 2-1   Speech Coding Techniques 38
Table 2-2   Selected Current Speech Products and Capabilities 40
Table 2-3   Four Stages of Speech Understanding 46

Table 3-1   Examples of Pocket PCs 61
Table 3-2   Examples of Handheld PCs 61
Table 3-3   Wireless PDA services 62
Table 3-4   Personal Area Networks Applications for the Home 64
Table 3-5   Compatibility of PAN Standards, API, and Protocols 67
Table 3-6   Related Wireless LAN-PAN Standards 75

Table 4-1   Evolutionary Path of Networks 98
Table 4-2   SONET/SDH Bit Rates 101
Table 4-3   Connection Access 106
Table 4-4   Examples of Wireless Application Service Providers 124
Table 4-5   Comparing Broadband Technologies 128
Table 4-6   Summary of Broadband Access Architectures 129

Table 5-1   Wireless Telecommunication Standard's Characteristics 139
Table 5-2   The Technologies of Each Generation 146
Table 5-3   Wireless Web Services in 2001 163

Table 7-1   Examples of XML Standards, Frameworks, and Schema 194
Table 7-2   Comparing J2EE and .NET 199

Table 8-1   Examples of Language Translation Software Tools 234

Table 9-1   Global Transformations 243

Introduction

Throughout history, there have been many important inventions, such as the locomotive, the airplane, and plastic. But few inventions have transformed the world in a revolutionary way. Revolutionary change occurs only when there is a dramatic improvement in the efficiency of human activities. Such improvements are realized over varying periods of time, as the impact of the revolution permeates society. Only change producing orders of magnitude improvement can produce a true revolution.

Is the current Information Age a force for revolutionary change? To place the Information Age in historical perspective, let's contrast it with two great transformational events: the agricultural revolution (beginning around 8000 B.C. and continuing through around A.D. 1700) and the industrial revolution (beginning around A.D. 1700 and still spreading across the world even today).

Ten thousand years ago, humans lived in migratory groups and fed themselves by hunting, herding, fishing, and foraging. The rise of agriculture at that time was a dramatic turning point in human social development. Farmers were able to use 1 acre of land to produce the equivalent food supply that a hunter-gather produced from 100 acres. This 100-fold improvement in land utilization fueled the agricultural revolution and not only enabled far more efficient food production but also provided the new ability of producing a surplus greater than the needs of subsistence. This excess resulted in a new era based upon flourishing trade.

The agricultural transition progressed throughout the world for thousands of years, but was still incomplete when, at the end of the seventeenth century, the industrial revolution unleashed the second global revolutionary transition. Societies up until this period used human and animal muscle to provide the primary energy necessary to run the economy. As late as the French revolution, 14 million horses and 24 million oxen provided the physical force that supported the European economy.

The industrial revolution introduced machines that could produce 100 times the power of a farmer and his horse. Thus the industrial revolution represented a second 100-fold increase in human productivity in terms of increased power in the hands of the laborer.

The latest historic turning point may be the Information Age. The Information Age can be traced to the 1950s with the emergence of the transistor as the initiation of a wave of innovative synergies. The resulting technological development brought microprocessor, computer, satellite, laser, and fiberoptic technologies. By the 1990s, these, in turn, fostered an enormous new capacity to disseminate information.

Although it is still to be determined whether the Information Age is actually a revolution comparable to the agricultural and industrial revolutions, it remains a strong candidate. Indeed, service workers today complete knowledge transactions many times faster through intelligent software using photons over IP packet switching compared with a clerk using electrons over circuit-switching technology just a few decades ago. Therefore the basis for the information revolution may be the falling cost of information-based transactions.

How does the Information Age save time and thereby improve worker productivity? Alan Greenspan, Chairman of the U.S. Federal Reserve, has suggested that the major contribution of Information Technology (IT) has been to reduce the number of worker hours required to produce a nation's output.[1] In addition, he has suggested that before this period of information availability, most twentieth-century business decisions were hampered by uncertainty about the timely knowledge of customers' needs, inventories, and materials. The remarkable surge in timely information has enabled business to remove large swaths of inventory safety stocks and worker redundancies. The dramatic decline in the lead times for the delivery of capital equipment has made a particularly significant contribution to the favorable economic environment of the past decade. That meant fewer goods and worker hours involved in activities intended only as insurance to sustain output levels. This emphasizes that the essence of information technology is the expansion of knowledge and the reduction in uncertainty.

Why do we suggest that intelligent wireless devices will mean further improvement in productivity over the next decade? The Internet has become the grim reaper of information inefficiency. For the first time, ordinary people have real power over

---

1. Alan Greenspan credited technology innovation with propelling the nation's economy into a record ninth year of expansion (CNNfn, July 11, 2000).

information production and dissemination. As the cost of information drops, the microprocessor in effect gives ordinary people control over information about consumer market production and distribution.

What has restrained the Internet from achieving its full potential has been the limited bandwidth and availability directly to the consumer, inadequate user interfaces, and software that is, at best, unhelpful. Eventually, cheap, fast Internet access will be available to every home and business, unleashing powerful effects. Eventually, the user interface will improve through the use of speech. And, eventually, software will deliver services that are credibly intelligent.

By applying the power of Moore's law to the chips that support the many and varied wireless technologies, wireless will change from an upscale market luxury technology into a necessity for mobile devices. Devices using the Intelligent Wireless Web will offer consumers, as well as businesses, access to products and services any time, anywhere.

Approximately half of today's $28 trillion world economy involves transactions related to office work, including buying and selling transactions, banking applications, insurance forms, government information processing, education forms, and business-to-business transactions.[2] From a global perspective, this information processing is currently being done mostly by specialized humans and secondarily by machines. And the Internet is only now beginning to touch the vast expanse of office work.

Banking, which typically involves straightforward, standardized transactions, could be one of the first major areas for widespread wireless access. The ubiquitous mobile phone is the new contender in financial services, and it carries with it the potential for very broad access. Unlike earlier experiments with smartcards and the first PC banking services, mobile devices look like a natural channel for consumer financial services. Mobile operators have built networks and technology capable of cheap, reliable, and secure person-to-merchant and person-to-person payments. Wireless telecommunication actually can compete with one of the banker's traditional greatest strengths—control of the payment system. Wireless service providers now have the capability of challenging credit card associations.

How much faster will the growth of intelligent applications over Wireless Web devices improve global productivity in the next decade? No one knows. But the

2. McInerney, F., and White, S. *FutureWealth*, Truman Talley Books, 2000.

Intelligent Wireless Web holds a vision that may significantly contribute to the information revolution through the use of

1. A growing number of mobile wireless devices for home and office providing broader access
2. Improvements to the user interface, including speech
3. "Nomadic" software from servers provided to our local devices as needed, including complete personal data and preferences
4. Intelligent software that could improve information transactions and productivity

◆ Statement of the Problem

Although progress is being made in many new technologies that are producing today's Information Age, there is one area that may become particularly influential—the Intelligent Wireless Web. This area includes wireless mobile devices, speech interfaces, and intelligent software. And as a result, the construction of an Intelligent Wireless Web requires the integration of advances in many disparate fields. Today, there is need for clarifying the "Big Picture" of how these many and varied fields of study fit together—where they touch, where they cooperate, and where they conflict.

◆ The Purpose of This Book

The purpose of this book is to provide insight into the "Big Picture" of how we may "build" an Intelligent Wireless Web. The book evaluates the compatibility, integration, and synergy of five merging technology areas that will lead to the Intelligent Wireless Web:

1. *User interface:* To transition from the mouse click and keyboard to speech as the primary method of communication between people and devices
2. *Personal Space:* To transition from connecting devices by tangled wires to multifunction wireless devices
3. *Networks:* To transition from a mostly wired infrastructure to an integrated wired/wireless system of interconnections

4. *Protocols:* To transition from the original Internet Protocol (IP) to the new Mobile IP

5. *Web architecture:* To transition from dumb and static applications to new applications that are intelligent, dynamic, and constantly improving

This book provides the background for understanding these merging technology areas. It provides an evaluation of the major advantages and disadvantages of individual technologies and the problems that must be overcome. Finally, the book provides a vision for building the Intelligent Wireless Web.

Yogi Berra once said, "Predictions can be tricky, especially when you're talking about the future." And certainly, making projections about competing technologies is more perilous than using hindsight to review history. However, the future of rapidly converging technologies is not so complex and uncertain that a few reasonable "trial solutions" about certain aspects of the Web's further development can't be put forward for examination. Indeed, several large advanced research efforts, such as MIT's $50-million Project Oxygen, demonstrate that concepts incorporating key elements of the Intelligent Wireless Web are being actively pursued.

Hopefully, the vision of technology development and convergence presented in this book will offer insights into the actual unfolding of the future of the Web. However, we fully acknowledge that there are competing visions for the development of various Web technologies and the actual winners are yet to be determined.

◆ Who Should Read This Book

The primary target audience for this book includes developers, engineers, innovators, research strategists, and IT managers who are looking for the "Big Picture" of how to integrate and deliver intelligent products and services wirelessly through Web services, software applications, and hardware devices.

The breadth and vision of this book offer synergistic perspective to many disciplines. This book should prove valuable to the technologists, innovators, integrators, computer science educators, and technical experts who are already contributing to the construction of the Intelligent Wireless Web in their own areas of expertise, including Intelligent Networks Designers, Internet Protocols Developers, Device Manufacturers, Wireless Communication Engineers, Standards Organizations, Knowledge-Base System Developers, Software Developers, Intelligent Agent Analysts, Speech

Recognition and Synthesis Developers, IT Research Managers, and IT Corporate Strategists.

Finally, this book provides a clear "mindset" for intelligent applications in the Wireless Web and is therefore a valuable reference for students of technology and managers requiring broad knowledge of leading technology issues.

◆ The Organization of This Book

This book is organized into three parts. Part I deals with communication from people to devices. Part II discusses interactions from device to device. Part III examines connections from devices to people. Within these three parts, we present the essential wireless communication relationships.

In Part I, we discuss how people communicate with devices. We start, in Chapter 1, by presenting an overview of the Intelligent Wireless Web, how the Web is becoming smarter, and how the five major technology components can come together as a framework for the Intelligent Wireless Web. Then, in Chapter 2, we show how speech recognition and understanding are growing more powerful and soon will be ready to become a central user interface between people and machines, replacing keyboards and mice wherever possible.

In Part II, we discuss how devices communicate with devices. We start, in Chapter 3, by presenting the specifics of your own Personal Space and its communication infrastructure of the wireless personal area network (WPAN). In Chapter 4, we preview the global communication infrastructure of interlacing networks and how wired and wireless networks are merging. Finally, in Chapter 5, we provide the basics of wireless protocols and standards between devices. This demonstrates how the mobile wireless networks and the Web are merging.

In Part III, we discuss how intelligent ways are being developed for communications from devices to people. We start, in Chapter 6, by discussing artificial intelligence, and we develop a thesis of growing intelligence for the Web. In Chapter 7, we explore current Web applications that are considered smart today, such as Enterprise Application Portals. Then we present the transition of Web architecture toward a Semantic Web with a logic layer. In addition, we explore concepts such as Web IQ. Then, in Chapter 8, we present speech synthesis and translation.

We digress in Chapter 9, to develop the economic basis for the rapid progress of an Intelligent Wireless Web. Finally, in Chapter 10, we weave a Big Picture of the likely progress over the next decade in actually "building" the Intelligent Wireless Web.

Within each chapter, the analysis includes the state-of-the-art technology and an evaluation of how that technology may evolve. We consider how intelligent applications and Web-smart devices work together within each particular area. In addition, each chapter provides a projection on how these relationships of the communication cycle will interface through standards that allow for intelligence to grow.

The sidebars within each chapter provide supplemental information of historical, illustrative, or explanatory nature. Additional advanced information is available in the appendices.

◆ Associated Resources

MIT's AI Laboratory hosts Project Oxygen, which is available online at http://oxygen.lcs.mit.edu/. The Semantic Web Organization has developer software resources at http://www.SemanticWeb.org.

Acknowledgments

We would like to acknowledge the helpful and constructive criticisms and recommendations of Michael Swaine of *Dr. Dobb's Journal;* Uche Ogbuji of Fourthought, Inc.; Minerva Tabtoco-Hobbs of Answerthink; Bill Pitzer of Divine, Inc.; and Michael Champion of Software AG.

We would especially like to thank Dominick Zingarelli, Doug Vogt, Mark Smith, Cassius Smith, Maynard Holiday, and Mariann Kourafas for their comments and suggestions during early drafts of this work. Their insights helped guide a complex effort.

Thanks also to our wives, Chris and Kathy, as well as our families for their feedback and advice on various drafts of this book and for their support during its preparation.

Finally, we would like to acknowledge the invaluable assistance of Mary O'Brien, senior acquisitions editor at Addison-Wesley, and the editorial, production, and marketing staffs, including Alicia Carey, Patrick Peterson, Kim Arney Mulcahy, Beth Hayes, Carol Noble, and Chanda Leary-Coutu.

About the Authors

H. Peter Alesso is an engineer with an M.S. and an advanced engineering degree from Massachusetts Institute of Technology, along with 20 years of research experience at Lawrence Livermore National Laboratory (LLNL). As Engineering Group Leader at LLNL, he led a team of computational physicists and engineers in a wide range of successful multimillion-dollar software development research projects. Peter has extensive experience with innovative applications across a wide range of supercomputers, workstations, and networks. His areas of interest include computer languages, algebras, graphs, and Web application software. He has published several software titles and numerous scientific journal and conference articles. H. Peter Alesso is the author of *e-Video: Producing Internet Video as Broadband Technologies Converge*, Addison-Wesley, 2000.

Craig Smith, Ph.D., is an engineer with 30 years of experience in research and development and application of advanced technologies. Dr. Smith received his Ph.D. in Nuclear Science and Engineering from the University of California, Los Angeles (UCLA) in 1975. He is currently a Deputy Associate Director of the Energy and Environment Directorate at Lawrence Livermore National Laboratory. He is responsible for a wide range of multimillion-dollar projects, and he is a collaborator on several international research initiatives. His areas of interest include sensors, robotics, and automated systems; information technology applications; and future energy systems. He has published numerous scientific journal and conference articles on advanced engineering topics.

PART I

Connecting People to Devices

In Part I, we present how people will communicate with devices. We begin in Chapter 1, by presenting an overview of the Intelligent Wireless Web, discussing how the Web is becoming smarter and how major technology components can be combined as a framework for the Intelligent Wireless Web. In Chapter 2, we show how speech recognition and understanding is growing more powerful and soon will be ready to become an important user interface between people and machines.

Developing a Framework
for the Intelligent Wireless Web

In this chapter, we define what we mean by the Intelligent Wireless Web and discuss compatibility, integration, and synergy issues facing the five central technology areas that we believe will form its framework:

1. *User interface:* Transitioning from the click of a mouse to speech
2. *Personal Space:* Transitioning from local systems connected by a tangle of wires to interconnected multifunction wireless devices
3. *Networks:* Transitioning from a predominately wired infrastructure to integrated wired/wireless systems
4. *Protocols:* Transitioning from the current Internet Protocol (IP) to Mobile IP
5. *Web architecture:* Transitioning from dumb and static applications to those that are intelligent and dynamic

Wouldn't it be great just to tap your "combadge" and be able to speak to anyone, any time, anywhere—the way they do on *Star Trek*? Or to say "Computer," followed by a perplexing question, and receive an intelligent answer?

It is not difficult to imagine that, in the foreseeable future, advances in information science, the Internet, and communications will continue at a very rapid pace and that technology convergence will begin to yield major improvements in the usefulness and productivity of technology. Science fiction may become reality as technology provides devices that increasingly mimic the features of the *Star Trek* "combadge."

In reality, advances in technology have frequently followed the imagination of futurists and science fiction writers, but it is much more difficult to chart the course of technology development than it is to imagine the end point. Building the Intelligent Wireless Web requires developing the framework in which a science fiction-like end point can be achieved through advancement in five technology areas—areas in which considerable ongoing work is being successfully performed so that convergence[1] will enable the next major advance in productivity.

To begin, it is important to describe what we mean by the "Intelligent Wireless Web." Let's take each term in turn, explain how we are using it, and indicate how each relates to the contents of this book. First let's consider what intelligence in the Wireless Web implies.

> ▶ **Intelligence:** Although most people have an implicit understanding of what is meant by the word *intelligence*, there is little agreement, even among experts, on precise definitions. This is true for both biological systems (that is, human beings) and machines. Intelligence usually refers to the ability to reason, solve problems, remember information, and learn and understand new things. A chess player who can conceptualize and evaluate large numbers of alternative positions for the next few chess moves is thought to demonstrate intelligence. A mathematician who can calculate a complex math problem in his mind demonstrates a different type of intelligence. The child prodigy who can memorize a vast number of facts shows yet a different form of intelligence. Yet each of these forms of human intelligence has been well demonstrated by modern computing systems. Computers are at their best when used as tools in solving complex problems that require brute-force calculation and prodigious amounts of memory. And we have all observed the dominance of Deep Blue, the chess-playing supercomputer from IBM that finally, in May 1997, beat the best chess master in the world, the reigning World Champion, Garry Kasparov.
>
> Notwithstanding the difficulty of defining intelligence (in humans or machines), it is worth recognizing that terms such as *artificial intelligence, intelligent agents, smart machines,* and the like refer to the performance of functions that mimic those associated with human intelligence. These topics are reviewed in Chapter 6. Although one can formulate the concept of an intelligence quotient (IQ) for humans as a surrogate measure of the phenomena we associate with human intelligence, a similar concept of "Web IQ" or "Web per-

---

1. Technology convergence is expressed in several different ways. We see hardware convergence of products such as pagers, cell phones, and personal digital assistants where the features found in different devices are gradually being incorporated into multifunction devices. Functional convergence is seen in the use of the personal computer for such functions as telephone communications, audio and video broadcast reception, and a player for DVD movies. Software convergence is seen in the interoperability of office software packaged as a suite of programs.

formance index" will someday likely be developed to provide measures of the effectiveness of hardware and software systems in achieving the goal of delivering intelligence through their applications and of learning and growing in time.

▶ **Wireless:** "Wirelessness" is the current rage. In a sense, the term *wireless* is self explanatory and obvious. Even so, the current emphasis on development of new wireless technology is a symptom of the present evolutionary trend in information technology toward convenient, mobile access to information systems any time and anywhere.

It's interesting to consider the development of telecommunications technologies over the past century and to note that hardwired connection has been the norm for communications for most of that time (for example, telegraph and telephone services), whereas, for broadcast information (for example, television, radio), wireless transmission has been the usual method. In the last few years, this arrangement has been dramatically altered. Both television and radio are frequently delivered to the home by hard wire (for example, coaxial cable) whereas telephone communications is rapidly shifting toward wireless delivery (that is, cell phone). In the rapid expansion of cell phone usage, we have become quickly accustomed to the idea of any time, anywhere connectivity. Expansion of this idea to include the full range of information services is the logical next step, and we are seeing the introduction of a variety of portable user devices (for example, pagers, personal digital assistants [PDAs], Web-enabled cell phones, small portable computers) that have wireless connectivity. Thus, although wireless connections among devices in our local area networks (LANs: see Chapters 4 and 5) are an important development, the extension of information services to the mobile user is perhaps even more exciting.

▶ **Web:** The word *Web* is another widely used but somewhat ambiguous term. Although it is usually used interchangeably with the term *Internet,* the distinction

---

The Internet and the World Wide Web

The Internet can be considered to be a huge network of networks. It links networks and users together through the use of a layered set of protocols known as Transmission Control Protocol/Internet Protocol (TCP/IP).

Computers connected to the Internet run software to access and view information. The Internet itself is the transport medium for the information stored in files or documents. Computers on the Internet may use any of the following Internet services:

- Electronic mail (e-mail) to send and receive mail or access e-mail based discussion groups
- TELNET or remote login to log onto another computer and use it remotely
- File Transfer Protocol (FTP) to rapidly retrieve complex files intact from a remote computer

The World Wide Web (WWW, the Web) is a set of protocols and standards for multimedia information exchange on the Internet. It includes the HyperText Markup Language (HTML), HyperText Transfer Protocol (HTTP), and Uniform Resource Locator (URL).

between these two terms is itself interesting. The historical development of the Internet extends back nearly 40 years to concepts that were introduced for a highly reliable, fault- and damage-tolerant network of interconnected computers. At a critical stage in the resulting evolution of the Internet as a network of networks, the World Wide Web was introduced (in 1989) as a set of tools (that is, programs, protocols, and standards) to permit the creation, display, and transfer of multimedia information. Many attribute the rapid growth of use of the Internet to this critical development.

Thus the term *Web* can be considered a shorthand term for the World Wide Web, but the common usage of the term is broader than this and is inclusive of the entire Internet, including the multimedia enhancements. The Web is what the Internet has become in its current form—a large, rapidly growing, multimedia-enabled network of networks.

But why do we suggest putting all three of these terms together into one concept—the Intelligent Wireless Web? It is certainly possible to develop intelligent applications for the Internet without media (that is, audio/video) Web features and/or wireless capability. It is our suggestion, however, that Web media, such as audio, can lead to improved user interfaces using speech and that small wireless devices, widely distributed, can lead to easier access to large portions of the world's population. The end result could be not just an intelligent Internet but a widely available, easily accessible, user-friendly, Intelligent Wireless Web.

As a result, the concept of an Intelligent Wireless Web weaves together important concepts related to the growing and evolving system of information technology software and hardware known as the Internet. Intelligence (in particular, the ability to learn) and "wireless" (with its attendant mobility and convenience) promise the delivery of increasingly capable information services to mobile users any time and anywhere.

Fundamentally, our vision for the future of an Intelligent Wireless Web is straight forward—an Intelligent Wireless Web is a network that provides any time, anywhere access to information resources with efficient user interfaces and applications that learn and thereby provide increasingly useful services whenever and wherever we need them.

What exactly do we want our future communications and information processes to become? How can we construct such a system? In the following sections, we will lay out the framework and building blocks for future communications and information resource processes that will enable the construction of the Intelligent Wireless Web.

◆ The Wireless Communication Process

Where were you the last time the stock market dropped? Chances are you were in a car, in a meeting, or walking to your next appointment. In other words, you were away from your personal computer (PC) and unable to check your portfolio or make vital trades.

Or how about the last time you opened up your notebook computer and were unable to readily connect to your company network to transfer that all-important business report you were sure would guarantee your next promotion.

Today, our desire for immediate satisfaction in conveying our message is growing exponentially. How fast we communicate is becoming as important as what we have to say. The challenge is that we urgently want our technology to provide communication at a distance as conveniently as we communicate face to face. From e-mail to paging, fast is just not fast enough.

As we enter the twenty-first century, the use of wireless communication technologies—cellular telephones, personal communication systems (PCSs), satellite phones, paging systems, wireless modems, and local area networks (LANs), plus local multipoint distribution services (LMDS) for wireless delivery of television and Internet service—is expanding rapidly. The proliferation of components and devices offers multiple options for communication development.

Ideally, we would like the future wireless communication process to start with a user interface based on speech recognition by which we merely talk to a personal mobile device that recognizes our identity, words, and commands. The personal mobile device would connect seamlessly to embedded and fixed devices in the immediate environment. The message would be relayed to a server residing on a network with the necessary processing power and software to analyze the contents of the message. The server would link to additional Web resources that could then draw necessary supplemental knowledge from around the world through the Internet. Finally, the synthesized message would be delivered to the appropriate parties in their own language on their own personal mobile device.

Sounds good, doesn't it? But how is it going to be constructed? The ideal future wireless communication process will require us to explore the following inherent relationships of communications along with their essential components:

Part I: Connecting people to devices—the user interface. Currently, we rely on the mouse, keyboard, and video display. Speech recognition and understanding deployed for mobile devices is a key component for the future.

Part II: Connecting devices to devices. Currently, hardwired connections between devices limit mobility and constrain the design of networks. In the future, the merging of wired and wireless communication infrastructure requires the establishment of wireless protocols and standards for the connection between devices. Future smart applications require the development and improvement of artificial intelligence (AI) methods. Ultimately, a method is needed to measure the performance and/or intelligence of the Internet so that we can assess advancements.

Part III: Connecting devices to people. To deliver useful information to the globally mobile user, future systems require advances in speech synthesis and language translation.

We will present these topics in the subsequent chapters of this book, arranged according to these three parts.

By addressing these relationships between and among people and devices, and in particular by addressing the identified essential components for future systems, current systems of information services and communications can be dramatically transformed from their current limitations to a future of spectacular broadband global delivery.

Several challenges exist to the development and deployment of scalable, production-level, Intelligent Wireless Web applications. These include

▶ Device proliferation

▶ Bandwidth and interface limitations

▶ Applications with limited capabilities

▶ Emerging wireless standards

But perhaps the most daunting challenge is the integration, synthesis, and interfacing of these elements.

So, just how can the Web become smart enough to fulfill the vision of a robust global mobile system providing increasingly relevant and intelligent applications? The development of the physical components and software necessary to implement the Intelligent Wireless Web requires insight into the compatibility, integration, and synergy of the following five emerging technology areas:

1. *User interface:* To transition from the mouse click and keyboard to speech as the primary (but not exclusive) method of communication between people and devices

2. *Personal Space:* To transition from connection of devices by tangled wires to multifunction wireless devices

3. *Networks:* To transition from a mostly wired infrastructure to an integrated wired/wireless system of interconnections

4. *Protocols:* To transition from the original IP to the new Mobile IP

5. *Web architecture:* To transition from dumb and static applications to new applications that are intelligent, dynamic, and constantly learning.

As the Web matures, the information technology community seems to be viewing the Web as a global database with a knowledge representation system. Although a database management system is simply a collection of procedures for retrieving, storing, and manipulating data, it is also possible to view the Web in terms of applied learning algorithms in which data is taken from a database as input and, after appropriate algorithmic operations (based upon statistics, experiment, or other approaches) are performed, an output statement is returned that contains enhanced data, thereby representing a form of learning. In building the Intelligent Wireless Web, we are seeking to create a Web that learns, yielding continuously improved applications and information.

In the next sections, we will highlight the innovative processes underway in each of these technological areas:

▸ *User interface:* From click to speech

▸ *Personal Space:* From wired to wireless

▸ *Networks:* From wired to integrated wired/wireless

▶ *Protocols:* From IP to Mobile IP

▶ *Web architecture:* From dumb and static to intelligent and dynamic

For each of these areas, we will introduce the technology requirements that are needed to achieve the objectives of the Intelligent Wireless Web. We also will identify the steps needed to advance the current state of technology. Finally, the results or attributes of the desired outcome will be indicated. Each of these topics then will be presented in greater detail in the subsequent chapters of the book.

◆ User Interface: From Click to Speech

Communication between humans and their machines has been the subject of considerable technical research. Work on the "human-machine interface" has been conducted since the development of complex machinery, such as locomotive trains, automobiles, and washing machines. The need to efficiently provide information to machines, control their functions, and receive information from them to inform human operators of their status has increased dramatically over many decades.

Language—both written and spoken—is the primary means of human communication. Yet, communication through language has many obstacles, from the simple and obvious differences between the tongues spoken in different countries to the "untranslatable" slang differences between cultures. And, even for a healthy listener, background noise can make normal speech perception difficult.

So, how should we converse with a computer, its connected devices, and the machines they may control? If talking is the most natural way humans communicate, why not communicate with computers through ordinary language? After all, we learn to speak before we learn to read and write. Speech is also a highly efficient form of communication—people speak about five times faster than they type.

However, there are significant problems. The human voice is unique to each individual—no two people have exactly the same voice—and many words that sound alike have a different spelling or meaning. Minor differences in meaning can lead to major misunderstanding of language. Nuances of meaning can frequently be interpreted only by considering overall context. These problems present challenges for speech recognition software and speech-enabled applications.

Today there are two basic approaches to deciphering spoken commands. One approach uses matching algorithms that compare bit patterns of the spoken commands to standard bit patterns stored in the speech recognition software's library of patterns. The commands and related bit patterns are matched for appropriate actions. This approach is most often used in discrete speech applications. A library of bit patterns is created by averaging the patterns of a large sampling of pronunciations for a specific vocabulary.

In the second approach, users "train" the speech software by providing speech patterns. This approach uses statistical modeling and libraries of word and grammar rules to increase the accuracy and responsiveness of the speech software. Most of today's speech recognition applications have vocabulary databases of up to 200,000 words with appropriate grammar rules

Speech recognition (speech-to-text) transforms human voice inputs into commands and characters. Speech recognition would be a highly desirable capability for handheld, mobile devices, if the many obstacles can be overcome, allowing machines to recognize the user's comments and respond in context. Two modes of speech recognition already exist: command-and-control and dictation.

Voice input to a command environment can trigger specific actions and can be used to navigate an application. For example, a user speaks the command "Call George" to launch the application that automatically dials George's cell phone number. Rather than speaking a single word or phrase to initiate an action, dictation transcribes the user's speech into text. The text file then can be saved just like any other file and sent as an attachment over the Web.

The demand for digital speech coding algorithms grows every day, fueled by applications such as streaming speech over the Web, digital cellular telephony, wireless teleconferencing, and various multimedia applications. As companies strive to continuously improve productivity, there are many applications in which speech-enabled computers present sound solutions.

It is readily discernible that speech recognition and understanding will play an expanding role in communicating with devices. In the following chapters, we explore the specifics of the transition from clicking commands at a workstation to speaking commands to a wide variety of small, wearable, handheld, or embedded devices.

The final element in completing the communication process is providing recognizable speech output to the recipient. This involves speech synthesis. Speech synthesis (text-to-speech) refers to audible responses from the computer, either as human speech or computer-generated responses. Voice responses can use recorded human speech phrases or units to produce a more natural human sound. However, a large amount of memory is needed to store the recorded voice vocabulary.

Voice responses that are computer-generated use speech units termed phonemes. Phonemes are the fundamental elements of pronunciation. Phonemes provide the building blocks to voice and combine to form syllables and words. Many applications use a combination of speech recognition and speech synthesis to create a natural interactive environment.

The Speech Interface Framework working group of the World Wide Web Consortium (W3C) is developing standards to enable access to the Web using spoken language (see www.w3.org/Voice/). The Speech Synthesis Markup Language (SSML) specification is part of a set of new markup specifications for voice browsers. It is an Extensible Markup Language (XML)-based markup language for assisting the generation of synthetic speech on the Web. It provides authors content to synthesize in a standard way and allows them to control aspects of speech such as pronunciation, volume, pitch, and rate across different synthesis-capable platforms. The VoiceXML Forum (see xml.coverpages.org/vxml.html) is an industry organization established to promote VoiceXML as the standard for speech-enabled Web applications. Speech synthesis is addressed further in Chapter 8. Figure 1-1 illustrates the complete cycle of communications envisioned for the Intelligent Wireless Web.

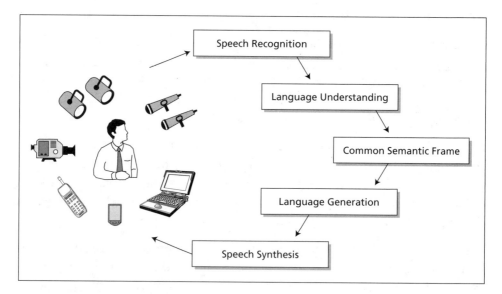

Figure 1-1   The communication process

Current computer systems use video displays and the keyboard or mouse (to point and click) as the primary methods for user interface. As small devices proliferate, what is needed to transition from the point-and-click method to the more natural use of human speech as a primary user interface? The main technology requirements are centered on speech recognition, speech understanding, conversion of text to speech, language translation, speech synthesis, and Speech Markup Language as well as greater available CPU processing power. These requirements, the current state of development, the steps needed to progress toward the Intelligent Wireless Web, and the expected results are outlined in Figure 1-2 and discussed in further detail in Chapter 2. Although we may expect speech interfaces to permeate society steadily, we anticipate that successful traditional interfaces, such as mouse and touch screen, will continue to be in operation for a very long time, particularly for such high-power applications as selecting data from detailed graphical representations.

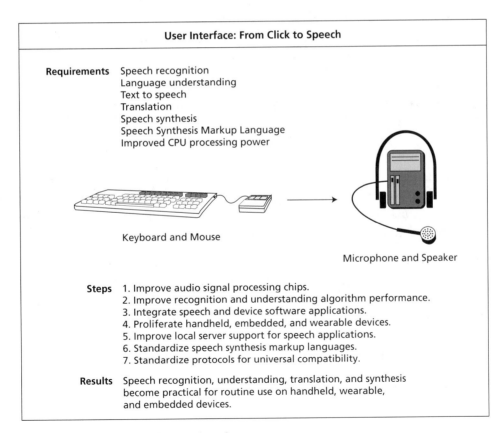

User Interface: From Click to Speech

Requirements Speech recognition
Language understanding
Text to speech
Translation
Speech synthesis
Speech Synthesis Markup Language
Improved CPU processing power

Keyboard and Mouse

Microphone and Speaker

Steps 1. Improve audio signal processing chips.
2. Improve recognition and understanding algorithm performance.
3. Integrate speech and device software applications.
4. Proliferate handheld, embedded, and wearable devices.
5. Improve local server support for speech applications.
6. Standardize speech synthesis markup languages.
7. Standardize protocols for universal compatibility.

Results Speech recognition, understanding, translation, and synthesis
become practical for routine use on handheld, wearable,
and embedded devices.

Figure 1-2 Transitioning the user interface

◆ Personal Space: From Wired to Wireless

Imagine living your entire life within the confines of your own Personal Space (PS). Let's define Personal Space as the immediate vicinity that you can visually inspect around you. If you were to look around such a space, how many electronic devices would you see? How many wires would exist? With every new electronic device, you add to the "cable tangle" around you both at the office and at home. Wireless technology offers connectivity among these devices within your Personal Space without that encumbering tangle.

In the year 2000, there were over 15 billion devices of various types worldwide and 30 percent of all communication was actually conducted as device to device.[2] By 2010, 95 percent of all communication will be between devices. To understand how the new and emerging wireless networks will change communications it is important to consider how expanding communications will allow people to talk to each other and also to control the many devices that run our world. Clearly, device-to-device communication must become more efficient and intelligent if we are to realize our expectations of increased productivity.

With billions of devices already in use today, developing multipurpose communications systems that can be programmed to receive and transmit many different types of signals is a daunting challenge. At one extreme, we must consider Personal Space device-to-device network interfaces at home and at work—the personal area network (PAN). At the other extreme, we must recognize the need to adapt to a global interlacing complex of networks with potentially interconnected devices that must accommodate a large number of possible device-to-device combinations. This in turn makes obvious the need to establish and implement worldwide standards for interconnection of Web devices.

The next generation of networking will be Web-centric but with the introduction of the mobility factor, extending to devices such as wireless phones or PDAs. Only recently, through standards and advances in computing and communications technologies, has the convergence of wireless networks and the Internet begun to take place. The model extends the Enterprises' reach to a disparate range of devices, such as wireless phones, PDAs, pagers, LAN phones, automobile PCs, and cable television.

---

2. McInerney, F., and White, S. *FutureWealth.* Truman Talley Books, 2000.

In a wireless network with many mobile devices, channel conditions vary unpredictably over time. In addition, running a variety of applications over a network introduces significant variability in required bandwidth, error rate, and security. For example, electronic-commerce (e-commerce) applications require encryption, whereas an entertainment application may not.

Conventional network interfaces are inflexible. They are designed to operate under the worst conditions, rather than to adapt to changing conditions. This leads to inefficient use of spectrum and energy. Although great effort has been expended to simplify connectivity at the office, it continues to be difficult to plug your camera or cell phone into your company network to exchange data and images. The problems range from wires and connectors to operating systems (OSs) with annoying incompatibility and difficult component integration. Currently, wireless standards for connecting local devices are competing for dominance. The three near-term standard leaders are Bluetooth, Jini, and Universal Plug and Play (UPnP).

The Bluetooth standard is a short-range wireless capability to beam documents easily from a Bluetooth laptop to a compatible printer or to transfer data from a PC to a cell phone. Powerful device-to-device communications via SUN's Jini into smart devices is also coming along, though more slowly than Bluetooth. Microsoft's UPnP is further behind. MIT's Oxygen concept, described below, is further out in the future.

Project Oxygen

While Bluetooth, Jini, and UPnP are near-term technologies, Massachusetts Institute of Technology (MIT) Artificial Intelligence Laboratory is embracing the next generation of computation with access from any location using interacting anonymous devices in a project named Oxygen.

Oxygen's vision is for there to be computation capability available all the time, everywhere, just as electricity is universally available from electric power sockets. Anonymous devices, either handheld or embedded in the environment, would personalize themselves in our presence by finding whatever information and software we need. We would communicate naturally, using speech, leaving it to the computer to locate appropriate resources and carry out our intent.

Project Oxygen's human-centric approach began in 1999 as a Defense Advanced Research Projects Agency (DARPA) project at MIT. A collaboration of MIT colleagues searched for radical new ways of deploying and using information. Their unifying goal was pervasive, human-centric computing. In May 2000, industrial partners joined MIT in the $50 million Project Oxygen. The Oxygen prototype devices and software will be completed in 2002, and the final testing by MIT will not be complete until 2004. The goal of the Oxygen system is to be pervasive, embedded, nomadic, and always on.

Oxygen rests on an infrastructure of mobile and stationary devices connected by a self-configuring network. This infrastructure supplies an abundance of computation and communication capabilities which are harnessed through several levels of software technology to meet user needs.

Devices in Oxygen, both mobile and stationary, will be universal communication and computation appliances. They would also be anonymous, not storing customized configurations to any particular user. In Project Oxygen, speech will replace keyboards and mice.

MIT's stationary devices are to be embedded in offices, buildings, homes, and vehicles to create intelligent spaces. They include interfaces to camera and microphone arrays and users will be able to communicate to the devices using speech.

MIT's handheld devices provide mobile points for users both within and without the intelligent spaces controlled. They will accept speech input, and they can reconfigure themselves for various protocols (see Chapters 3, 4, and 7 for more on Oxygen).

So, how do we transition from our present situation of fixed, wired Personal Spaces to the flexibility and efficiency of the Intelligent Wireless Web? Some of the key technology requirements are adaptable wireless devices and the establishment, acceptance, and development of wireless protocols, wireless small-screen applications, and "nomadic," or mobile, software for devices. These requirements, the current state of development, the steps needed to progress toward the Intelligent Wireless Web, and the expected results are outlined in Figure 1-3 and discussed in greater detail in Chapter 3.

◆ Networks: From Wired to Integrated Wired/Wireless

The earliest computers were stand-alone, unconnected machines. To transfer information from one system to another, it was necessary to store the data in some form, physically carry it to the second compatible system, and read it into the computer. During the subsequent decades, mergers, takeovers, and downsizing have

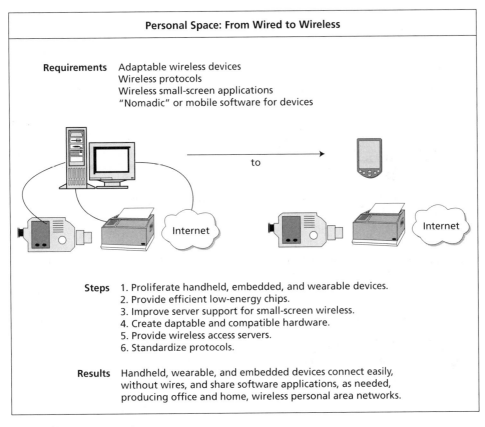

Personal Space: From Wired to Wireless

Requirements   Adaptable wireless devices
Wireless protocols
Wireless small-screen applications
"Nomadic" or mobile software for devices

to

Internet

Internet

Steps   1. Proliferate handheld, embedded, and wearable devices.
2. Provide efficient low-energy chips.
3. Improve server support for small-screen wireless.
4. Create daptable and compatible hardware.
5. Provide wireless access servers.
6. Standardize protocols.

Results   Handheld, wearable, and embedded devices connect easily,
without wires, and share software applications, as needed,
producing office and home, wireless personal area networks.

Figure 1-3   Transitioning your Personal Space

led to a need to consolidate company data in fast, seamless, integrated databases for corporate information. With this consolidation acting as a driving force, intranets and local networks began to increase in size, and this required new ways for devices to interface with each other.

Over the past decade, enterprise models and architectures, as well as their corresponding implementation in actual business practices, have changed to take advantage of new technologies. Network computing has become the means to increased efficiencies in knowledge management—systematically finding, selecting, and organizing information. As knowledge management improves, employees, partners, and customers become better connected within an enterprise. As a result, mundane tasks can be easily relegated to computers while corporations focus on more important tasks.

One of the big lures of wireless networks is the potential for implementing architectures that can send packets from people with small personal devices, such as cell phones, to conduct e-commerce transactions. The number of wireless subscribers is expected to grow globally to more than 400 million by 2005. Although these prospects are attractive, the burst in growth demands that the wireless architecture proceed wisely.

For corporations that are heavily invested in legacy systems, however, deploying new wireless applications could mean that they must find a way to build on the existing infrastructure.

Networks are built upon three necessary elements that must be balanced:

1. Bandwidth
2. High-speed switching
3. Network intelligence

Many of us are already familiar with optical fiber developments expanding bandwidth and the contest between IP packet switching verses asynchronous transfer mode (ATM) circuit switching, but network intelligence is only recently showing its importance.

Intelligent Networking (IN) is a concept that is leading to new technological development, as user demands become more sophisticated. IN is more than just network architecture: it is a complete framework for the creation, provisioning, and management of advanced data transmission services.

The characteristics and quality of data transmission are determined by both the nature of the media and the signal. For wired media (copper wire, coaxial cable, and optical fiber), the medium itself is as important in establishing its limitations as the signal.

For wireless media, transmission and reception are achieved by antenna. To transmit, the antenna radiates electromagnetic waves into the air and the receiving antenna picks up the waves from the surrounding media.

Communication satellites compete with fiberoptics in delivering broadband signals for television, long-haul telephone, and private business networks. Direct broadcast satellite (DBS) uses satellites to directly distribute programming to the home. Satellite transmission is also used for point-to-point trunks between telephone exchanges. In addition, satellite transmissions are used for business data applications over private networks.

Wireless LANs have come to occupy a growing niche in the LAN market. Wireless LAN is viewed as a satisfying adjunct to traditional wired LAN, meeting the requirements of mobility, relocation, ad hoc networking, and coverage of locations difficult to wire. Until recently, wireless LANs suffered from high prices, low data rates, and licensing requirements.

Early wireless LAN products of the 1980s were marketed as substitutes for wired LANs. A typical wireless LAN configuration includes a backbone wired LAN, such as an Ethernet, that supports several servers, workstations, and one or more bridges or routers to link to other networks. A control module interfaces to a wireless LAN that regulates access by polling or token passing schemes.

Wireless wide area network (WAN) technologies include packet radio, analog cellular data, cellular digital packet data, satellite communications, meteor burst communications, and combining location devices with wireless WANs.

So, what are the key needs to enable transition from our present wired LANs and WANs to integrated the wired/wireless systems of the Intelligent Wireless Web? Some of the key technology requirements are the wireless LAN, the wireless WAN, satellite communications technology, commercial spectrum allocation, and wired/ wireless Interfaces. These requirements, the current state of development, the steps needed to progress toward the Intelligent Wireless Web, and the expected results are outlined in Figure 1-4 and discussed in greater detail in Chapter 4.

◆ Protocols: From IP to Mobile IP

Over the years, several protocols have been defined by various players in the market for various types of applications. In the beginning, Unwired Planet had its Handheld Device Markup Language (HDML), a protocol for Internet access to be used over cellular digital packet data (CDPD) networks. In 1997, Nokia launched a protocol named Tagged Text Markup Language (TTML), a protocol with a focus similar to that of the HDML protocol but designed to be used in the global system for mobile communications (GSM) world. Ericsson, in turn, was in the process of launching a protocol mainly focusing on telecommunications-related and messaging applications to be used inside the GSM networks, named Intelligent Terminal Transfer Protocol (ITTP).

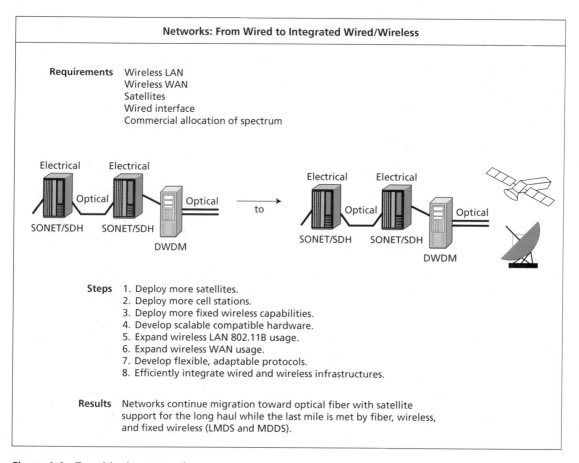

Networks: From Wired to Integrated Wired/Wireless

Requirements   Wireless LAN
Wireless WAN
Satellites
Wired interface
Commercial allocation of spectrum

Steps   1. Deploy more satellites.
2. Deploy more cell stations.
3. Deploy more fixed wireless capabilities.
4. Develop scalable compatible hardware.
5. Expand wireless LAN 802.11B usage.
6. Expand wireless WAN usage.
7. Develop flexible, adaptable protocols.
8. Efficiently integrate wired and wireless infrastructures.

Results   Networks continue migration toward optical fiber with satellite
support for the long haul while the last mile is met by fiber, wireless,
and fixed wireless (LMDS and MDDS).

Figure 1-4   Transitioning networks

These three protocols represented only a fraction of the different wireless protocols defined by different organizations and available in the marketplace. This fragmentation limited the market growth for wireless applications. To clean up this fragmentation, forces were joined in defining a common platform and protocol and embracing Internet access and messaging.

The first joint meeting to consider wireless standards took place in June 1997. The intention was to broaden the group of companies working with the Wireless Application Protocol (WAP). In December 1997, WAP Forum Ltd. developed WAP. WAP is designed to provide data-oriented (nonvoice) services any time and anywhere (see www.wapforum.org).

The WAP microbrowser can be compared to a standard Internet browser. The applications must be written in the new markup language defined within WAP, named Wireless Markup Language (WML). WML is structured rather similarly to HTML.

In addition to specialized protocols, such as WAP, Internet Protocols themselves are undergoing transition. The Mobile IP Working Group of the Internet Engineering Task Force has developed routing support to permit IP nodes (hosts and routers) using either IP version 4 (IPv4) or IPv6 to seamlessly "roam" among IP subnetworks and media types. The Mobile IP method supports transparency above the IP layer.

Normally, IP routes packets from a source to a destination by allowing routers to forward packets from incoming to outbound network interfaces in accordance with routing tables. The routing tables maintain the next-hop (outbound interface) information for each destination IP address. The network number is derived from the IP address.

To maintain existing transport-layer connections as the mobile node moves from place to place, it must keep its IP address the same. However, in Transmission Control Protocol (TCP), the connection is indexed by a quadruplet IP address with port numbers for both endpoints. Changing any of the four numbers will cause the connection to be lost. The problem is that delivery of packets to the mobile node's current point depends on the network number contained within the mobile node's IP address, which changes at new points of attachment.

Mobile IP has been designed to solve this problem by allowing the mobile node to use two IP addresses. In Mobile IP, the home address is static to identify TCP connections. The "care-of" address changes at each new point of attachment and can be thought of as the mobile node's topologically significant address. This address shows the network number and identifies the mobile node's point of attachment.

Whenever the mobile node is not attached to its home network, the home unit gets all the packets destined for the mobile node and delivers them to the mobile node's current point of attachment.

Whenever the mobile node moves, it registers its new "care of" address with its home unit. The home unit delivers the packet from the home network to the care-of address.

So, what are the key needs necessary to enable transition from the present system of Internet protocols to the additional protocols needed to bring about the promise of

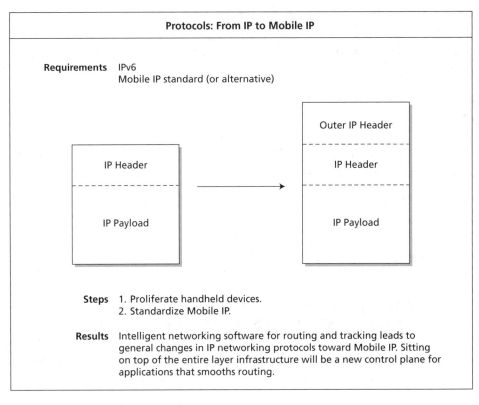

Figure 1-5 Transitioning protocols

the Intelligent Wireless Web? The primary technology requirement is the development and establishment of the Mobile IP to enable the same kind of information system access—any time, anywhere—that we enjoy with our current cellular phone technology. This requirement, the current state of development, the steps needed to progress toward the Intelligent Wireless Web, and the expected results are outlined in Figure 1-5 and discussed in greater detail in Chapter 5.

◆ Web Architecture: Dumb and Static to Intelligent and Dynamic

We have said that fundamentally our vision for the future of an Intelligent Wireless Web is very simple—it is a network that provides any-time, anywhere access to information resources with efficient user interfaces and applications that learn and thereby provide increasingly useful services whenever and wherever we need them.

For the Web to learn, it requires learning algorithms and mechanisms for self-organization of a hypertext network. It needs to develop algorithms that would allow the Web to autonomously change its structure and organize the knowledge it contains, by "learning" the ideas and preferences of its users.

One way to move toward these goals has been suggested by W3C through the use of better semantic information as part of Web documents and of the use of next-generation Web languages such as XML and RDF. The Semantic Web Architecture will enable movement from IP to Mobile IP in addition to providing an XML layer, an RDF schema layer, and a logic layer.

Facilities to put machine-understandable data on the Web are becoming a high priority for many communities. Tomorrow's programs must be able to share and process data even when designed totally independently. The Semantic Web is one vision of having data on the Web defined and linked in a way that it can be used by machines not just for display purposes but for automation, integration, and reuse of data (Figure 1-6). An alternative to the Semantic Web is the successful development of Intelligent Web Services through Microsoft Net and Java2 Enterprise Edition (J2EE).

> **XML and RDF**
> XML stands for Extensible Markup Language. The key feature of XML in comparison with HTML is that it provides the ability to define tags and attributes, not allowed under HTML. XML is part of the Standard Generalized Markup Language (SGML) designed for use on the Internet. It supports all the features of SGML, and valid XML documents are therefore valid SGML documents.
>
> XML is designed to be very easy to implement so that application vendors can provide XML support internally or as plug-ins or downloadable applets. XML provides a ready entry point to structured markup for HTML users.
>
> RDF stands for Resource Description Framework, which integrates a variety of Web-based metadata activities, including site maps, content ratings, stream channel definitions, search engine data collection (Web crawling), digital library collections, and distributed authoring, using XML as the interchange syntax.

So, what are the key needs to enable transition from the current dumb and static systems to the intelligence and flexibility of the Intelligent Wireless Web? One key is the Semantic Web. Key technology requirements include XML schema, RDF schema (and its converging competitor, Topic Maps), logic layering, and distributed AI and AI service providers. In addition, information registration and validation will be an essential global service to support activities such as financial transactions. These requirements, the current state of Web Services development, the steps needed to progress toward the Intelligent Wireless Web, and the expected results are outlined in Figure 1-6 and discussed in greater detail in Chapters 6, 7, and 10.

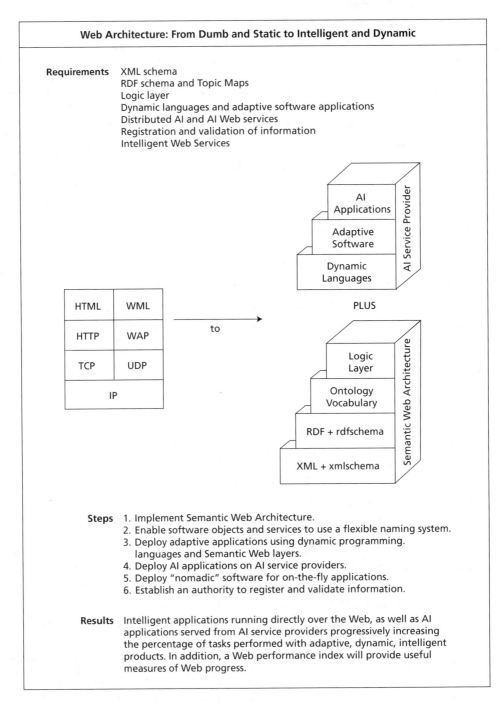

Figure 1-6   Transitioning Web architecture

Self-Organizing Software and Adaptive Protocols

Traditional software development was based on principles such as exact specification, complex maintenance, and high levels of abstraction. Today software is expected to do more for us because of our increasingly complex environments. The complexity comes from users, systems, devices, and goals. Programmers are accustomed to a trade-off of time versus memory. Now they have to worry about bandwidth, security, quality of information, resolution of images, and other factors.

The problems with existing software are that it takes too much time and money to develop and it is brittle when used in situations for which it was not explicitly designed. Various software design methodologies can alleviate this problem.

The Web needs a significantly higher degree of dynamism and mobility, as well as a robust network infrastructure and protocols. Self-organizing software, adaptive protocols, and object-oriented dynamic languages can provide the Web with the tools it needs to learn.

Self-organizing software means the ability of networks to organize and configure themselves. Adaptation means the ability of protocols and applications to learn and adapt to the changing conditions in the network, such as levels of congestion and errors. The next generation of programming languages will support intelligent, adaptive, complex software systems. "Reflection," or reasoning, will be built into the language's own structure, performance, and environment, along with support for dynamic modification of behavior. Adaptive software will use information from the environment to improve its behavior over time.

Today, adaptive programming is aimed at the problem of producing applications that can readily adapt in the face of changing user needs and environments. Adaptive software explicitly represents the goals that the user is trying to achieve. This makes it possible for the user to change goals without a need to rewrite the program. A typical application is an information filter.

Adaptive software adds a feedback loop that provides information based on performance. The design criteria itself becomes a part of the program, and the program reconfigures itself as the environment changes.

Static languages, such as C, require the programmer to make a lot of decisions about structure and the data. Object-oriented dynamic languages form a higher level of abstraction and reflection. MIT's Dynamic Language (Dylan) and Common Lisp

Object System (CLOS) allow these decisions to be delayed and thus provide more responsive programming.

How will this produce significant change to improve the intelligence and efficiency of the Web? First, we must think of the Internet in terms of information instead of data packets. Instead of establishing TCP connections to some server, think of the device as a client of the information, rather than a client of the server. It becomes a distributed application that is running on some machine that requires some functionality or some service that exists somewhere in the network. As a result, large networks have a set of consumers and a set of providers of information. The network task is to match consumers and providers (one way to accomplish this is through the use of Intelligent Web Services or AI service providers).

Second, the network becomes efficient by learning about conditions on the network, such as changes in bandwidths, error conditions, and failure modes. And, finally, it begins to adapt.

Adaptive protocols can achieve this when they become a core component in the future Internet infrastructure. They will enable distributed applications that can be designed to organize themselves. So how do we architect a system to do this?

Deployable intelligence mechanisms can be associated with Learning Algorithms, including pattern recognition algorithms and data mining algorithms. And different applications can reuse the same algorithm-level software. It is important to be able to guide the automation process and to override decisions. Software areas under development include

- ▶ Agent technology acting for a user's preferences
- ▶ Data mining
- ▶ Decision theory providing terminology for expert systems for preferred outcomes
- ▶ Reinforcement learning finding actions to perform
- ▶ Probabilistic networks providing algorithms for computing optimal actions
- ▶ Expert systems: Computer applications making decisions in real-life situations that would otherwise be performed by a human expert
- ▶ Neural networks: Systems simulating intelligence by reproducing the types of physical connections found in animal or even human brains

Major research challenges are ahead in expanding intelligence offered as Web Services. The first is the problem of scaling to large networks and to large numbers of applications. The second issue is an end-to-end adaptation framework with underlying layers of the protocol stack to applications. This will allow learning about what's going on in the network and enabling new algorithms and new protocols to react. One method to achieve this is through a new protocol layer (see Chapter 7).

Web IQ

To achieve an Intelligent Wireless Web that learns we need an intelligence or performance measure for the Internet to measure progress. Basically, to be of value, such a measure need only provide a crude estimate of Internet progress toward an improving capability.

In seeking to evaluate Web IQ or Web performance, we are not specifically looking to pass Turing's test. But we are asking for an evaluation of the Internet's progress, as it grows more capable. Certainly the following elements play a role: data storage capacity, data transmission speed, device interface, protocols, database searching, data sorting and filtering, speech recognition and synthesis, video object recognition and tracking, object linking, expert systems, AI applications, and communication standards. How can we put it all together to find a useful measure to track the growth of expanding Web IQ? We believe this will be a continuing topic of interest as the capabilities and scope of the Web continue to expand.

Artificial Intelligence

In 1947, shortly after the end of World War II, English mathematician Alan Turing started to seriously explore intelligent machines. By 1956, John McCarthy of MIT contributed the term *artificial intelligence* (AI). And by the late 1950s, many researchers were working in the area of AI, most basing their work on programming computers. Eventually, AI became more than a branch of science—it has expanded far beyond mathematics and computer science into such fields as philosophy, psychology, and biology.

Today AI is still a developing science with great potential, but it has not yet achieved the success expected. As a result, the introduction of AI applications to the Web is a prospect met with both skepticism and hope.

◆ Conclusion

In this chapter, we provided an introduction to what we mean by the Intelligent Wireless Web, a survey of how it may develop using wireless applications, and a discussion of how it will provide optimized performance while packaging knowledge in ways that are increasingly beneficial.

We have begun to consider what is necessary to produce a "learning" Web. It requires designing applications with Learning Algorithms and mechanisms for the self-organization of a hypertext network. We suggested that we need to develop algorithms that would allow the Web to autonomously change its structure and organize the knowledge it contains, by "learning" the ideas and preferences of its users. In addition, we suggested that intelligent applications would find their way onto the Web as Web Services through Enterprise Information Portals and through the evolution of Semantic Web Architecture.

We highlighted the compatibility, integration, and synergy issues facing the five merging technology areas that will build the Intelligent Wireless Web:

- ▶ User interface
- ▶ Personal Space
- ▶ Networks
- ▶ Mobile protocol
- ▶ Web architecture

Ten technological questions about the future of the Intelligent Wireless Web that we will specifically seek to address in subsequent chapters are as follows:

1. What is the status of developing speech recognition, understanding, synthesis, and translation?
2. What devices are being developed as handheld, wearable, and embedded devices that will contribute to Ubiquitous Computing?
3. What are wireless personal area networks and what role will they play in the office and at home?
4. How are wired and wireless infrastructures merging and performing together?
5. How will intelligent networking software for routing and tracking change from current IP networking protocols to address mobile requirements?
6. Will wireless devices play a central role in producing a dialog with the Web?
7. How will Enterprise Information Portals and Web Services contribute to the Intelligent Wireless Web?
8. What is Semantic Web Architecture and will it offer opportunities for intelligent applications?

9. How will intelligent applications using Learning Algorithms and AI be deployed on the Web in combination with either Web Services or Semantic Web Architecture?

10. Is the Intelligent Wireless Web the catalyst that will change the Information Age into the information revolution?

2

Speech Recognition and Understanding

In this chapter, we discuss issues related to speech recognition and understanding, including:

- Man-machine communications
- Voice analysis and language
- Speech/sound recording, compression, and analysis
- Progress and innovations in speech recognition and understanding
- Future directions in speech recognition

How should we communicate with our computer systems to realize maximum efficiencies in information transactions? If talking is the most natural way humans communicate with each other, why not communicate with computers through ordinary speech? After all, we learn to speak before we learn to read and write, and speech is a highly efficient form of communication.

We face a wide range of needs to communicate not only with computers but also with other machines at home and in the work place; and the number and variety of these needs are increasing rapidly. For many different purposes, the use of natural speech greatly improves the effectiveness of our communications. This is especially true for wireless applications because mobile devices are small and awkward to manipulate and have limited capacity for receiving and delivering text or graphical information.

Is this to say that future systems will rely exclusively on the speech interface to wireless handheld devices? Of course not. Future systems should be expected to implement a variety of user interfaces and terminal devices. The mouse and its associated graphical displays will be with us for some time, and there will always be the need to display highly data-intensive visual outputs. Speech-based interfaces represent a new dimension that does not exclude but rather builds upon the methods currently used to interact with computer systems and networks.

◆ Man-Machine Communications

Communication between humans and their machines not only has been the subject of a large amount of technical research but also has provided a topic of choice for many science fiction writers. Work on man-machine interfaces have been carried out since the early development of complex machinery. The need for efficient interface between humans and machines has increased dramatically as machines have become more complex and refined. Today's complex machines, from nuclear reactors to space shuttles and modern computers, require sophisticated interactions with their operators.

Communications with computers, from the earliest days, required input commands that are fashioned from human language. FORTRAN, COBOL, BASIC, C, and so on are referred to as programming languages because they encode computer commands (programming instructions) in word sequences that imitate human language. The vocabulary of these languages is generally taken from spoken language, and the command syntax, though more structured and unambiguous than human language, shares some of its characteristics. No one, however, would confuse a programming language with natural human speech.

Voice Recording and Analysis

The use of real human speech to actively communicate with machines is a relatively recent development. However, voice recording systems for telephone communications represent an interesting precursor to the use of voice to communicate with electronic devices, and voice recording has a long history of development (see the sidebar on page 33).

High-quality voice recorders and voice messaging systems have been with us for several decades. Such systems serve the simple function of providing voice messages to recipients who are not available at the time of the original call.

Initially, many voice recording systems were based on local recording devices using magnetic tape cassettes. Over the years, primarily in business settings, these systems have migrated to local telephone networks that allow more effective message distribution, routing, and storage. More recently, telephone companies have offered centralized voice mail services to corporate as well as private-party customers. New applications have emerged in which voice messages are automatically sent to selected individual telephone subscribers for purposes such as product advertising, soliciting support for political candidates, and requesting charitable contributions.

The use of the human voice to command or provide direction to a machine, however, represents a major departure from these voice recording and messaging systems. In addition, the technical challenges of voice recognition and understanding are substantially greater than those encountered in voice messaging. Over the past several years, several such applications have been commercially produced and are now in regular use. These include voice-activated telephones, automated answering systems with voice activation, and computer software that enables voice-to-text interpretation and text-to-voice synthesis.

Voice-activated telephone systems have been developed and deployed effectively; although, for the most part, they have remained somewhat of a novelty application. The main function of voice activation has been to recognize the name of the individual or location to be called and automatically retrieve and dial the number associated with that name. The use of voice activation for automatic dialing is particularly useful in car phones, where a great benefit is achieved by "hands-free" operation. The distraction caused by manual dialing and operation of cell phones by drivers can be a significant safety hazard to everyone on the road.[1] Voice-activated telephones for

---

1. On June 25, 2001 the New York State Assembly gave final approval to a measure that would make New York the first state to ban the use of handheld cell phones while driving.

Highlights in the History of Voice Recording Technology: From Tinfoil to Digital Magnetic Media

- The recording of sounds in general, and the human voice in particular, dates back at least to the 1870s, when, in 1877, Thomas Edison created his first recording of the human voice on a phonograph using a tinfoil cylinder: "Mary had a little lamb."
- Phonograph (and the related gramophone) recording media evolved over the succeeding decades, progressing from tinfoil to wax, to hard rubber to shellac, to celluloid, and finally to artificial plastics. Cylinders gave way to disks. Vinyl records remained the most popular means of distributing recorded music well into the second half of the twentieth century.
- The use of magnetic media dates back to the first magnetic recorder based on steel wire, patented in 1898 by the Dane Valdemar Poulsen. In the late 1920s, the German Fritz Pfleumer patented the use of magnetic powders on paper, or filmstrips, opening the way for magnetic tape recording.
- The Vocoder was developed and implemented during World War II to allow voice compression, digitization, and encryption. This technology was kept secret for the subsequent 30 years.
- The invention of pulse code modulation (PCM) was a key enabling technology for future digital sampling applications.
- The transition to digital recording took place in the 1980s, with audio compact discs in 1982 and digital audio tape players in 1987.
- As we begin the twenty-first century, digital technology has become commonplace, from telephones to music, voice, and video recording, to electronic data transfers of all types.

home use have found limited success; the primary benefit is the convenience of having the phone system remember and dial preprogrammed numbers. Generally these systems recognize a limited library of prerecorded names and are limited to recognizing the voices of the individuals originally recorded when the library of names was established. Voice activation is now becoming a common feature on new phones.

We are all familiar with interactive telephone system features offered by most businesses that conduct customer interactions by phone, from banks to computer technical support to the telephone service providers. In fact, in many cases, the entire communication is with automated systems and a human operator is not involved at all. At first, these automated systems required the use of the telephone keypad to indicate a choice: "press 1 for option A, or 2 for option B." More recently, voice activation has been added, and a simple "yes" or "no" or "one" or "two" response is solicited and processed for recognition. These simple, one-word or short-phrase voice inputs have proved to be a straightforward substitute for the keypad entry of simple numerical options. The problem of voice recognition is greatly simplified when the range of responses is well defined and limited in number.

Computer software that allows text generation from dictation is readily available and is being rapidly enhanced in the competitive commercial environment. The ability to dictate to a computer or other device and have the dictation instantly converted to text is of particular value to the handicapped, but it is also finding widespread use in many other areas, including the fields of medical and legal practice. Such systems offer interpretation of continuous, natural speech with large vocabularies of words and considerable flexibility and capability to interpret voices from different individuals with significantly different frequency characteristics. For example, some systems are able to adjust to female versus male voice characteristics. Most systems offer the ability to define voice macros that allow insertion of blocks of text from a single command (for example, a complete address based on a simple command), and many permit voice commands for text formatting on the fly (for example, "bold and italicize this word"). In Chapter 8, we will present voice-to-text Web browser technology, including the Speech Synthesis Markup Language (SSML).

Language

Most human communication is through natural language, either written or spoken. Although we easily use language to communicate with each other, there are many obstacles that must be overcome for it to be effective. Differences in dialects, accents, and idiomatic usage are a few of the more obvious problems. Background noise represents another common obstacle to spoken communication. Although the human hearing process is well adapted to discerning meaning from different human voices (no two voices are exactly the same), machine interpretation of human language must deal with these differences. These problems, and others like them, present major challenges for speech recognition software and speech-enabled applications.

Researchers and technology industry leaders have been testing the use of the human voice as a computer interface for many years. Significant research has already been conducted on advancing speech technologies. A new generation of speech-based interfaces for high-performance systems is now beginning to emerge.

Computer stores are now carrying consumer speech-recognition software for dictation. Several available applications allow voice commands for browsers and other programs. And speech-activated phone attendants are used to prompt navigation through menu trees.

The goal of the next generation of speech-based interfaces will be to enable us to communicate with computers in much the same way that we communicate with each other. But this goal must be tackled in two steps. The natural language process is divided into understanding and generation. Understanding involves working out the meaning of the spoken words, starting with word recognition and understanding of the individual words, continuing with interpretation of word combinations and their context, and, finally, comprehending special usages such as colloquial language (see sidebar). Generation is concerned with taking a formal representation of a concept or response and expressing it in a language, such as English. (In this chapter, we focus on language understanding, including speech recognition. We will take up the problem of language generation, including speech synthesis, in Chapter 8 after we discuss device-to-human communication).

Figure 2-1 highlights the requirements of changing our user interfaces from keyboard and mouse to speech-oriented devices such as the microphone headset.

The Process of Going from Speech to Understanding Includes

- Sound-to-word recognition
  - Recognizing voice differences among individuals
  - Isolation and recognition of individual words in continuous speech
  - Discrimination of speech from noise
- Word understanding
  - Resolution of word ambiguity
- Phrase and sentence interpretation
  - Identification of word relationships
  - Resolution of phrase ambiguity
  - Context
- Consideration of idiomatic, colloquial, and slang usage
- Tolerance for human language error

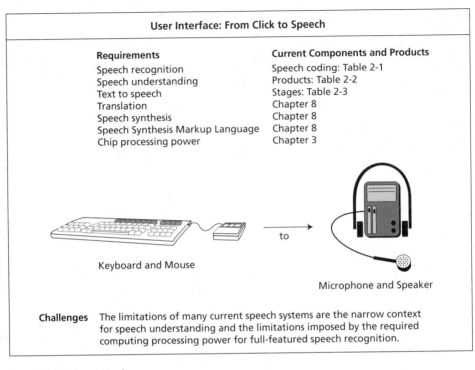

User Interface: From Click to Speech

Requirements	Current Components and Products
Speech recognition	Speech coding: Table 2-1
Speech understanding	Products: Table 2-2
Text to speech	Stages: Table 2-3
Translation	Chapter 8
Speech synthesis	Chapter 8
Speech Synthesis Markup Language	Chapter 8
Chip processing power	Chapter 3

Keyboard and Mouse

to

Microphone and Speaker

Challenges   The limitations of many current speech systems are the narrow context for speech understanding and the limitations imposed by the required computing processing power for full-featured speech recognition.

Figure 2-1   User interface

Speech/Sound Recording, Compression, and Analysis

The actual beginning of digital speech was kept under wraps until 30 years after World War II. During the war, a secret telephone link named Vocoder was established between Winston Churchill, Franklin Roosevelt, and Allied military headquarters on five continents. The Vocoder allowed sufficient compression of speech signals that it could be digitized at 1,551bps and subsequently encrypted. The Vocoder has spawned many other methods of speech compression, such as linear predictive coding (LPC) and code excited linear prediction (CELP). See sidebar on page 37.

Today, digital signals can be processed by a sensor and recognized by a computer. The treatment of sensor data is termed *signal processing*. The computer tries to "understand" what a natural signal "means" through the process of pattern recognition and analysis. Emergence of fast algorithms, such as the Fast Fourier Transform, transistors, integrated circuits, and the computer chip, have made sophisticated signal processing a present reality.

The term *speech coding* refers to the process of representing speech signals either directly as a waveform or indirectly as a set of parameters resulting from some analysis of the input waveform. In digitizing speech, the signal (which is continuous in time and amplitude) is sampled at a certain rate and each sample is represented using a certain number of bits. Speech energy falls off dramatically for frequencies above 4KHz; for practical purposes, virtually all the speech information is carried at frequencies below 3.5KHz. Because of this, a speech sampling rate of 8KHz is typical for use in digitized speech applications.

The two major types of speech coding are the waveform coding methods and the parametric coding methods. Waveform coders attempt to represent speech in a digitized form that is close to the original signal on a sample-to-sample basis. The earliest and most widely used form of waveform coding is the technique known as *pulse code modulation* (PCM). Speech sampling for today's telephone landline networks typically use the PCM method with 8-bit sampling and a transmission rate of 64kbps.

To address the problem of bandwidth limitations in the world's growing telecommunications systems, especially for satellite links, it was recognized that it would be beneficial to reduce the 64kbps transmission rate required for PCM transmission. This need for a lower bit rate speech sampling led to the development of new

LPC and CELP Speech Analysis Algorithms

- Linear predictive coding (LPC) and code excited linear prediction (CELP) are techniques for speech recording, representation, compression, and analysis that have been widely used in applications that require low bit rate transfers (2,400 and 4,800bps).
- LPC is based on a model of human speech in which the glottis (the space between the vocal cords) emits basic sounds defined in terms of intensity (loudness) and frequency (pitch); these sounds are then subjected to resonances as they pass through the vocal tract. These resonances are known as *formants*.
- LPC analyzes speech by estimating the formants, removing their effect from the speech signal (through a process termed *reverse filtering*), and recognizing the remaining signal as a residue. The analysis results in the decomposition of the speech signal into two components, formants and residue. This representation of the speech (formants and residue) can then be transferred, stored, or processed.
- The reverse process then recreates LPC speech: the residue is the basis for the source signal; the filter is based on the formants; and speech results from the process of running the source through the filter.
- To capture the rapidly varying sounds that are characteristic of speech, LPC speech analysis is carried out on small time clips of speech, known as *frames,* usually at rates of 30 to 50 frames per second.
- The desire to encode the residue more efficiently than in LPC, without significantly increasing the bit rate, has resulted in the development of methods that use a code book to define codes for typical signals instead of sending the residue itself. Such methods use the decoded residue to "excite" the formant filter; these methods are therefore termed *code excited linear prediction* (CELP).
- U.S. Federal Standard 1015 (NATO STANAG 4198) is the standard for the LPC algorithm. U.S. Federal Standard 1016 addresses CELP.
- Modifications to CELP have been implemented to increase the bit rate substantially beyond the 4,800bps standard, up to 16kbps.

techniques that encoded the difference between adjacent samples or the difference between the current sample and a predicted value of the current sample based on previous samples. Adjacent speech samples are highly correlated; therefore predicted values tend to have a small error. This approach is termed the *differential PCM* (DPCM) approach. The DPCM and the PCM successor, *adaptive differential PCM* (ADPCM), methods offer good speech coding quality with substantially lower bandwidth requirement. Even so, this is not used extensively by landline.

Parametric speech coders analyze the speech signal to extract parameters that are appropriate to represent the speech with sufficient quality for a given bit rate. Generally these methods are based on a biological model of speech (see the sidebar on page 37) and use predictive models to estimate the characteristics of the vocal tract function and thereby obtain the spectral envelope of the speech signal.

By far the most popular parametric speech coding technique is the CELP technique. Table 2-1 provides information on CELP and several other speech coding techniques in use.

Table 2-1 Speech Coding Techniques

Type of Use	Method	Transmission Rate	Quality
Wireline communications	PCM: Pulse code modulation	64kbps	Telecommunications or wireline quality
	ADPCM: Adaptive differential pulse code modulation	32kbps	
Cellular communications	VSELP: Vector sum excited linear predictor (North America cellular)	8kbps	Cellular quality
	RPE-LTP: Residual pulse excited long-term predictor (GSM full rate standard)	13kbps	
Minimum for communications	CELP: Code excited linear predictor	4.8kbps	Communications quality (perceptible degradation)
	LPC: Linear predictive coding	2.4kbps	Intelligible quality (loss of speaker identity and naturalness)

◆ Speech Recognition and Understanding

IBM, Lernout & Hauspie,[2] Dragon Systems,[3] Philips, and AT&T Bell Labs pioneered the use of speech recognition systems. Major research efforts are ongoing at various institutes, including MIT, SRI, Microsoft, and Bell Labs. The current commercialized technology is employed in such applications as speech-to-text document preparation and virtual assistant services that allow users to request news and stock quotes. Table 2-2 summarizes some of the current products, research projects, and capabilities. The broad variety of different offerings, capabilities, and research directions is evident from the number and types of products and is indicative of the major emphasis being placed on speech technology. It is expected that the speech recognition industry will be a multibillion-dollar industry by 2003. Speech recognition can be expected to be seen in virtually every segment of consumer technology, from car navigation systems, to television voice control, to control of devices for household security and comfort.

However, significant difficulties remain in the development of speech systems of the future. The human voice is distinctive, and many words sound alike but have different spellings and meanings. These problems present challenges for speech recognition software and speech-enabled applications.

The problem of determining the meaning of spoken commands is a difficult one. As mentioned in Chapter 1, two approaches have commonly been used to address this problem. The first uses matching algorithms to evaluate the digitized bit patterns that represent speech utterances and compare them with standard bit patterns stored in a library maintained by the speech recognition system. This approach is used most often in discrete speech applications. The library of bit patterns is created and maintained by averaging the patterns of a diverse set of pronunciations of a given vocabulary.

Near-term and Current Speech Technology Applications

- Messaging
- Voice-activated speakerphone (home, cell, automobile)
- Dictation
  - Text preparation
  - Medical record keeping
  - Legal document preparation
- Language translation
- Commands to structured software systems
  - Web browser
  - Window navigation
  - Spreadsheets
- Automated travel arrangements
- Voice-activated banking
- Speaker identification/verification
- Car navigation
- Voice-activated frequency selection for aircraft navigation
- Voice-activated computer-aided design (CAD)
- E-mail generation and response
- Voice-activated control of home security and comfort
- Stock quoting and other financial transactions

---

2. Lernout & Hauspie filed for bankruptcy protection in November 2000.
3. Dragon Systems, Inc. was acquired by Lernout & Hauspie in June 2000.

Table 2-2 Selected Current Speech Products and Capabilities

Developer/ Supplier	Application/ Product	Highlights and Web Locations
Apple	Macintosh Operating System	Speech recognition features are incorporated into the Mac OS, including speaker independence, flexible vocabulary that can be customized, the ability to function accurately in real-world environments using a "push-to-talk" feature, and recognition of continuous speech. http://www.apple.com/macos/speech/
AT&T- Lucent- Bell Labs	Lucent Speech Server/ VoiceXML Interpreter	Speech server capability offering automatic speech recognition, text-to-sound, and speaker verification. Subscribers interact, with the VoiceXML interpreter creating a bridge between the voice network and the Internet. VoiceXML interpreter allows Web content to be provided over the telephone. http://www.lucent.com
	AT&T Network Watson	AT&T Network Watson is a software product that supports client/server automatic speech recognition, speaker verification, and text-to-speech synthesis. Network Watson is available under license from AT&T to selected network platform suppliers. http://www.research.att.com/projects/watson/
Automated Voice Systems, Inc. (AVSI)	Mastervoice Butler-in-a-Box	Provides voice control for home electrical and electronic devices, including lights, stereo, TV, coffeemaker, heating and cooling systems, and security systems. Can be trained in any language; distinguishes which of up to four users is speaking. B System also serves as a voice-activated speakerphone/telephone with stored numbers and call waiting. http://www.mastervoice.com/
Canadian National Research Council	Direct Voice Input	Speech recognition technology allows helicopter pilots to issue voice commands (such as radio frequency [RF] changes) without manually keying in commands. Designed to operate in high-noise environment with limited vocabulary (approximately 300 words) and speaker dependence.
Command Corp. Inc.	IN CUBE Voice Command	Voice macro command software for performance of repetitive tasks. Continuous speech recognition engine used for window navigation, CAD, and publishing applications. http://www.commandcorp.com/cci/incube_welcome.html
Daimler- Chrysler Research Institute	TEMIC Speech Processing	TEMIC provides speaker-independent recognition using Hidden Markov Models (statistical approach). No user profiles or preceding training sessions are necessary. It also provides speaker-dependent recognition using dynamic time warping algorithms for user-trainable vocabularies. Noise reduction is achieved through integrated signal preprocessing to reduce the influence of noise and other sources of interference and to improve the quality of recognition.

Table 2-2   Selected Current Speech Products and Capabilities (*continued*)

Developer/ Supplier	Application/ Product	Highlights and Web Locations
Daimler-Chrysler Research Institute (*continued*)	TEMIC Speech Processing	TEMIC also provides for "break in" to allow for intentional interruption of a dialog during a voice output. The software adapts itself to the characteristics of the speaker's voice, the telephone line, or the acoustic background within vehicles and is able to recognize keywords in a naturally spoken sentence (word spotting). http://www.starrec.com/
Dragon Systems (recently purchased by Lernout & Hauspie)	Naturally Speaking	Speech recognition software for continuous speech recognition. Incorporates high accuracy rates, large vocabularies, and special features for correction, editing, and spelling out words not in the vocabulary. Different versions of the software are designed for different markets such as medical, legal, and so on. http://www.dragonsys.com/
DVI	VoicePower VoiceWave SpeechPower	DVI was the first major digital dictation vendor to market a product designed specifically for Windows NT, VoicePower. Their VoiceWave product is used by medical centers, transcription services, and law enforcement agencies. In September 2000, DVI entered into an alliance with Philips for integration of digital dictation and speech recognition. http://www.dvi.com/
IBM	Via Voice	Software for document creation from voice input. Provides for utilization of standard document formats and specialized vocabularies. Also allows voice commands for Web browsing and other software applications. http://www-4.ibm.com/software/speech/
Kurzweil (Kurzweil was acquired by Lernout & Hauspie in 1997)	VoicePlus/ VoicePro	The first commercially marketed large vocabulary speech recognition application. Provided discrete speech recognition at 60 to 80 words per minute. Provided voice control for many Windows applications, including word processing, spreadsheets, e-mail, menu and dialog boxes, and Windows desktop commands. VoicePro is the professional (medical, legal, engineering) version of VoicePlus.
Lernout & Hauspie (Currently under bankruptcy protection)	Elan text-to-speech (TTS)	Elan TTS translates text into speech; it reads texts out loud, with the flexibility and richness of natural-sounding speech. Provides for multilingual voice-enabled services such as e-mail reading over the phone, interactive games, car navigation aids, and traffic information. http://www.elantts.com/
	L & H Voice Xpress	Voice Xpress is a family of continuous speech recognition products providing natural language voice dictation for control of word processors, spreadsheets, e-mail, calendars, money management online programs, and Web browsers. http://www.lhsl.com/voicexpress/

Table continued on next page.

Table 2-2   Selected Current Speech Products and Capabilities (*continued*)

Developer/ Supplier	Application/ Product	Highlights and Web Locations
Microsoft Research	Dr. Who WhisperID WhisperLM	Technology projects supporting and leading to the vision of a fully speech-enabled computer. Dr. Who uses continuous speech recognition and spoken language understanding. Dr. Who is designed to power a voice-based pocket PC with a Web browser, e-mail, and cellular telephone capabilities. Whisper speech recognition system is a current state-of-the-art speech recognizer. WhisperLM is a language-modeling project; WhisperID is a speaker identification module. http://www.research.microsoft.com/research/srg/
Philips Speech Processing	Free Speech 2000, SpeechMagic, and a variety of other speech processing products	Includes a PC-based speech recognition package enabling keyboard-free document creation; application control and navigation of the PC desktop with natural language commands; multilanguage dictation capability, including a range of languages; and Web surfing with voice feature. Philips Speech Processing has 22 languages available for the SpeechPearl and SpeechMania products. http://www.speech.philips.com/
Sensory, Inc.	VoiceActivation	Noise-tolerant speech recognition, including speaker-independent or speaker-dependent, speech prompting, speech verification, and audio record and playback. Word spotting recognizes words embedded in sentences in parallel or series and allows the creation of a natural language user-friendly voice interface. http://www.sensoryinc.com/
SRI Speech Technology and Research Laboratory	DECIPHER	Ongoing research efforts in speech recognition. DECIPHER system is capable of recognizing natural, continuous speech without requiring the user to train the system in advance (that is, speaker-independent recognition); it provides modeling of variations in pronunciation and tolerance of background noise to enable recognition of spontaneous speech of different dialects. Other projects address machine translation, securities trading by speech, and voice banking. http://www.speech.sri.com/
United Research Labs	Voice Action	Wave-to-text, text-to-wave, and e-mail answering machine products. http://www.research-lab.com/
Voxware	Voice Logistics Suite	A noise-robust speech recognition engine that is language, accent, and dialect independent. Includes an innovative client-server software and a distributed, scalable Web-based architecture that grows with the customer's operations. Also includes a rugged, portable hardware platform with a built-in 2.4GHz wireless LAN radio that supports full worker mobility on the warehouse floor. http://www.voxware.com/

Table 2-2 Selected Current Speech Products and Capabilities (*continued*)

Developer/ Supplier	Application/ Product	Highlights and Web Locations
Wizzard Software	Interactive Voice Assistant (IVA) and related products	Uses speech recognition and other intelligent interface technologies; allows user to talk to personal assistant and hear its immediate response with information such as stock quotes and e-mail dictation. Includes dictation and translation capabilities. http://www.wizzardsoftware.com/

The second approach involves "training" of the speech software to recognize speech patterns of the individual users. It also employs statistical modeling and libraries of word and grammar rules to increase its accuracy and responsiveness. Such speech recognition applications require vocabulary databases that may incorporate 60,000 to 200,000 words and grammar rules.

The accuracy of speech recognition has increased dramatically over the past several decades (see Figure 2-2). Current speech recognition software providers claim accuracies of up to 95 percent; however, this is generally under ideal conditions.

Although the objective of speech recognition is accuracy as close to 100 percent as possible, the highly variable nature of human speech makes this impossible. In fact, even human speech recognition falls short of this goal. When considering the diversity of confounding factors (speaker characteristics, vocabulary size, noise, accents, and dialectic differences, etc.), it is not surprising that achieving accuracies greater than 90 percent usually requires that the speech situation be constrained in one or more ways. When highly constrained, accuracies of 99 percent may be accomplished; where speech recognition is limited to a single individual's voice with a large vocabulary, accuracies between 90 percent and 95 percent may be seen in commercial products. For situations involving multiple different speakers using different recording channels (and associated noise background) and large vocabularies, accuracies below 90 percent should be expected, and processing times can be much greater than the real-time duration of speech.

Speech Recognition

Early speech recognition efforts focused on identification of words spoken in isolation, which is termed *discrete speech recognition*. Where words are spoken discretely

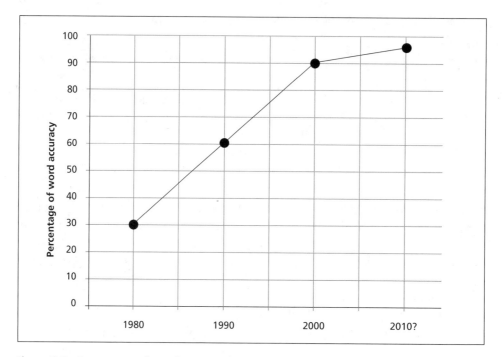

Figure 2-2   Percentage of word accuracy by speech recognition

by a single speaker and are limited to a small vocabulary of a few hundred words chosen to avoid similar sounds, highly accurate recognition is relatively easy to achieve. The difficulty of speech recognition increases greatly when multiple speakers are allowed, when large vocabularies are included, and, of course, when continuous speech is encountered.

Several approaches have been used to recognize speech in these more challenging circumstances. In cases in which speech is being directly converted to text (i.e., "speech-to-text" or dictation), each word must be individually recognized and correctly represented, and this demands a word-based approach. Other applications may focus on the basic sounds, or phonemes, that make up speech. Word spotting allows the identification of particular words in speech, and this is especially useful when the application involves dialog in which the speech is structured as keywords interspersed among "noise." Because much of natural speech comprises meaningless sounds such as "um" and "uh," other unintended sounds or false starts, and words that are not crucial to the task, word spotting ignores this part of the speech and is therefore very tolerant of relaxed speech styles.

One of the most important factors in understanding speech is the context within which the speech is being used. Highly structured dialogs channel and simplify the recognition problem by constraining responses to limited numbers of possibilities. Before general-purpose speech recognizers are practical, there will undoubtedly be many separate systems that are implemented for particular purposes. For example, a speech-enabled calculator provides a useful and limited sample application for speech recognition. With such an application, the commands are limited to a very few possibilities (numbers and arithmetic function commands).

Another limited application that has been considered for many years and may be approaching practical commercialization is the speech-enabled travel agent. As long ago as 1980, Bell Laboratories set up a demonstration system to illustrate the potential for a future commercial airline reservation service based on speech recognition;[4] more recently, Michael Dertouzos[5] illustrated the Massachusetts Institute of Technology (MIT) vision of future voice-operated systems using a travel reservation system currently under development and nearing commercial viability. The reason the travel reservation process is likely to be one of the earliest examples of commercialized speech recognition is that the dialog is fairly well constrained and is therefore amenable to near-term implementation.

Speech Representation, Storage, Transmission, and Analysis

A key factor in the use of voice in communicating with computers is the technology for representing, storing, transmitting, and analyzing speech. From the early years of voice recording, the only option for representing speech was to store the voice signal in its analog form. The storage of analog voice on magnetic media, such as magnetic tape or drums, was a commonly used method. Storage on photographic film also has a long history, especially with sound for motion pictures. Digital representation has radically improved options for storage, transmission, and analysis of speech.

Speech Understanding

Four stages are involved in understanding or deciphering spoken language. The first stage is speech recognition. It is the process of translating the speech signals into a sequence of recognized words. Once this sequence of words has been obtained, the

---

4. S. E. Levinson and K. L. Shipley. "A Conversational-mode Airline Information and Reservation System Using Speech Input and Output." *Bell System Technical Journal* 59(1):119–137, 1980.
5. M. Dertouzos. *The Unfinished Revolution: Human Centered Computers and What They Can Do for Us.* HarperCollins, 2001.

understanding process proceeds, with three subsequent stages: syntactic analysis, semantic analysis, and pragmatics. We summarize these stages in Table 2-3.

The speech recognition process starts with an analog signal from a microphone or other input device that can be split into different frequencies using special filters. The energy in each frequency can be measured and plotted on a frequency spectrogram against time. The next step is matching the frequency spectrogram with corresponding words. All human languages use a small number (40 to 50) of basic sounds termed *phonemes* (for example, the "a" sound in cat); thus we can obtain a complete library of frequency spectrograms, or templates, for each phoneme. The process is now to match speech fragments with the library templates. If two sounds are spoken at different speeds, a process called dynamic time warping (DTW) is used to correct for differences.

Then we use the phonemes to build words. Finding which words are spoken involves statistical analysis to determine between possible phonetic similarities. These statistical methods usually involve a technique named Hidden Markov Modeling. See sidebar on page 47.

The main difficulty is that there is no simple mapping between speech signals and words, because different speakers may pronounce a given word differently. In addition, because there is virtually no gap between words in normal speech, it is difficult to distinguish beginnings and endings of words.

The output of a speech recognizer is just a sequence of words. Syntactic analysis helps to understand how the words are grouped into meaningful phrases and sentences. This process uses syntactic rules to deduce the proper structure of the sentence. Rules of syntax specify possible word organizations and lead to determining the most likely

Table 2-3   Four Stages of Speech Understanding

Stage	Description
Speech recognition	Converts the raw speech signals into a sequence of words spoken.
Syntactic analysis	Analyzes the sequence of words using language grammar and sentence structure.
Semantic analysis	Uses information about sentence structure and word definitions to form partial meaning of the whole sentence.
Pragmatic analysis	Uses context—when, who, and where—to form a representation of the sentence meaning.

sentence structure. This set of rules is referred to as a grammar for the language. In addition, a parser is used to break the sentence structure up into possible organizations focusing on the most appropriate grammar formalism. The parse tree organizes the structure groupings.

The remaining stages of analysis are semantics and pragmatics. These final stages are concerned with getting at the *meaning* of a sentence. Semantics seeks a way to give meaning to the entire sentence, and pragmatics evaluates context. In the first stage (semantics), the possible syntactic structure(s) of the sentence and the meanings of the words in the sentence are used to establish a partial or tentative representation of the meaning. In the second stage, the meaning is further pinned down based on evaluation of connecting or *contextual* information.

Examples of Voice Activation

Many people use cell phones today, and thanks to advances in speech recognition, text-to-voice, and XML technology, voice portal applications are entering the business and consumer markets. These services bring the power of the Internet and corporate networks to the telephone. For example, cell phones today can access the Web, retrieve e-mail, and check stock quotes.

Several voice portals are available that are geared toward consumers, offering data such as information for movies and driving directions. Tellme (www.tellme.com) provides information such as listings of local restaurants, entertainment content, and stock quotes via a menu. By dialing the toll-free number, you can obtain verbal driving directions, weather reports, and sports updates—all available in a variety of voice patterns. BeVocal (www.bevocal.com) is a voice-activated service similar to Tellme. The virtual operator can provide flight information and other conveniences. These speech recognition capabilities still require patience. Both Conita PVA (www.conita.com) and SANDi (www.soundadvantage.com) provide voice messaging services, retrieval of stock quotes, and weather information.

Hidden Markov Modeling

The Hidden Markov Model is a widely and successfully used tool in statistical modeling and statistical pattern recognition. Over the years, it has become the predominant speech model used in automatic speech recognition. The main reason for this success is its ability to characterize speech signals in a way that can be represented mathematically.

In a typical Hidden Markov Model–based speech system, the voice signal undergoes a preprocessing (parameter extraction) stage. The resulting output is a discrete time sequence of parameter vectors, and this is the input to the Hidden Markov Model process.

The Hidden Markov Model uses a finite set of *states*, each of which is associated with a (generally multidimensional) probability distribution. Transitions among the states are governed by a set of probabilities termed *transition probabilities.* Given a particular state, an outcome or *observation* is assigned according to the associated probability distribution. It is only the outcome, not the state, that is visible to an external observer, and therefore states are "hidden"; hence the name Hidden Markov Model.

◆ Future Trends

Speech recognition and understanding technologies have received a high level of attention and have been the focus of considerable research and development over the past several decades. The advances to date have been substantial, but the complexity of automatic speech recognition when conditions are not highly constrained represents a significant continuing challenge.

Improvement of speech recognition technologies is being supported in a large number of research initiatives in the United States and internationally with private and public funding. For example, research at the University of Washington is addressing speaker tracking and other issues associated with the recording of meetings; Carnegie Mellon University is studying intelligent speech interfaces to enable complex problem solving with voice as the man-machine interface.

The large number of commercial products that are now on the market and the diversity of research initiatives that are underway testify not only to the great interest that speech technology generates but also to its importance as a critical feature of future consumer products. On the other hand, we seem to be at a turning point, where many specialized applications are available but the technology has not yet entered the mainstream. We can expect this to change dramatically over the next few years as new technologies are introduced (for example, chips with expanded processing power) and, more importantly, as the results of key projects are released by research organizations at MIT, Microsoft, and other major laboratories. As processor chips achieve speeds of 2GHz or more they are only beginning to offer the processing power required by quality speech recognition. Nanotechnology will extend the life of existing silicon technology for another decade. By 2007, Intel expects to have a 1-billion-transistor chip making complex voice commands and language translation readily accessible.

Speech recognition and understanding must be viewed as something more than just a novel and limited interface. When the use of natural speech is seen as a primary means to achieving the goal of information technology access any time, anywhere, speech recognition will move to the center stage of essential technologies. This implies that speech recognition will become a prominent feature in mobile wireless devices that connect individuals on the move to computational devices at remote locations.

In considering the present popularity of mobile wireless communications and computing, it is clear that we are currently experiencing a phenomenon of technology expansion and radiation. From Palm Pilots to Web-enabled paging devices; pocket computers; and voice-activated, Internet-enabled cell phones, we are being inundated with a growing selection of specialized devices. Technology convergence has begun to appear as cell phones become Web enabled and pagers provide e-mail access. Ultimately, it is likely that multipurpose personal, mobile, wireless devices will emerge to provide the any time, anywhere access of the future. But what does this imply for speech recognition?

The problem of how to obtain speech recognition functionality in a handheld device is quite challenging. Certainly, it is not an intractable problem for a handheld device (for example, a cell phone) that performs limited speech recognition activities (for example, voice-activated dialing). But as the demands for speech functionality grow with the greater complexity of the speech recognition tasks, it becomes increasingly difficult to provide these capabilities on a small, mobile wireless device with limited capabilities. Therefore the problem becomes one of distributing the capability for speech ability between the local wireless device and a remote processing system to which it is connected.

This problem is currently being addressed in far-reaching research at several places, most notably at the MIT Laboratory of Computer Science and at Microsoft Research. The Microsoft effort is directed at technology projects supporting and leading to the vision of a fully speech-enabled computer. Dr. Who uses continuous speech recognition and spoken language understanding. It is designed to power a voice-based pocket PC with a Web browser, e-mail, and cellular telephone capabilities.

Perhaps the most promising initiative, however, is the MIT Laboratory for Computer Science initiative named Oxygen. This visionary effort is developing a comprehensive system to achieve any time, anywhere computing. In this concept, a user carries a wireless interface device that is continuously connected to a network of computing devices in a manner similar to the way cell phone communications maintain continuous connection to a communications network. The local device is speech enabled, and much of the speech recognition capability is embedded in the remote system of high-capability computers.

At the MIT Laboratory for Computer Science, systems for conversional interface are being developed. The machines are currently capable of communicating in several languages and can answer queries in real time. The speech-based applications use an architecture named Galaxy. It is a distributed architecture that can retrieve data from several different domains of knowledge to answer a query. Galaxy has five main functions: speech recognition, language understanding, information retrieval, language generation, and speech synthesis.

Speech recognition may be an ideal interface for the handheld devices being developed as part of Project Oxygen. But Project Oxygen will need far more advanced speech recognition systems to achieve its ultimate objective of enabling interactive conversation with full understanding.

◆ Challenges and Opportunities

Speech recognition technology has advanced considerably over the past several decades. Interest in speech recognition evidenced by ongoing research activities and the introduction of a broad expanse of commercial products attests to the fact that automated speech recognition remains a topic of great interest and potential. For the full promise of speech recognition to be realized, several challenges must be overcome, including the limitations of many current systems that require narrow context for speech understanding and the limitations imposed by the required computing processing power for full-featured speech recognition. This latter limitation is especially important as we attempt to introduce speech recognition into small, mobile, handheld devices that are by their nature limited in size and computational capability.

The opportunities for speech recognition are both technical and commercial. The remaining technical limitations of speech recognition, in addition to the hardware challenges of supplying adequate computational capabilities in small devices (see Chapter 3), involve the software aspects of speech recognition technology. The development of speech understanding capabilities (as opposed to the simpler task of recognition) remains a challenging area that is open to technological creativity. Commercial opportunities follow the technology innovations, but we should expect that speech technology will be increasingly used and accepted over the next five to ten years through diverse applications that include telephone transactions, speech-based dictation and report generation, automobile navigator systems, and speech control of home appliances and security systems.

◆ Conclusion

In this chapter, we presented man-machine communications; speech/sound recording, compression, and analysis; and progress and innovations in speech recognition and understanding. In addition, we reviewed future directions in speech recognition. Although we may expect speech interfaces to permeate society steadily, we anticipate that successful traditional interfaces will have continued use for a considerable time, particularly for high-power applications. From this chapter, you may conclude that

▸ The technologies for speech coding and analysis developed for digital communications have become the norm.

▸ Speech recognition and understanding have been implemented in a broad variety of commercial applications. These applications, however, are generally limited in scope.

▸ We can expect, within the next few years, that speech recognition and understanding applications will become increasing capable, enabling their use as part of the Intelligent Wireless Web.

PART II

Connecting Devices to Devices

In Part II, we present how devices will communicate with other devices. We can think of the focus shifting from being person-centric to being machine-centric—in other words, focused upon machine-to-machine communications.

We start in Chapter 3 by presenting the specifics of your own Personal Space and its communication infrastructure within the wireless personal area network. In Chapter 4, we preview the global communication infrastructure of inter-lacing networks and how wired and wireless networks are merging. Finally, in Chapter 5, we provide the basics of wireless protocols and standards between devices. This demonstrates how the mobile wireless networks and the Web are merging.

3

Wireless Personal Area Networks

In this chapter, we present the concepts of Personal Space, "nomadic" or mobile software, and Ubiquitous Computing as the ingredients for developing wireless personal area networks (WPAN), and we address the related questions:

- How will we use small handheld and embedded devices in the office and at home?
- How available and widespread will computer resources become?

With billions of various devices already in use today, developing multipurpose communications that can receive and transmit compatible signals is a daunting challenge. At the local level, Personal Area Networks (PANs) form device-to-device interfaces at work and at home. At the global level, we must adapt an interlacing complex of networks to connect compatibly to a large number of possible device-to-device combinations.

◆ Personal Space

Imagine living your entire life within the confines of the region that surrounds you. You could call this region your Personal Space. As you travel from home to work, this region travels with you, just like a bubble. If you look around this space, how many electronic devices would you see? How many wires would exist? With every new electronic device, you add to the "cable tangle" at both the office and home. Wireless technology offers connectivity among these devices within your Personal Space without the encumbering tangle.

Wirelessly connected devices create a promising new network infrastructure termed a Wireless Personal Area Network (WPAN). In the hierarchy of networking that includes wide area network (WAN), metropolitan area network (MAN), and local area network (LAN), the WPAN's scope is the smallest and least developed.

In March of 1999, the Institute of Electrical and Electronic Engineering (IEEE) 802.15 was formalized by the WPAN Working Group. The working group's goal was to define a wireless communications standard for a PAN, focusing on low power consumption, small size, and low cost.

The first obvious application of a WPAN is in the office workspace. With this technology, your essential workspace electronic devices will be wirelessly networked together. These could include your desktop computer, portable computer, printer, handheld device, mobile phone, pager, and so on. Your personal devices will wirelessly update your appointment calendar on your office personal computer (PC). You will have greater flexibility in arranging your office because peripherals will not need to be within cable length of the PC. The less obvious applications of a WPAN are uses outside of the office such as at your home and public places. The growth of home automation and smart appliances will require WPAN applications just as in the office. And public places with embedded devices will seek to connect to your mobile devices as you pass by.

In today's environment, information is one of our most valuable commodities. In an electronic future with smaller, cheaper, and more powerful devices, the speed and convenience at which information is accessible will become increasingly more important. Creating a WPAN of our immediately available devices will enable a future in which a lifetime of knowledge may be accessed through gateways worn on the body or placed within our Personal Space.

WPAN will also allow devices to work together and share each other's information and services. For example, a Web page can be called up on a small screen and then wirelessly sent to a printer for full-size printing. A WPAN can even be created in a vehicle via devices such as wireless headsets, microphones, and speakers for communications. Additional wireless devices may eventually be embedded throughout public places to provide continuous connectivity as you travel within your Personal Space from one location to another.

As envisioned, WPAN will allow the user to customize his or her communications capabilities, enabling everyday devices to become smart, tetherless devices that spontaneously communicate whenever they are in close proximity. We will come back to our discussion of Personal Space later in this chapter, within the context of Ubiquitous Computing.

Proliferating Personal Devices

Paradoxically, the more the demands of modern life encourage us to move about, the more we need to stay in touch with the people and places we leave behind. The wireless devices emerging today will help keep us connected in an increasingly mobile future.

Consumers have been skeptical about introducing new "labor-saving" converged devices into their computer systems because it seems that they are simply replacing the complexity of the multiple appliances and applications with increased complexity of their PC system. Why introduce something new when things work well in the old configuration? A compelling case for changing can be made only when the new configuration and capabilities are significantly better than the old configuration and the difficulty of implementation is minimal. Until such obstacles can be overcome, it will continue to be difficult to achieve the promise of new devices that, in theory, offer significant improvements in performance and ease of use.

A variety of companies have come up with appliances that combine functions for access to the Internet, digital video disc (DVD), and television. But the question about these devices is whether they do any one thing exceptionally well. Although most American homes have many appliances, there is little evidence to date that people want to replace them with combination appliances representing technology convergence.

It appears that the Japanese consumer tends to embrace converged devices, partly because space is at a premium in Japanese homes. The success of the Japanese Internet-capable I-mode cell phones has led product designers to attempt to combine Internet functionality, videoconferencing, games, and everything else into devices resembling old-style cell phones. But the success of these devices in Japan should not necessarily be seen as indicative of broader, automatic, global acceptance.

Aside from design flaws, converged devices used for access to e-mail and other Internet applications generally operate at slow speeds and are not well matched to devices such as cell phones. As a result, access to such applications on cell phone-like devices can be very frustrating to the user. The United States is moving slowly in establishing standards for high-speed wireless Internet while awaiting improved bandwidth capabilities.

The current selection of personal devices offering wireless connectivity includes pagers, cell phones, handheld computers, personal digital assistants (PDAs), and notebook PCs. As wireless technology evolves, these devices are converging in appearance and function. You can find pagers with keyboards, handheld devices that function as phones, phones that function as PDAs, and notebooks that do it all.

With the limited space on a cell phone keypad and display, putting more functions into the same space is a recipe for greater complexity. Web-capable cell phones might be important in the future, particularly when they are combined with the features of PDAs such as Palm devices; however, the user interface issues must be carefully considered. Indeed the user interface cries out for supplementing the keyboard and mouse with touch-screen display and microphone headsets systems capable of speech recognition.

Internet-enabled cellular phones, often referred to as Internet phones, place the Internet in your palm. Sprint PC and Verizon currently offer services that can deliver news articles, access Web sites, provide stock information, check airline schedules, and order items. To connect to the Internet, you launch the phone's minibrowser, usually at 14.4kbps. The minibrowser implements a simple text menu for compatibility with the limitations of the phone's capabilities for input and output.

Pagers also connect to the Internet to send and receive digital messages, thereby becoming two-way communication devices. Incoming messages generate a ring or other message notification alarm and show an onscreen message. Outgoing messages transmit across wireless networks, typically at 6kbps. Many wireless paging networks partner with content providers to deliver sports and stock information. Many pagers have built-in keyboards. Manufacturers such as Motorola and Compaq sell the devices, and wireless Internet service providers (ISPs), such as GoAmerica, PageNet, or SkyTel, offer connection services for monthly fees.

Internet connectivity is finally becoming a feature of handheld computers and PDAs in two ways. The device either contains an integrated wireless modem or it provides for an external connector to a wireless modem. For example, the Palm VIIx provides an integrated wireless modem. Just turn on the device and open the application to establish an active Internet connection. On the other hand, the iPAQ H3600 from Compaq supports a proprietary PC card expansion pack for an external modem connection. No dial-up is needed, and the transmission speed is typically at up to 19.2kbps. Monthly service providers, such as GoAmerica and OmniSky, support these wireless devices.

The communication applications on a notebook computer are typically more sophisticated than those of other mobile handheld devices. Unfortunately, the present state of wireless Internet access at 19.2kbps greatly limits Web site access functionality. The Sprint PCS enhanced Internet connection service uses compression technology to mimic 56kbps transmission speeds. The Metricom Ricochet network is developing speeds up to 128kbps in 41 U.S. cities in 2001. We will present evolving bandwidth capabilities in Chapters 4 and 5.

Many individuals are continually juggling multiple career and lifestyle responsibilities and schedules. Mobility dictates a constant need for access to organizational tools and resources. The need to use the power of a computer can occur in the street, at home, on travel overseas, in a classroom, in a car, or just about any time and anywhere.

If you lead the life of a mobile professional, you need to access e-mail, write memos, and check the status of business matters on the run rather than from behind your desktop PC or from a static location where hard-wired access is available. Professionals in a variety of fields, including doctors, managers, lawyers, healthcare workers, educators, journalists, sales representatives, and consultants, have a compelling need for mobile access. The convenience of handheld devices provides one of the first steps toward the new mobile freedoms that all workers can enjoy.

Figure 3-1 illustrates how requirements for your future Personal Space are related to elements of WPANs, as presented in the tables in this chapter and discussion further in this book. It relates the requirements and challenges of Personal Space with the products and components being developed.

A wide variety of devices will continue to evolve into a spectrum of capabilities to inhabit our future Person Space. We would like to present a few categories of these devices at their current state of technology, both to gauge their limitations and to provide perspective, as time makes them increasingly obsolete. Table 3-1 provides examples of Pocket PCs and Table 3-2 shows examples of handheld PCs. Table 3-3 presents wireless PDA services. Table 3-4 (on page 64) lists home applications. In addition, there are embedded (e.g., MIT Project Oxygen) and wearable devices under development (see http://www.xybernaut.com; a lightweight computer includes built-in digital-signal processors [DPSs] from Texas Instruments Inc., for

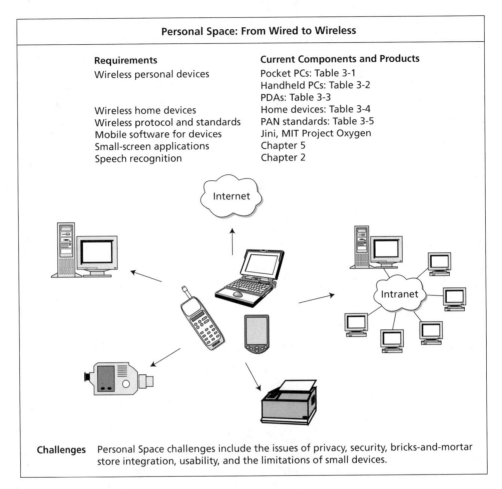

Personal Space: From Wired to Wireless

Requirements	Current Components and Products
Wireless personal devices	Pocket PCs: Table 3-1
	Handheld PCs: Table 3-2
	PDAs: Table 3-3
Wireless home devices	Home devices: Table 3-4
Wireless protocol and standards	PAN standards: Table 3-5
Mobile software for devices	Jini, MIT Project Oxygen
Small-screen applications	Chapter 5
Speech recognition	Chapter 2

Challenges Personal Space challenges include the issues of privacy, security, bricks-and-mortar store integration, usability, and the limitations of small devices.

Figure 3-1 Personal Space

more processing power, a longer-lasting battery, and lighter headgear). Together these tables illustrate the current devices available. The specifications and key characteristics are offered only as a point of departure, because these devices are expected to undergo rapid evolution.

Two problems with all of the devices shown in Tables 3-1 and 3-2 are that not only are their screens small but their resolution remains low. One solution may be larger screens. The extra space could come from a flexible screen that unfolds like a map. Plug it into a pocket PC and you have a workable product. But pocket-size, foldable screen technology is still a few years away. An alternative is "electronic

Table 3-1 Examples of Pocket PCs

	Display (pixels/ inches)	CPU/RAM	Battery/Life/ Operating System	Size (in)/Weight
Askey Piccolo PC010 www.askey.com.tw	240 × 320	8MB RAM	2 AA NiMH/NA	4.9 × 3.35 × 1/8.8 oz
Casco Cassiopeia www.casio.com	240 × 320/8"	150MHz 32MB RAM	L-ion/7 hr/ Windows CE	5.13 × 3.25 × 0.75/ 9 oz
Compaq iPAQ www.compaq.com	240 × 320/3.8"	206MHz 32MB RAM	L-ion/14 hr/ Windows CE	5.13 × 3.11 × 5 / 5.3 oz
HP Jornada www.hp.com	240 × 320/3.8"	133MHZ 16MB RAM	L-ion/8 hr/ Windows CE	5.2 × 3.1 × 0.6/ 9 oz
Symbol PPT www.symbol.com	240 × 320/3.6"	16MB RAM	L-ion/NA	7 × 3.5 × 1/11.6 oz

Table 3-2 Examples of Handheld PCs

	Display (pixels/inches)	CPU/RAM	Battery/Life	Size (in)/Weight
HP Jornada www.hp.com	640 × 240/7.5"	128MHz 16MB RAM	L-ion/ 8 hr	7.4 × 3.7 × 1.3/1.1 lbs
Hitachi HPW www.hitachi.com	640 × 480	128MHz 16MB RAM	L-ion/8 hr	8.7 × 1.2 × 6.3/1.8 lb
Itronix www.itronics.com	640 × 240	74MHz 16MB RAM	L-ion/8–12 hrs	7.5 × 6.1 × 1.4/1.75 lb
NEC Mobile Pro www.neccsd.com	800 × 600	168MHz 32MB RAM	L-ion/8 hr	9.6 × 7.5 × 1/2.6 lb
NTS Dreamwriter It.dreamwriter.com	640 × 480	80 MHz 16MB RAM	NiMH/8 hr	15 × 11 × 2.5/4 lb
Sharp Mobilon www.sharp.com	640 × 480	129MHz 16MB RAM	L-ion/8 hr	9.3 × 7.7 × 1/2.7 lb
Mainstream www.vadem.com	640 × 480/9.4"	168MHz 32MB RAM	L-ion/10 hr	11.25 × 8.75 × 1/3.2 lb

Table 3-3   Wireless PDA services

Device/Service	Portal Used	Type of Modem	Size (HxWxD)	Weight (Ounces)
Palm Vx 800/881 www.palm.com	OmniSky Software	OmniSky	4.96 × 3.0 × 0.9	8.5
Palm VII 800/881 www.palm.com	Palm.Net www.palm.net	Built-in	5.25 × 3.25 × 0.8	6.7
RIM Blackberry 957 www.blackberry.net	GoAmerica	Built-in	4.6 × 3.1 × 0.7	5.3

ink" technology being developed at E. Ink of Cambridge, Massachusetts. Electrostatic charges orient white microscopic particles suspended in tiny spheres. Unfortunately, electronic ink is also several years from practical use. Another approach keeps the display small but offers good resolution using magnifying lenses mounted on monocular units or goggles. Sony's Glasstron and Eye-Trek from Olympus both give the viewer an image equivalent to a 132-cm screen seen from two feet away.

If output over small screens looks troublesome, input is even harder. Just think what it's like using keypads from your cell phone to send typed messages. Certainly several cellular phone manufacturers, including Motorola and Nokia, are trying fledgling speech recognition already, in the form of simple "yes" or "no" responses or in the form of one-word names of stored phone numbers.

Speech recognition and speech synthesis offer attractive solutions to both the input and output limitations of small mobile devices, if their own memory and processing power limitations can be overcome (see Chapters 2 and 8).

Personal Area Networks for the Home

A PAN is composed of the personal devices around us and in our immediate environment. In the office, these devices are work productivity devices that enable us to access to applications, data, text, and images related to performing our jobs. At work, we are more likely to find wireless LAN components and standards (see Chapter 4). At home, however, there is also the need to plug into our work-related problems. But beyond doing office work at home, our home can be a central part of our PAN in the control of home devices and personal applications.

It is amazing how many wireless PAN-type devices we already use. Remote controls for televisions and video cassette recorders (VCRs) can be considered PAN devices. The remote control for your garage door is another. Unfortunately, few of these devices are built to interoperate.

Universal remote controls for televisions or VCRs come with either a list of special codes or a procedure for teaching it how to send commands. This is necessary because there is no way for it to determine what it is talking to, and each device has its own special language for the same commands. This has happened because manufacturers have developed them to proprietary standards rather than agreeing on a common set of communication standards. This is changing, however. Standards are being developing that will allow these devices to speak a common language at the lowest level, and industry-wide standards for command interfaces will allow these devices to finally truly become universal.

Now let's consider what is happening in home networks today and how they will integrate with WPANs in the near future. Most of the subsystems and devices in and around the home can be connected and automated on a home network, and there is increasing growth in this industry. Soon, even appliances will communicate on the home network. In the near future, appliances and devices will be manufactured with intelligence built-in so that they can send status information on the home network.

> **IEEE 1394/Firewire**
> The introduction of digital video and the rapid growth of multimedia applications on the Web naturally led to the need for standards and systems capable of integrating digital video with the PC. One of these is the IEEE 1394 standard, commonly referred to as Firewire. Firewire is a high-speed method of interconnecting peripherals and consumer electronics products. Originally developed as a specification by Apple Computer, Firewire was adopted as an industry standard by the IEEE in 1995. Some of its features include
>
> - Multiple data streams
> - Connection of up to 63 devices without the need for additional hardware
> - High data transfer rates of up to 400Mbps (1.2Gbps speeds in development)
> - Plug-and-play operation
>
> Firewire is provided on Apple computers and can be implemented on PC systems with additional hardware.

The most common types of home networks today are Powerline, radio frequency (RF), IEEE 1394 (see sidebar), PhoneLine, Security, infrared (IR), Digital Audio/Video, HVAC, RS232, RS485, USB, and Ethernet. Several standards are available today that provide a communications protocol for these home networks.

Table 3-4 lists some of the most common subsystems and devices that can be automated in the home environment.

A home internal and external automation system consists of devices and appliances networked for the use of whole-house control, monitoring, security, convenience,

Table 3-4 Personal Area Networks Applications for the Home

Home Automation			Home Security			Web System		
Heating and Cooling Control	Electrical Device Control	Entertainment Control	Alarms	Monitoring	Surveillance	Communications	Computing	Internet
Heating	Lighting	Television	Motion sensor	Cameras	Outdoor areas	Telephone	Multimedia	Electronic library
Cooling	Appliances	Cable	Vibration sensor	Indoor areas	Internet recorded	Voice mail	Television	E-mail
Humidity	Doors and gates	Stereo	Driveway sensor	Access through the Internet	VCR taped	Intercom	Recipes	News
Hot water	Blinds and drapes	Compact disc	Triggers paging and Internet upload of video surveillance		Flood lights	Paging	Schedule events	Sports
Monitoring of power consumption	Pumps and filters	VCR			Monitoring service	E-mail	Checkbook	Weather
Control of power consumption	Sprinklers	Home theater A/V	Gas leak sensor		Remote control	Video conference	Bill payment	Stock data
	Fans		Smoke sensor		Panic buttons		Photography and video editing	Shopping mall
	Pool and spa		Heat sensor				Home database	Grocery store
	Garage doors						Picture album	Video surveillance
							Medical records	Internet uploads
								Investments
								Maps
								Travel

entertainment, and future gateway services. A house system could be designed or retrofitted to provide the interoperability of the home's devices, systems, and networks. The components of a home automation system could include

1. *Computing—Internet* (with home network): The PC oversees the automation systems, and logs and reports any problems. The PC uses access to the automation systems to monitor and control any aspect of the system through the home network.

2. *Home automation* (energy management, environmental control systems, audio/visual [A/V] and IR distribution, home theater and entertainment control): The system communicates through the home network status and controls information to maintain comfort, safety, and energy efficiency.

3. *Home security* (with video surveillance): Security systems communicate through the home network status information.

4. *Infrastructure* (structured wiring or wireless): The infrastructure of the home network must be compatible with the automation systems.

5. *System access*: Access to the whole-house automation system is ubiquitous and secure from unauthorized access.

The benefits of home networking include access, convenience, personalized control over the environment, proactive maintenance/servicing, communications, home management, and security. In addition, as we integrate our home network into a home Personal Space with our personal embedded devices, we are taking the first steps toward Ubiquitous Computing.

Building codes, technological standards, and public needs are changing the home building industry. A home built on past wiring standards is becoming inadequate because the subsystems and devices the home contains are smarter and new services cannot be implemented with older standards.

Basically, new homes could be wired with a structured cabling system meeting CEBus[1] standards or when a remodeling project makes this economically and

---

1. CEBus is an open standard for home automation, also known as EIA-600. Through implementation of CEBus, the home's 120V, 60-cycle electrical wiring can be used to transmit messages and interconnect household devices.

physically feasible. Existing homes could be installed with "no new wires" (using Intellon,[2] HomePNA[3]) or wireless RF.

Today's technologies are generally converging into a meaningful, stable set of standards that should apply for the next decade. For the components of different systems to seamlessly interact and communicate with each other, a careful consideration of the standards and protocols of the home networking and automation systems is necessary.

Table 3-5 provides a list of the current standards, application programming interfaces (APIs), and protocols and how they are implemented in today's home technologies to achieve interoperability.

PAN Technologies and Standards for the Home

In this section, we will briefly review some of the PAN technologies and standards for the home along with comment on key features.

- ▶ *LonWorks:* The LonWorks system is a leading, open, networked automation and control solution for buildings and homes. In a LonWorks network, software controls nodes, which communicate with each other using a common protocol.

- ▶ *Home RF:* Wireless home networking–Shared Wireless Access Protocol (SWAP)–compliant products can share and communicate voice and data in and around the home in a peer-to-peer configuration without wires.

- ▶ *IEEE 1394:* IEEE 1394 provides a popular digital interface for A/V and a software standard for transporting data at 100, 200, or 400Mbps.

- ▶ *Sharewave:* Sharewave Digital Wireless is a portfolio of technologies that enable real-time multimedia-capable digital wireless connections among various devices throughout the home.

- ▶ *CEBus:* CEBus uses the home's 120V, 60-cycle, electrical wiring to transport messages between household devices. CEBus Powerline Carrier uses spread spectrum technology to overcome communication impediments found within the home's electrical power line. Spread spectrum–signaling works by

---

2. Intellon Corp. provides power-line home communication through its Power Pocket technology. It enables speeds of up to 14Mbps using existing home power lines.

3. HomePNA is a specification that enables the use of existing phone lines to implement home networking.

Table 3-5   Compatibility of PAN Standards, API, and Protocols

Communication Networks	Distribution Media	Automation Devices	Interoperability
CEBus	Powerline, twisted pair, coaxial cable, RF, infrared, fiberoptic	CEBus	HomePNA, Intellon
Bluetooth	Point-to-point 10 m, 2.45Ghz RF	Short-range data	N/A
HomeRF / SWAP	Peer-to-peer RF data network 2Mbps, 50 m, 2.4GHz FHSS	Wireless voice and data	TCP/IP, HomeRF, USB
LonWorks	LonWorks and other media	LonWorks	LonTalk
X-10	Powerline	X-10 Compatible	All
Jini	IP networks	Jini	OSGi
HomePNA	Phoneline 1Mbps	PCs / Internet	Ethernet
HAVi	IEEE 1394 Up to 400Mbps	IEEE 1394 entertainment and A/V devices	HAVi
HomePNA	Powerline, RF, HVAC comfort, A/V, security, and phone line networks	N/A	CEBus
UPnP	IP networks	All	HomeAPI, LonWorks
OSGi	WAN/LAN HTTP using JAVA	Jini	Jini, HomePNA, X-10, CEBus, Bluetooth, HomeRF, HAVi
Sharewave	2.4GHz RF DSSS 4Mbps	Data, voice, A/V	
Intellon	CEBus Powerline 1Mbps RF 7kbps	RF—spread spectrum carrier for two-way 900MHz and 2.4GHz unlicensed communication	CEBus / HomePNA
HomeConnex	Proprietary	1Mbps USB	N/A
HomeAPI	All LAN networks	All	All
CAT 5 Ethernet	LAN, phones 10Mbps–100Mbps	Phones, PC	N/A
Coaxial RG6	130 channels (frequencies)	A/V RF signals	N/A

N/A = Not applicable.

spreading a transmitted signal over a range of frequencies, rather than using a single frequency. The CEBus Powerline Carrier spreads its signal over a range from 100Hz to 400Hz during each bit in the packet. However, instead of using frequency hopping or direct sequence spreading, CEBus Powerline Carrier sweeps through a range of frequencies as it is transmitted.

▶ *HomePNA:* The Home Phone Network Alliance (HomePNA) is developing a PhoneLine network standard to connect home network devices.

▶ *HAVi:* The Home Audio/Video interoperability (HAVi) defines a protocol for interconnecting and controlling A/V electronic appliances connected in the Audio/Video Home Network based on IEEE 1394.

▶ *LonTalk:* LonTalk protocol was designed to meet the unique and demanding requirements of control applications and is optimized and tuned specifically to allow for the creation of networked control systems.

▶ *X-10:* X-10 facilitates control of household devices over the existing home wiring system using Powerline Carrier (PLC) technology.

▶ *Home Plug-and-Play:* Home Plug-and-Play is a common application language designed to promote interoperability among multiple communication protocols and home networking standards (Powerline network, RF network, HVAC comfort network, A/V network, security network, PhoneLine network).

▶ *HomeAPI:* These software services and programming interfaces enable applications to discover and control home devices. The development of this standard is necessary to communicate to different home networking protocols. It establishes one common means of communicating to home devices independent of the protocols on which they are based.

▶ *OSGi:* OSGi defines a set of APIs and provides a sample implementation of service gateway architecture. This service gateway is inserted between the external network and internal network and devices.

An immediate option for deployment of short-range communications that is available today is the IrDA standard for PAN. This infrared communications capability is standard on many laptops and handheld devices and is based on the same technology that is used on a device for a plug to accept a wire. Infrared light can be a very useful way of sending information wirelessly. Television remote controls and other devices have used this cheap, effective medium for years. The biggest problem with it is that there is no standard for this communication. An "On" command to a Sony television is very different than the same command to a Panasonic television. The IrDA standard was defined to fix this problem, among others. It lets devices talk to each other by just allowing a clear path between them. The advantages are simplicity and universality, because the IR band is not regulated anywhere in the world. However, in 2001, IrDA seems to be losing market share to new competitors, such as Bluetooth, Jini, and Universal Plug-and-Play (UPnP), which are described briefly here and discussed later in this chapter.

Bluetooth is a technology specification for small, low-cost, short-range radio links between mobile PCs, mobile phones, and other portable devices. The Bluetooth Special Interest Group is an industry group consisting of leaders in the telecommunications and computing industries that are driving development of the technology and bringing it to market.

Jini is another competitor. The Java programming language is the key to making Jini technology work. Devices in a network employing Jini technology are tied together using Java Remote Method Invocation (RMI). The discovery and join protocols, as well as the lookup service, depend on the ability to move Java objects, including their code, between Java virtual machines. It will enable users to connect a wide range of computing and telecommunications devices easily and simply, without the need to connect cables. It delivers opportunities for rapid ad hoc connections between devices.

UPnP is a Microsoft initiative to bring easy-to-use, flexible, standards-based connectivity to consumer networks, whether in the home, in a small business, or attached to the global Internet. It embraces the zero-configuration peripheral connectivity of plug-and-play but is more than just a simple extension of the plug-and-play peripheral model. UPnP is an evolving architecture that is designed to extend the zero-configuration mantra to a highly dynamic world of many networked devices supplied by many vendors.

Just as we concluded that small, mobile devices found speech recognition and speech synthesis attractive solutions to both the input and output limitations, home PANs can equally benefit from speech controls and reporting.

Important protocols involved include

▶ *TCP/IP*: The Transmission Control Protocol and Internet Protocol defines Internet communication format (see Chapter 5).
▶ *WAP*: The Wireless Application Protocol (WAP) is an open, global specification that empowers mobile users with wireless devices to easily access and interact

with information and services instantly (see Chapter 5). WAP is both a communications protocol and an applications environment. It can be built on any OS, including PalmOS, EPOC, Windows CE, FLEXOS, OS/9, JavaOS, and so on. It provides service interoperability even between different device families, including handheld digital wireless devices such as mobile phones, pagers, two-way radios, smart phones, and communicators. In addition, WAP is designed to work with most wireless networks such as CDPD, CDMA, GSM, PDC, PHS, TDMA, FLEX, ReFLEX, iDEN, TETRA, DECT, DataTAC, and Mobitex.

In addition to the challenges of network interactions between static devices, in a wireless network with many mobile devices, channel conditions can vary considerably and unpredictably over time. Also, the need to run a variety of applications over a network introduces significant variability in required bandwidth, allowable error rate, and security requirements for device interactions. For example, electronic commerce (e-commerce) applications require encryption, whereas an entertainment application may not. Instead, the bandwidth requirements for entertainment applications are frequently much greater than what is needed for many commerce applications.

Conventional network interfaces are inflexible and conservative in design. They are designed to operate under the worst conditions, rather than to adapt to changing conditions. This leads to inefficient use of spectrum and power, which is reflected in suboptimal performance.

Although great effort has been expended on simplifying local connectivity at the home and office, it continues to be difficult to introduce new devices and capabilities into existing systems. For example, with current systems in place, it can be quite challenging to plug a device such as a digital camera or cell phone into the company network to exchange data and images. The problems range from compatibility of wires and connectors, to software conflicts and incompatible OSs.

◆ Mobile Software

Today, there aren't any good options for widespread, high-bandwidth, low-power wireless connectivity. Networks for mobile devices are difficult to design because of the problem of routing packets across networks characterized by constantly changing topology. A wireless network serving a population of frequently changing mobile nodes presents a moving target. Any scheme for managing routing across such a network has to be sufficiently flexible to adapt to continuous and unpredictable change in three fundamental characteristics—overall density, node-to-node topology, and usage patterns.

Next-generation networks will be predicated on the idea that networks can be made more flexible and useful by embedding code mobility deep into their infrastructures. Active networking researchers are building systems consisting of highly configurable routers and smart packets.

Mobile software has become an active area of study using contemporary tools, such as the Java programming language. It has made mobile agent systems easier to implement and deploy.

Mobile software has become particularly interesting for applications at the network infrastructure layer. The use of simple, cooperative, highly distributed building blocks to organize connectivity makes good technical sense for heterogeneous networks. Moreover, mobile software agents serve as a powerful cognitive tool, allowing system designers to think about complex, macro-level interactions through clear and useful abstractions.

As we develop a need for more specialized services within our Personal Space, we will want to have wireless devices that are small and light. The result will be a growing need for mobile software that provides the equivalent service of "just in time" software applications, in a fashion similar to the way "just in time" inventory control provided a major boost the manufacturing industries in the 1980s.

In other words, devices that are easy to carry will require a minimum amount of preinstalled software. Instead, they will look to have real-time software delivery—in effect, software with its own mobility. Software will be called to a device on an as-needed basis only. A technique termed *application streaming* is being adapted for Palm Pilots and cell phones connected to wireless networks to run large applications without storing the software locally. It is an updated version of mainframe networks in which the central server contained the programs that were accessed from "dumb terminals" with very little computational power of their own.

The technique can work in several ways. Citrix Systems of Fort Lauderdale, Florida, for example, places all of an application's calculation work on a server so that only the screen image is compressed and sent down to the client device and only clicks and keystrokes are sent upstream. Nevertheless, it takes a powerful server to keep up with the back-and-forth data flow. Alternatively, the application can be broken down into components (or Web Services: see Chapter 7) and sent to the user as

Software Control of Wireless Applications

The idea of controlling operations of wireless reception and transmission with software started during the Cold War. The U.S. military needed receivers that could scan the spectrum, sense incoming signals from enemy aircraft and ships, and react to countermeasures on the same frequencies. After the Cold War ended, one developer, E-Systems in Dallas, Texas, started to exploit the potential commercial applications of these ideas. And DARPA began a project named SPEAKeasy to see how reprogrammable software could help the myriad of military radio systems talk to each other. DARPA also started a related project at MIT called SpectrumWare.

We will return to SpectrumWare on page 81.

needed. AppStream of Palo Alto, California attempts to predict the user's needs based upon past decisions using Java applications. In contrast, Nortel Network's Application Management Solutions of Chelmsford, Massachusetts breaks the application into small chunks that will "see" what the running application will need next and that is based upon using Windows CE.

Wireless devices that morph through different applications and features to respond to the immediate need of their users are an attractive technology (see sidebar).

In the following section, we will examine today's leaders in merging wired and wireless mobile standards—Bluetooth, Jini, and UPnP. In addition, we explore the prospects for the next-generation WPAN technology. We will identify the use of mobile software within the mobile device environment.

The three standard leaders in device interconnectivity are Bluetooth, Jini, and UPnP. Whereas Bluetooth is exclusively a wireless standard and technology, Jini and UPnP integrate wired and wireless network capabilities.

The Bluetooth standard is designed to support a short-range wireless capability to beam documents easily from, for example, a Bluetooth laptop to a compatible printer or to transfer data from a PC to a cell phone.

Powerful wired and wireless device-to-device communications via SUN's Jini standard for smart devices is also coming along, though more slowly than Bluetooth, and Microsoft's UPnP is further behind.

Bluetooth

Most current computer systems implement short-range digital communications using cables. These cables connect to a multitude of devices using a wide variety of connectors with many combinations of shapes, sizes, and number of pins, which has become quite burdensome. With Bluetooth technology, these cable connections are eliminated and devices communicate using radio waves to transmit and receive data. Bluetooth wireless technology is designed for short-range (nominally

10 m) communications. One result of this design is very low power consumption for use with small, portable personal devices powered by batteries.

The Bluetooth Special Interest Group was formed in 1998 as an open standard publicly available and royalty free. Bluetooth uses low-power two-way radio link built into a microchip to offer data speeds up to 1Mbps at a frequency of 2.4GHz. Bluetooth enables devices such as laptops, phones, printers, pagers, and PDAs to communicate without wires. Voice communications are now commonly transmitted and stored in digital formats. Voice appliances such as mobile telephones are also beginning to be used for data applications such as e-mail access and Internet browsing. Through speech recognition, computers can be controlled by speech; through speech synthesis, computers can produce audio output in addition to visual output. Some wireless communication technologies are designed to carry only voice, whereas others handle only data traffic. Bluetooth wireless communication makes provisions for both voice and data.

Originally, wireless networks were designed loosely in compliance with IEEE 802.11 standard (see sidebar), which allowed for 2Mbps data rate using either direct sequence spread spectrum (DSSS) or frequency hopping spread spectrum (FHSS) (see Chapter 4). The DSSS method, used in most of the faster wireless networks, breaks each bit of data into a pattern of "chirps." Each chirp is sent at a different frequency, and the pattern of switching frequencies is known and set in advance. When they are received, the chirps are made back into the original data. The ratio of the number of chirps for each bit of data is the spreading ratio.

Most DSSS schemes switch frequency often and use a small spread ratio. This produces accurate transmission of data. Most of the lower-speed wireless networks use the second method, FHSS. It also switches frequency, but it transmits data more or less uncoded when the

IEEE 802.11

IEEE 802.11 is one of two standards today that form the basis for the commercial 2.4GHz wireless LAN market, the other being the OpenAir 2.4 standard.

IEEE 802.11 specification was developed by a committee of the Institute of Electrical and Electronic Engineering (IEEE) to specify an "over-the-air" interface between a wireless client and a base station or access point, and among wireless clients.

There are two layers addressed in IEEE 802.11 specification: the physical (PHY) and media access control (MAC) layers. At the PHY layer, there are three physical approaches for wireless LANs: diffused infrared, direct sequence spread spectrum (DSSS), and frequency hopping spread spectrum (FHSS). The infrared PHY operates at the baseband, and the other two PHYs operate at the 2.4GHz band. For wireless devices to be interoperable, they must conform to the same PHY standard. All three PHYs specify support for a 1Mbps and 2Mbps data rate.

The 802.11 MAC layer addresses rules for accessing wireless media. Two network architectures are defined: the infrastructure network and the ad hoc network. an infrastructure network provides communication between wireless clients and wired network resources. The transmission of data between wireless and wired media is through an access point.

receiver and transmitted are locked on the same frequency. The newer version of IEEE 802.11 is 802.11a which runs at 11Mbps.[4]

Bluetooth is based on a completely different standard. Most cellular phones, notebooks, and handheld computers offer Bluetooth as an integral part of the device. Bluetooth products are also being developed using the 5.8GHz band (as opposed to the 2.4GHz band). Moving into this band provides full integration with all forms of wireless local area networks and enables smaller devices and faster data speeds. Table 3-6 summarizes three key standards and their current status.

Although skeptics have questioned Bluetooth products, Ericsson is shipping a mobile phone and headset that are linked by Bluetooth, and Toshiba plans to release a PC card that puts Bluetooth in laptops.

Much debate has ensued over whether Bluetooth competes directly with IEEE 802.11. The standards overlap in some areas: creating wireless LANs, operating in the unregulated 2.4GHz frequency band, and ability of each to interfere with the other's transmissions.

The IEEE 802.11 wireless LAN protocol standard transmits data about 100 times as far and 15 times as fast as Bluetooth. Yet, as a result, it costs more to build and uses more battery power than its so-called competitor. The speed and range of 802.11 make it useful for laptops on large corporate campuses; the power and cost savings of Bluetooth make it better for mobile phones and handheld computers. In the end, the technologies may prove to be complementary.

Intel's recent decision to abandon the HomeRF platform in favor of IEEE 802.11B may be an important step toward standards convergence.

Jini

Jini

The Jini technology was developed under the leadership of Bill Joy and Jim Waldo. The team included Ann Wollrath, the inventor and designer of Java Remote Method Invocation (Java RMI); Ken Arnold, the designer of Java-Spaces technology and coauthor of the book *Java Programming Language* with James Gosling; and Bob Scheifler, a principal of the X Consortium and designer of Jini lookup and discovery.

Jini technology (see sidebar) is an architecture for the interconnecting of objects to all types of networks (both wired and wireless). Jini technology provides a simple infrastructure for delivering services in a network and for

---

4. Another standard SWAP from HomeRF Working Group is also a frequency-hopping method with 50 hops per second at 2.4GHz band.

Table 3-6   Related Wireless LAN-PAN Standards

	IEEE 802.11B Wireless LANs	HomeRF	Bluetooth Wireless PANs
Speed	11Mbps	1.2–10 Mbps	30–400 kbps
Use	Office LAN	Home/office	Personal area network
Types of terminals	Notebooks, desktop, palm, Internet gateway	Notebooks, desktop, palm, Internet gateway, phone, mobile device	Notebook, palm, phone, pager, car, appliance
Types of configuration	Multiclient per access point	Point-to-point or multiple devices per access point	Point-to-point or multiple devices per access point
Range	20 to 1000 m	50 m	10 m
Frequency sharing	Direct sequence spread spectrum (DSSS)	Wideband frequency hopping spread spectrum (FHSS)	Narrowband frequency hopping (FHSS)
Backers	Cisco, Lucent, 3Com WECA	Apple, Compaq, Dell, HomeRF, Motorola, Proxim	Bluetooth, Ericson, Motorola, Nokia
Status	Shipping	In development	Shipping
URL	Wirelessethernet.com	Homerf.org	Bluetooth.com

creating spontaneous interaction between programs that use these services regardless of their hardware and software implementations. Any kind of network made up of services (applications, databases, servers, devices, mobile appliances, printers, etc.) and clients can be easily assembled, disassembled, and maintained on the network using Jini technology. Services can be added or removed from the network, and new clients can find existing services.

Jini technology simplifies interactions on a network. It follows the Java platform. Software written to the Jini specification allows the ability to dynamically add and manage network services. The Jini architecture is also designed to handle the network outages and changes of configurations that happen in real networks over time.

RMI

RMI stands for Remote Method Invocation and relies on a protocol called the Java Remote Method Protocol (JRMP). Java relies on Java Object Serialization, which allows objects to be transmitted as a stream. Because Java Object Serialization is unique to Java, both the Java/RMI server object and the client object must have been written in Java. Java/RMI can be used on diverse operating system platforms, from mainframes to UNIX boxes, to Windows machines, to handheld devices, as long as there is a Java Virtual Machine (JVM) implementation for that platform.

CORBA

The CORBA is an emerging open distributed object framework proposed by a consortium of over 600 companies known as the Object Management Group (OMG). CORBA automates many common network programming tasks. Since its inception in 1991, CORBA has existed in some form as an adopted technology of the OMG's open standards-setting process.

The Jini architecture lets programs use services in a network without knowing anything about the wire protocol that the service uses. One implementation of a service might be Extensible Markup Language (XML)-based, another RMI-based, and a third Common Object Request Broker Architecture (CORBA)-based (see sidebar). The client is, in effect, taught by each service how to talk to it. A service is defined by its programming API, declared as a Java programming language interface.

When a service is plugged into a network of Jini technology–enabled services and/or devices, it advertises itself by publishing a Java programming language object that implements the service API. The client finds services by looking for an object that supports the API. When it gets the service's published object, it will download any code it needs in order to talk to the service, thereby learning how to talk to the particular service implementation via the API. The programmer who implements the service chooses how to translate an API request into bits on the wire using UPnP, RMI, or CORBA. In other words, the Jini architecture uses objects that move around the network.

The Jini architecture integrates legacy systems as long as somewhere in the network there is a Java virtual machine (JVM) that will execute the required Jini technology on the legacy system's behalf. To use a service, a person or a program locates it using the lookup service. The lookup service acts as a switchboard to connect a client looking for a service with that service. Compatibility requires no central repository of drivers because each service provides everything needed to interact with it.

Devices in a network are tied together using Java RMI. The discovery and join protocols, as well as the lookup service, depend on the ability to move objects written in the Java programming language, including their code, between Java Virtual Machines.

Jini technology defines a set of protocols for discovery, join, and lookup to provide resilience in a dynamic networked environment. The underlying technology and service architecture is powerful enough to build a fully distributed system on a network of workstations. And the Jini technology infrastructure is small enough that a community of devices enabled by software written to the Jini specifications can be built out of the simplest devices. As a result, a device can take charge of its own interactions. It can self-configure, self-diagnose, and self-install.

The API that defines a service is simply a list of what the service does. Existing technologies rely on agreeing, not only on what remote objects will do but also on how requests are transmitted on the wire. The Jini architecture makes the details of how a service uses the network into an implementation detail that can differ between implementations of the same service without changing the client code.

Many complementary technologies can take advantage of the capabilities of the Jini architecture. Because the Jini technology hides the details of how a service API is implemented, the Jini architecture can be used with a variety of network technologies to integrate them into a single network of services that clients use without any modification. For example, UPnP is a protocol for data transmission focused on developing XML standards for home networking, operating primarily at the connectivity level of a network stack focusing on devices. Once devices connect to a network, there is a need for an advanced service delivery architecture that can deliver services and a higher order of interoperability to networked devices. This is where Jini technology and UPnP work together.

In a Jini technology–enabled network of services or devices, an UPnP device would be published as a service that implements the relevant API by translating method requests into appropriate XML on the wire and translating any returned results into the terms of the API.

UPnP works in static systems where every client can be told, in advance, how to talk to every service implementation. Because the Jini architecture relies upon telling the client how to talk to a new service via downloaded code, a network of Jini technology–enabled services or devices is able to accommodate changes over time with greater flexibility.

Any connectivity scheme, including UPnP, can interoperate with Jini because Jini technology is wire-protocol and transport-protocol neutral. The Jini architecture also allows UPnP devices to work in the same network as devices using other protocols.

Service Location Protocol (SLP) is a mechanism for dynamically finding services on the network, based on a particular wire protocol. SLP defines services in terms of string names. As with UPnP, SLP does not use mobile code, and so clients must know, in advance, how to talk to any service they will ever use. A bridge could publish SLP services into a Jini technology–enabled network.

Bluetooth can be used as a transport mechanism in a network of Jini technology–enabled services or devices transparent to clients who connect to services via Bluetooth.

Universal Plug-and-Play

Microsoft's UPnP is a combination of hardware and software support that enables a computer system to recognize and adapt to hardware configuration changes with little or no user intervention.

UPnP is a rival to Sun's technology Jini; however, it is behind both Jini and Bluetooth. Both technologies, which are still being developed, allow devices such as printers and scanners to be connected easily to networks and then to electronically "announce their presence" on the network so that users can tap into their services.

In Windows 2000, UPnP support is optimized for laptop, workstation, and server computers. In addition, Microsoft Windows Driver Model (WDM) provides plug-and-play device driver support. Windows 2000 provides the following support for plug-and-play:

▶ Automatic and dynamic recognition of installed hardware

▶ Hardware resource allocation (and loading of appropriate drivers)

▶ An interface for driver interaction with the UPnP system

▶ Interaction with power management

An example of interoperability is Atinav Inc. (www.atinav.com). Atinav is a software company that provides integrated Internet communications software to a translator between the Internet and any communication device, providing the ability to access and translate Internet or network resource data in real time over any global network carrier. Atinav integrates the leading protocols and standards, such as Bluetooth, Jini, UPnP, and I-Mode.[5]

---

5. Note: We will discuss and compare the Java 2 Platform, Enterprise Edition (J2EE), and Microsoft.Net technologies in Chapter 7.

◆ Ubiquitous Computing Research

Advances in computer power, storage, speech recognition, the Web, and, especially, wired and wireless networking integration, are bringing the concept of an Intelligent Wireless Web within reach. Although wireless network integrating technologies, such as Bluetooth, Jini, and UPnP, are more near-term solutions, advanced research is ongoing at such places as IBM's Pervasive Computing, SUN's Public Utility Computing, and MIT's AI Laboratory.

For example, IBM has committed $500 million over the next five years to move toward a new, mobile, networked world, IBM's Pervasive Computing. It sees that services will grow from a 24/7 world to a 24/7/360 one, in which the 360 represents the degrees around the globe. The drive will push computational power into objects (laptops, handheld and wearable devices) with a smaller footprint. IBM has committed to building an "intelligent" infrastructure of chips, mainframes, servers, databases, and protocols for supporting data-rich mobile environments.

SUN's Public Utility Computing shares IBM's 24/7/360 view and aims to create dynamic virtual networks or supernets. The PUC technology could store and retrieve data and access database services to analyze customer trends. The catch comes in making it secure. The notion of procuring computer services from a utility, much the way we get water, electricity, and phone service, is not new. The idea at the center of the public utility trend in computer services is to allow firms to focus less on administering and supporting their information technology and more on running their business. The infrastructure is a key to integrating and enabling such "remote access" constituencies as business-to-business, outsourcing vendors, and workers who telecommute.

However, the most forward-looking research that comprehensively addresses the vision of the Intelligent Wireless Web is currently being carried out by MIT's AI Laboratory in Project Oxygen.

MIT's Project Oxygen

MIT's AI Laboratory is embracing the next generation of computation everywhere with interacting anonymous devices in the MIT Project Oxygen.

The human-centric approach formally began in September 1999 as a DARPA Information Technology project at MIT. A collaboration of MIT colleagues M. L. Detouzos, A. Agarwal, R. Brooks, F. Kaashoek, and V. Zue searched for radical new ways of deploying and using information. A unifying goal emerged as pervasive, human-centric computing. In May 2000, Acer, Delta Electronics, HP, Nokia, NTT, and Philips become industrial partners in the $50 million project. The Oxygen prototype will be completed in 2002, and the final testing by MIT should be complete in 2004.

The goal of the Oxygen system is to be pervasive, embedded, nomadic, and always on. The MIT vision is computation that is available all the time, everywhere, just as electricity is available from electric power sockets. Anonymous devices, either handheld or embedded in the environment, would personalize themselves in our presence by finding whatever information and software we need. Person-centered devices would provide universal personal appliances that would be equipped with transducers such as a microphone, speaker, and display. In response to speech commands, they would reconfigure themselves through software into many useful appliances, such as a two-way radios, cell phones, geographical positioning systems, and PDAs, thereby replacing the many dedicated devices we usually carry with us, reducing overall weight, and conserving power. As a result, we would communicate naturally, using speech and phrases, leaving it to the computer to locate appropriate resources and carry out our commands.

Project Oxygen rests on an infrastructure of using both mobile and stationary devices built with new Reconfigured Architecture Workstation (RAW) chip designs and connected by a self-configuring network. This infrastructure supplies an abundance of computation and communication, which is harnessed through software technology.

Project Oxygen consists of three key components all tagged as 21, referring to the twenty-first century:

- ▶ Handy 21 (H21): Handheld device
- ▶ Enviro 21 (E21): Environmentally embedded device
- ▶ Network 21 (N21): Networking device

The H21 is battery powered and contains a microphone and speaker, a small screen to see text and pictures, a miniature camera, and an antenna for communication with wireless networks. This small device using mobile software can change functions whenever there is a software download to provide a new function. It can be a high-speed node on a network when you enter an office, or a slower node when you are outside and farther from resources.

When H21 cannot find a computer network nearby, it shifts into a cellular phone mode to call into a wireless network in that system's protocol. An H21 can be a two-way radio to talk to another H21 or it can turn itself into an AM/FM radio or even a television with the right software download.

The H21 takes a step beyond the handheld fixed devices of today—high-powered cell phones that access the Web or the palm devices (see Table 3-3) to handle e-mail. The H21 can implement any of these functions with the right software through mobility and flexibility. In effect, the H21 can in turn assume the functionality of various individual small handheld devices. It can be a cell phone, a PDA, a pocket PC, a pager, and so on, changing as the need arises and the appropriate software is downloaded.

How will this device accomplish the many transformations required? A new functional approach, developed by SpectrumWare, is being implemented in the H21 with digital, programmable circuitry. To change from one function to another, the H21 loads new software that gives it varied capabilities. Some of the software flows into it only when in use; the software is termed *nomadic* or *mobile* because it travels where needed.

For now, H21 is being built with off-the-shelf hardware, but a new breed of microprocessor is being developed, named Reconfigurable Architecture Workstation (RAW), pioneered by A. Agarwal and A. Amarasinghe.

Today's chips process signals the way city streets process cars. Each signal checks at every intersection to see whether it should turn right or left to get to its destination. RAW software logically rearranges the internal circuitry so that each signal knows ahead of time all the turns it must make and can zip through without having to slow down.

Chip technology (see sidebar) is approaching a billion transistors on a chip, and computer designers face three converging forces:

1. Keeping internal chip wires short for clock speed
2. Economic constraints of quickly verifying new designs
3. Changing application workloads, such as stream-based computations

The Transmeta Chip

A new chip start-up company that has attracted a lot of attention is Transmeta. The Transmeta chips are designed to have reprogrammable microcode. It's somewhat reminiscent of the RAW project out of MIT. Linus Torvalds, the originator of Linux, has joined the Transmeta organization to make an embedded version of Linux for one of the chips.

Transmeta designs platform solutions for the mobile Internet computing market. Transmeta's x86-compatible Crusoe processor is designed for a new class of ultra-light mobile computers. Crusoe is built to combine PC and Internet software compatibility with high performance and extremely long battery life.

Transmeta's technology is the combination of a VLIW engine and Code Morphing software (see Figure 3-2).

However, Transmeta is currently concentrating on low-power technology devices.

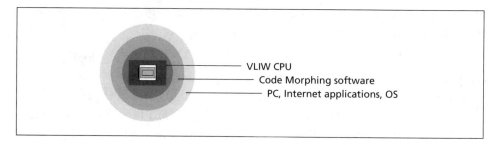

Figure 3-2 Transmeta chip

A RAW machine offers a software-exposed, or configurable, highly parallel VLSI architecture comprising a replicated set of processing tiles with a compiler system that schedules fine-grain parallelism across the tiles. These architectures require only short wires supporting efficient pipelined and data-level parallelism for stream-based multimedia and signal processing applications.

The hardware architecture is exposed fully to the compiler and the software system. In traditional multiprocessors, large communication latencies and synchronization costs limit them to exploiting coarse-grained parallelism across processors. Bit- or byte-level parallelism and instruction-level parallelism can be exploited up to only a very limited extent on modern superscalar architectures. The RAW architecture exploits a much more extensive fine-grained parallelism.

In addition, dynamic support can be provided in the software runtime systems. In this case, the compiler can identify threads that can be executed in parallel. Compilation in RAW is fast because it binds into commonly used hardware mechanisms such as Arithmetic Logic Units (ALUs) and memory paths. As a result, each software application can reconfigure the RAW chips in the H21 to optimize the calculations that software needs to make.

By exposing the chip's "wiring" to the software, the RAW chips allow themselves to be customized to suit the needs of any application. The result should be an H21 device that has high performance for low power requirements. H21 also trades off computation and power consumption to manage wireless transmissions by adjusting power, frequency, and data rate.

H21 devices provide mobile points for users both within and without the intelligent spaces controlled by Enviro 21s (E21s). The H21s can accept speech and visual input, and they can reconfigure themselves by various protocols. For example, when a user uses an anonymous H21, the device could customize itself to the user's preferred configuration. The H21s contain board-level antennas that enable them to couple with a wireless network or nearby H21s. H21s leverage the same hardware components as the embedded devices E21s, but differ in

- ▶ Connections to the physical world
- ▶ Computational power they provide
- ▶ Software that runs on the devices

H21s come equipped with a few perceptual and communication transducers, plus a low-power network, in order to remain small, lightweight, and power efficient. H21s are not equipped with keyboards and large displays, although they may be connected to such devices. Through the N21 network, an H21 handheld device can connect unobtrusively to nearby, more powerful embedded devices, which provides additional connections to the physical world. H21 initial prototypes are based on StrongARM processors (see sidebar), but plans exist to use stream-efficient RAW microprocessors to provide better performance and more efficient use of power.

Unlike the H21, E21 is an embedded computer within the walls of the office, home, or car, wherever you go. The purpose of E21 is to provide ample computer power and communication resources within your Personal Space. In effect, the E21 units can be installed in the office or the home with specialized or general functions. They can be a desktop PC, a printer, a fax, a video camera, a home security system, an AV control system, or an auto GPS, with network connectivity and mobile software to offer a specific functional capability.

E21 has the same capabilities as H21 but is capable of having greater resources in power and computational ability, allowing it to provide the necessary speech recognition for sophisticated interaction. The relationship between H21 and E21 is envisioned to be similar to that of a battery and an electric wall socket.

MIT's embedded or stationary device, E21, is to be embedded in offices, buildings, homes, and vehicles to create intelligent spaces. E21s include interfaces to camera and microphone arrays, and users would be able to communicate to E21s using speech recognition.

The StrongARM Processor

Progress in innovative chips is continuing and offers significant steady improvement as is evident by the StrongARM processor, produced by Intel. It is a high-performance, low-power "system on a chip" for portable wireless multimedia devices. It incorporates Application Specific Standard Product (ASSP) to provide performance, integration, and low power for palm-size devices, PC companions, smart phones, and other emerging wireless multimedia devices.

A high-speed, 100MHz memory bus and a flexible memory controller provide design flexibility, scalability, and high-memory bandwidth.

Like the H21, E21 will eventually be built from RAW chips and be connected via wireless networks. E21 will off-load power-hungry computations from the H21 and process them. In the home, E21 will be connected to heating, air-conditioning, phones, lights, and other devices (see Table 3-4). Wall-mounted touch-sensitive displays with microphones, speakers, and cameras will be connected to E21 for system-human interaction.

N21 is a set of network protocols that will reside in H21 and E21 to help them cope with mobility, interrogation, collaboration, and adapting to changes in the environment. N21 is seen as an additional set of capabilities on top of the protocols that handle the Internet (see the Semantic Web in Chapter 7).

N21s would connect dynamically changing configurations of self-identifying mobile and stationary devices to form collaborative regions. The N21s would support multiple communication protocols. One of the goals of Oxygen is to introduce a new scheme for interrogation known as Intentional Naming System (INM), invented by H. Balakishnan. To address a resource, you specify the property that you want the resource to meet, for example, "Nearest available printer." The N21 approach uses an electronic location support system to help machines locate the resource. These sources periodically broadcast at a simultaneous RF and ultrasound signal that H21 can sense.

Being able to access devices by intent is very important. N21 would also adapt to changing communication conditions. N21 is capable of rapid self-organization of a handful of H21s and E21s into a secure collaborative region (see Self-organizing and Adaptive Software in Chapter 7).

In Project Oxygen, speech and touch screens would replace keyboards and mice. The spoken language is the primary user interface for Oxygen's infrastructure. Four components, with well-defined interfaces, interact with each other and with Oxygen's device, network, and knowledge access technologies.

1. The speech recognition component converts the user's speech into a sentence of distinct words by matching acoustic signals against a library of phonemes. The component delivers a ranked list of candidate sentences, either to the language-understanding component or directly to an application. This component uses acoustic processing (for example, embedded microphone arrays) and application-supplied vocabularies to improve its performance.

2. The language-understanding component breaks down recognized sequences of words grammatically and systematically represents their meaning. It gener-

ates limited vocabularies and grammars from examples, and it uses these to produce input commands.

3. The language-generation component builds sentences that present data in the user's preferred language.

4. A commercial speech synthesizer converts sentences into speech.

An H21 uses local or downloaded software to reconfigure itself into particular communication devices (for example, cell phones or radios). It receives input from its antenna, processes the input in software, and outputs sound from its speakers.

The Oxygen software system includes a user OS, a machine OS, and a bridge OS. The software is loaded into each H21 and E21 device on an as-needed basis.

The user OS provides the interface for speech recognition and understanding. The machine OS is similar to today's OS, without the icon and mouse interface. It is a collection of low-level calls and directives performing machine functions. While the user OS supports user's needs and the machine OS supports central processor unit (CPU) requirements, the bridge OS ties the two parts together. It translates and implements.

MIT's Project Oxygen offers a clear direction for intelligent wireless devices that may be realized within the next decade.

◆ Challenges and Opportunities

For Personal Space to untangle network connections, several challenges must be overcome. These challenges include the issues of privacy, security, bricks-and-mortar store integration, usability, and the limitations of small devices:

▸ *Privacy:* With so much personal information transiting through the air, privacy safeguards are important. When consumers use handheld devices as wallets, entertainment platforms, and communication centers, they will expect information to be inviolable.

▸ *Security:* Macro viruses and denial-of-service attacks at e-commerce sites will include wireless developers. Brokers such as Ameritrade, E-Trade, and Suretrade; banks such as Harris Bank and Chase Manhattan; and bill-payment services such as CheckFree already offer consumers wireless stock trading, banking, and bill-payment services in the United States. For most devices, their security includes a user name and password for authentication, and some form of scaled-back secure sockets layer encryption technology to prevent eavesdropping (see Appendix E).

▶ *Integration:* Online and offline businesses need to be tightly integrated to provide customer satisfaction.

▶ *Usability:* The designers of new devices need to invest in learning how to make the customer interface usable. Ease of use will continue to influence the drive for mass adoption of the wireless technology.

▶ Limitations of small devices:

- They use slower processors.

- Their memory sizes range from a few hundred kilobytes in the smallest devices to a few megabytes in the larger devices.

- Their wireless connections typically run at narrowband speeds.

- Many limitations arise because of the devices' batteries.

- The small, mobile wireless device computing environment will not run large, complex OSs and applications. Instead, distributed applications, which gain their capabilities from collections of separate devices working in concert, will be necessary. Unlike desktop computers, small, mobile wireless devices use a variety of processors and OSs and are programmed in a variety of languages.

Important opportunities for small devices will develop if the right balance is achieved for the client-server relationship between small devices and their fixed or embedded server resources. The essential components for achieving this balance are new chip designs coupled with open, adaptive software. The goal for new chips is to provide hardware for small devices that is small and lightweight and that consumes little power while having the ability to perform applications (such as speech recognition) by downloading adaptive software as needed. The efforts of Transmeta, StrongARM, and RAW chip designs are possible examples, but it remains to be seen if a successful balancing act will occur.

Wireless Internet devices are developing as additions to the cell phone and may represent another opportunity as consumer-to-consumer communication channels. As an example, consider that today in Japan millions of people use wireless devices to pass something to a friend by just beaming it over. Wireless devices communicate to one another, constantly exchanging information.

◆ Conclusion

In this chapter, we introduced concepts and elements of Personal Space, mobile software, and Ubiquitous Computing as the components for WPANs. We presented the collection of personal handheld devices and the emerging home devices that are currently looking to sever their wire tether. We presented the need for mobile software that provides the equivalent of "just in time" software applications and reduces the memory, storage, and computational requirements for the small, handheld devices.

We examined emerging leaders in wireless network integrating technologies, such as Bluetooth, and network integrating technologies, such as Jini and UPnP, which offer near-term technologies. Advanced research at IBM's Pervasive Computing and SUN's Public Utility Computing was identified.

We reviewed the most forward-looking research that comprehensively addresses the Intelligent Wireless Web, MIT's Project Oxygen.

From this chapter, you may conclude that:

1. The demands for untethered Personal Space and the requirements of new services will trigger an explosive growth in mobile software. The results will be WPANs focused around near-term standards, such as Bluetooth, Jini, and UPnP.

2. Speech recognition and speech synthesis offer attractive solutions to overcome the input and output limitations of small mobile devices, if they can overcome their own limitation of memory and processing power through the right balance for the client-server relationship between the small device and nearby embedded resources. The essential components for achieving this balance are new chip designs coupled with open adaptive software. The new chips may provide hardware for small devices that is small and lightweight and that consumes little power while having the ability to perform applications by downloading adaptive software as needed.

3. Research projects, such as MIT's Oxygen, will offer a clear direction for intelligent wireless devices that is both comprehensive and realistic over the next decade.

Merging Wired and Wireless Networks

In this chapter, we present the basic components, characteristics, and features of wired and wireless networks. We address the questions and concerns about merging wired and wireless technologies.

We present the wireless LAN standards and the background for transitioning to 3G mobile wireless.

Early computers were stand-alone, unconnected machines. For transfer of data from one system to another, the user stored the data in some form, carried it to a second compatible system, and then read it into the computer. During the 1980s, corporate mergers, takeovers, and downsizing led to consolidation of company data into fast, seamless, integrated databases for corporate information. Moreover, as companies discovered that their data could be moved from expensive mainframes to small machines on more economical LANs and WANs, their executives started pressuring the information technology (IT) organizations to port applications and databases. With these driving forces, intranets and local networks began to increase in size, and this established further demand for ways to expand networks to interface with each other.

Simultaneously over the past decade, enterprise information portals (EIPs) and architectures have changed to take advantage of new technologies. Now network computing has become the means to increase efficiencies in knowledge management—systematically finding, selecting, and organizing information from around the world. But large-enterprise businesses have found that connecting to far off lands with very different network structures has not been an easy task.

◆ Wired Networks

The Internet is a vast configuration of transmission channels, control mechanisms, copper wires, fiberoptic lines, satellites, and an assortment of infrastructure devices, the composite of which can be viewed as a network of networks. One way to think of the Internet is analogous to our system of highways. Instead of highways, the Internet has transmission channels; instead of intersections, it has interconnecting access points. The transmission channels, like highways, come in a variety of sizes with different speed limits. The roads are owned and operated by various parties.

In general, the transmission channels can be classified by their basic characteristics in several ways. For example, channels can be characterized by their transmission media:

▶ Wired networks, such as the telephone and cable television networks, transmit signals through copper wires, coaxial cable, or fiber.

▶ Wireless networks, such as cellular, broadcast, and satellite systems, transmit signals on radio waves of different frequencies.

Or they can be characterized by their information flow:

▶ Interactive networks, such as the telephone system, carry information in both directions.

▶ One-way networks, such as TV cable and broadcast, deliver signals in only one direction, from the transmitter to the individual user.

Networks can also be distinguished by whether they transmit information in analog or digital form. Simply speaking, analog signals are continuous waves, whereas digital signals are pulses that form strings of ones and zeros, or bits, which are the common language of computers.

In digital form, all telecommunications signals are interchangeable. This means that voice, video, text, graphics, and data can all be transmitted over any kind of digital network. For the major industry players, the goal is to provide a full-service network that offers customers one-stop shopping for local and long-distance phone calling, cable television, mobile communication, and high-speed data communications for interactive services.

The growing complex of network architectures and protocols are reaching out to access homes and businesses. However, bandwidth is still the principal constraint that limits residential access to Internet data.

Network computing at a basic level consists of three main components: a server, a client, and a communication medium. A client is a program that requests services or information; a server is the provider of the services or information. The communication medium connects clients and servers. A server can request information from other servers and hence become the client for those servers.

In the early 1990s, the client-server model was the basis of network computing. The client-server architecture is a versatile, message-based, and modular infrastructure that is intended to improve performance, usability, flexibility, interoperability, and scalability, compared with the previous centralized mainframe, time-sharing computing.

Originally, in the client-server model, information and business logic resided on the mainframes or UNIX servers accessed by fat (that is, resource-intensive) clients on proprietary or private networks. Although these systems were secure, they were very expensive and problematic. Client software required installation at every terminal, which made system rollouts and installations tedious and costly.

The Web has changed the way people think about information sharing. The central theme of this second generation of network computing is ease of communication between machines and humans. As a result, the limitations of proprietary networks have vanished. Client software has been standardized in the form of Internet browsers.

The browser acts as a client, and the Web server acts as the server responding to the browser's request. Advantages of the Internet model are

- ▶ Rapid, nearly instantaneous propagation of information
- ▶ Virtual and global organizations
- ▶ Reduced infrastructure and deployment costs
- ▶ Equal benefits for government, commercial organizations, and private individuals

Web-enabled networking expanded the potential of Internet computing. A significant drawback to this model, however, has been lack of mobility. The key capability of accessing information and applications any time, anywhere is missing from 2G networking for information. The question now becomes shouldn't information be as mobile as humans? To present networks that offer greater mobility, we will first review fixed networks and discuss both their interface and compatibility with the new wireless networks under development. Then we will review how wired and wireless are merging together.

Essentially, networks are built upon three elements:

▶ Data flow (bandwidth)

▶ High-speed switching

▶ Network intelligence

The deployment of optical fiber technology expanded bandwidth and resulted in the contest between Internet Protocol (IP) packet switching and asynchronous transfer mode (ATM) circuit switching. Recent advances in ATM have facilitated using IP over ATM.

However, network intelligence is only recently showing its importance. Intelligent Network (IN) is a concept that is leading to new technological development as user demands become more sophisticated. IN is more than just network architecture: it is a complete framework for the creation, provisioning, and management of advanced data transmission services.

The characteristics and quality of data transmission are determined by the characteristics of both the media and the signal. The vast system of interconnecting networks that comprise the Internet is composed of several different types of transmission media, including

1. Wired
   - Fiberoptic
   - Twisted pairs (copper)
   - Coaxial cable

2. Wireless
   - Radio waves
   - Microwave

- Infrared (IR)
- Laser

For wired media, the medium itself is the most limiting factor. The two dominant media for data transmission are fiberoptic cabling and unshielded twisted pair (copper). The fiber is considerably faster. Fiberoptic cable provides higher speed and greater capacity because of its nonelectric medium. In contrast, not only is copper slower but it also is vulnerable to noise and interference because it has many of the properties of a radio antenna. The advantages of fiber include

▸ Security—resistance to electromagnetic taps

▸ Small size

▸ Light weight

▸ Low attenuation

▸ High bandwidth

The disadvantages of fiber include

▸ Local power required

▸ Fiber not as flexible for bending around corners

In addition, new electronics in fiberoptic networks, termed *dense wave division multiplexing* (DWDM), are further improving capacity. DWDM produces many colors of light on each fiber thread. This new, lambda-based (that is, wavelength-based) network can create end-to-end connections. The network could link the world over many colors of light in a way similar to the way voice network connected billions of customers over copper wires. The potential for a single-mode fiber is to provide every terminal with a unique wavelength address. Nortel is now producing a cable capable of 80Gbps on 80 wavelengths or 6.4Tbps on a single fiber.

Today, the key issue is connectivity rather than bandwidth, and the defining test of technology is the total number of lambda addresses, or light-paths. However, light-paths require a tunable system with wavelengths convertible into other wavelengths. In optics and electronics, the key to such a tunable system is resonance—a sharp peak of output or gain at a particular frequency.

In the past, tunability has implied selection using a dial such as on an ordinary radio receiver. In a broadcast and select system, radio stations broadcast in an assigned band of electromagnetic frequencies. The radio's antenna picks up all frequencies, but the receiver rotates to a point of resonance (where capacitance and inductance cancel out), until it selects the desired radio signal. At the resonant frequency band, the chosen resonating channel tunes in. Similar techniques are used in broadcast television, both over cable or the air.

The early proponents of all-optical networks envisaged a broadcast and select system as the most promising optical topology. Each transmitter would employ a different lambda, and at the other end users would tune their photodetector receivers to a desired wavelength station. An optical filter would invoke resonant tuning by altering the distance between mirrors in a cavity and thus the wavelength that is amplified. In a Fabry-Perot interferometer, the coupled mirrors play the role of the tunable resonator in an ordinary radio receiver. This system was unsuccessful because of a crucial difference between electronic technology and fiberoptics.

Although broadcast and select is impractical, the abundance of wavelength circuits possible on a single fiber still is appealing. But to achieve this goal, tunable lasers are required. If the sender of a message finds a particular light-path blocked by another user, he must be able to use a remaining open light-path. In a national network, this means an astronomical number of tunable lasers.

In 1999, the dominant lasers used to transmit signals down fiberoptic lines were only able to emit a single frequency band. Shifting to another required invoking a different laser, which was permanently tuned to another light-path. In 2000, however, companies began to develop lasers that could be tuned over an increasingly wide band of potential "colors" of IR light. They are now using a diversity of tunable technologies. Today, we are still not ready for end-to-end fiber networks. Instead, we have a mixed optical and electrical infrastructure, where optical signals enter electrical switches to be distributed over fiber, copper, or radio waves through a plethora of network structures and protocols.

Now we must ask, how is the vast interlacing structure of fiber and wire organized? To answer this question, let's start by differentiating the network types into a hierarchy based on bandwidth and physical extent, as follows:

▶ Personal Area Network (PAN) interconnects devices within the immediate vicinity of a person, ranging from 10 to 30 m.

▶ Local Area Network (LAN) typically interconnects computers within a small area of 5 km to 10 km, such as a building or campus, at speeds from 10Mbps to 100Mbps.

- Metropolitan Area Network (MAN) connects many LANs in a larger geographical area of 10 km to 100 km at speeds of 1.5Mbps to 150Mbps.
- Storage Area Network (SAN) switch vendors that integrate DWDM capabilities over a fiberoptic network core.
- Wide Area Network (WAN) interconnects computer systems over 100 km to 1,000 km at speeds from 1.5Mbps to 24Gbps.
- Global Area Network (GAN) connects networks between countries, across continents, and around the globe at speeds ranging from 1.5Mbps to 1000Gbps.

It is typical to find a modern computer facility with LAN links to other systems. LANs are commonly used for small areas but can run over copper wire, fiberoptic cable, infrared waves, or radio waves. A diversity of operating systems (OSs), such as UNIX, Linux, or Windows, administer the LAN server systems.

Intranets are networks connecting computing resources at a school, company, or other organization, but, unlike the Internet, they restrict users. On a broadcast network, such as Ethernet, any systems on the cable can send a message. Typically, Ethernets can support 10Mbps, but traffic usually reduces this capability. When messages collide and become garbled, it causes a problem. The extra load on the system because of collisions affects transmission rate. The high-speed Ethernets include

- Fast Ethernet, which is a shared protocol that reaches speeds of 100Mbps, ten times the standard Ethernet used by most LANs.
- Switched Ethernet, which is a nonshared service. Devices are given their own dedicated paths within a LAN.
- Gigabit Ethernet, which works with existing LAN protocols at 1,000Mbps and requires fiberoptic cabling. On LANs, it is mainly used by high-speed servers.

On a token ring network, such as fiber distributed data interface (FDDI), only one system can send a message at a time. A token is constantly being passed from one host to another around the ring to establish whose turn it is to send. This prevents collisions. If the ring is large, however, its performance can be degraded. The peak data rate of FDDI networks is 100Mbps.

FDDI was the first 100Mbps transport protocol for LANs and is a significant departure from IEEE 802 specifications. FDDI uses a frame type different from that of IEEE 802.3 (Ethernet) or IEEE 802.5 (token ring) standards. FDDI is an expensive protocol to implement; however, it is highly scalable.

LANs typically connect to WANs through a gateway. A gateway is a computer or device with multiple network connections. It converts data traffic to the appropriate format to and from networks.

Routers play an important role by communicating with one another dynamically, passing information about which computer routes are up or down, and providing directions for messages to reach destinations. Routers connect and translate protocols between LAN to WAN and determine the best path for data traffic to take to reach a destination.

Most connections on a WAN are through point-to-point links, using cable, radio, satellite, or wire links. The advantage of point-to-point links is that they are limited and well understood. The disadvantage is that each system can typically be equipped for a small number of links. They often use serial lines and modems or parallel ports.

The Internet has recently been upgraded to accommodate demand. Transfer rates of gigabits per second on experimental networks already exist and will soon be put into use.

Figure 4-1 shows the requirements and current status of the transition of networks from wired to a more integrated wired/wireless infrastructure. The requirements for successfully integrating the Internet over wired and wireless infrastructure includes expanding existing wired networking; additional deployment of wireless LAN, WAN, and satellites; redistribution of existing spectrum to favor commercial use; adaptive and self-organizing software; and Intelligent Web Architecture improvements. Figure 4-2 is a hierarchical illustration of the Internet from the perspective of networking interconnection.

Table 4-1 demonstrates a progression of networking development, from electrical analog technology to electrical digital technology for each category (that is, data, voice, video), progressing through networking development from the top of the table to the bottom. In addition, the integration of electric technology with optical technology (for example, DWDM and fiberoptics [see Figure 4-2]) is included. In the following sections, we present background information for the various technologies shown in this table.

Routers and Switches

Routers and switches are a lot like an information guide or reference map for crossing the Internet. Both device types help packets move to their destinations by using

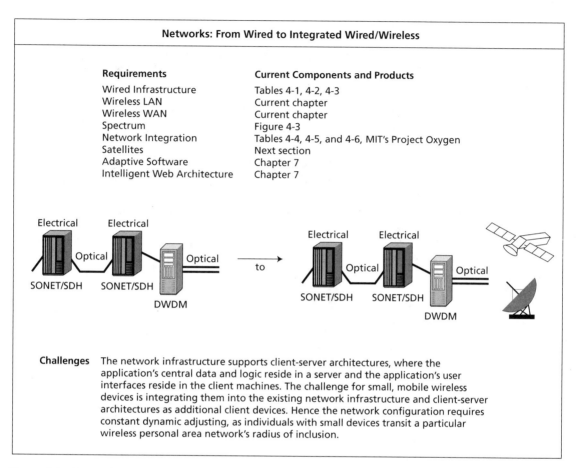

Networks: From Wired to Integrated Wired/Wireless

Requirements	Current Components and Products
Wired Infrastructure	Tables 4-1, 4-2, 4-3
Wireless LAN	Current chapter
Wireless WAN	Current chapter
Spectrum	Figure 4-3
Network Integration	Tables 4-4, 4-5, and 4-6, MIT's Project Oxygen
Satellites	Next section
Adaptive Software	Chapter 7
Intelligent Web Architecture	Chapter 7

Challenges   The network infrastructure supports client-server architectures, where the application's central data and logic reside in a server and the application's user interfaces reside in the client machines. The challenge for small, mobile wireless devices is integrating them into the existing network infrastructure and client-server architectures as additional client devices. Hence the network configuration requires constant dynamic adjusting, as individuals with small devices transit a particular wireless personal area network's radius of inclusion.

Figure 4-1   Networks

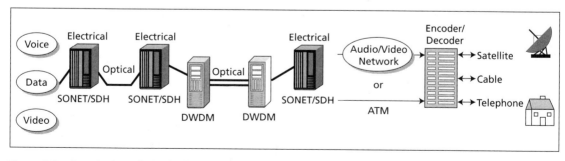

Figure 4-2   Connections from the backbone of the Internet to your home

Table 4-1   Evolutionary Path of Networks

ANALOG TECHNOLOGY		
Data Services	**Voice Services**	**Video Services**
Modems enable analog lines to carry data from digital computers	Analog technology POTS (plain old telephone service) —3 Khz	Analog coax-based video network Cable TV: 700MHz Broadcast local and satellite TV and Internet data

DIGITAL TECHNOLOGY		
Data Services	**Voice Services**	**Video Services**
Frame-relay–based network: T-1, T-3—up to 45Mbps—frame relay fiberoptics or digital microwave	x-DSL up to 6Mbps Digital subscriber line Residential and small business access	Fiber and coax-based switched network (HFC) Cable modem 1.5Mbps Residential and small business access
Fast Ethernet (100Mbps)	ATM/SONET network ATM: up to 13.22Gbps Asynchronous transfer mode: voice, data, and video	
Gigabit Ethernet (1Gbps)	SONET: up to 13.22Gbps— synchronous optical network	
	SONET with DWDM—480Gbps and more	
IP/Ethernet over ATM/SONET	ATM/SONET network	Fiber and coax-based switched video network
Fiberoptic-based broadband (data/voice/video) network IP/Ethernet over ATM/SONET		

data contained within the packet to help select a route for it to travel from one segment to another. As it travels to its destination, information over the Internet usually passes through at least a few segments, commonly referred to as hops.

Routers are often described as being traffic cops for the data. The information the routers use to make decisions is stored in a routing table, a database in the router that is built upon information maintained by different algorithms. Typically, algorithms feed a routing table the relationship between destinations and paths.

In static routing tables, packets are routed in a fixed manner, so particular addresses are always routed on certain paths. This means packets are not always sent along the optimal path. For example, in a static router, packet A's address is read and packet A follows the routing table indication to travel via path B. Static routing tables are generally used in small networks.

In a dynamic routing table, pathways are flexible. The routing table is continuously updated as the network changes. This means a packet can be routed around network congestion problems. For example, for packet A's address, the routing table indicates that path B and C are overloaded with traffic and therefore sends packet A over path D.

The routers and switches used for Internet communication today are high-end machines that operate rapidly. For example, Cisco's gigabit switch routers have a switching capacity ranging from 80Gbps to 320Gbps.

Some of the most common types of routing protocols include Routing Information Protocol (RIP), Open Shortest Path First (OSPF), and Interior Gateway Routing Protocol (IGRP). Routing protocols are different from routed protocols, which are protocols that are routed over a network (for example, IP, Netware, and AppleTalk).

◆ Asynchronous Transfer Mode

In 1995, the Internet backbones were becoming crowded and a new technology and ATM looked like a promising solution. It reused the older FDDI fiberoptic lines but operated at 155Mbps and offered expandability to 620Mbps. Most of the long-haul fiber was converted to ATM by 1997.

ATM is a dedicated-connection switching technology that organizes digital data into 53 cells or packets and transmits them over a medium using digital signal technology. Individually, a cell is processed asynchronously relative to other related cells and is queued before being multiplexed over the line. Because ATM is designed to be easy to implement by hardware (rather than software), faster processing speeds are possible.

Ethernet, or FDDI workstations, use Transmission Control Protocol/Internet Protocol (TCP/IP) to communicate over ATM switches. Like ATM, Switched Multimegabit Data Service (SMDS) is another cell-based service provided by the Regional Bell Operating Companies (RBOCs).

Network Clustering

Network clustering connects independent computers to work together in a coordinated fashion. The hardware configuration of clusters varies substantially depending on the networking technologies.

One approach to clustering utilizes central input and output (I/O) devices accessible to all computers (nodes) within the cluster. These systems are shared-disk clusters because the I/O involved is typically disk storage but does not require shared memory. Shared-disk cluster technologies include Oracle Parallel Server and IBM's HACMP.

Because all nodes may concurrently write to or cache data from the central disks, a synchronization mechanism must be used to preserve coherence of the system. An independent piece of cluster software referred to as the distributed lock manager assumes this role.

A second approach to clustering is dubbed "shared-nothing" because it does not involve concurrent disk accesses from multiple nodes. Shared-nothing cluster solutions include Microsoft Cluster Server (MSCS).

Clustering offers a high-performance computing alternative to massively parallel systems (see Chapter 7). Aggregate system performance aside, cluster architectures also can lead to more reliable computer systems through redundancy.

SONET Networks

Today, the synchronous optical network, SONET, offers greater capacity for the Internet. SONET is the U.S. standard for synchronous data transmission on optical media. It consists of a WAN interface to the public network carriers, with an internationally supported physical layer transport scheme. The international equivalent of SONET is synchronous digital hierarchy (SDH). Together, they ensure standards so that digital networks can interconnect internationally. New ways of networking on a global scale include network clustering (see sidebar).

SONET currently provides standards up to the maximum line rate of 9.953Gbps. Actual line rates approaching 20Gbps are possible. ATM runs as a layer on top of SONET, as well as on top of other technologies.

Traditional SONET solutions require numerous network nodes to handle traditional voice-centric traffic. Transparent optical networking offers service providers a way to migrate to a new transport foundation and will enable the transport of high-speed access services to the large bandwidth pipes of the core networks.

Ethernet Networks

The 1000Base-T is the fiber-based version of Gigabit Ethernet that will have a dramatic impact. It has long been acknowledged that Ethernet dominates the desktop. The availability of inexpensive Gigabit Ethernet connections running over Category 5 copper will cement Ethernet's dominance of the LAN. However, Gigabit Ethernet over long-haul fiber will take Ethernet into WANs and MANs.

Ethernet will be competitive with ATM, SONET, and other traditional MAN technologies for data-oriented applications. Gigabit Ethernet's low cost and ease of operation relative to other MAN technologies make it appealing to enterprises that want to extend their LANs across a metropolitan or wide area.

The Gigabit Ethernet MANs deployed to date have been private networks. Certainly, private Gigabit Ethernet MANs offer benefits, but the market for Ethernet-based MANs will really take off when public services are readily available.

Ethernet's ability to continue to scale in terms of bandwidth is crucial to its long-term viability in multiple markets, particularly compared with ATM. Currently, carriers and service providers are the main targets for this technology. WAN equipment makers would like the speed to match SONET OC-192 (9.95Gbps, see Table 4-2), thus allowing them to use existing technology and presumably reduce the complexity of connecting Ethernet LANs to MANs and WANs.

Although some industry players would like Ethernet to evolve to be more SONET-like, others want Ethernet to remain the relatively simple technology it has always been. Indeed, Ethernet's simplicity has been its key strength.

Wired Multiplexors

Network multiplexors play a fundamental role in networking by maximizing the use of expensive lines by connecting them together. A multiplexor has a high-speed line and multiple slow lines and transfers information from the slower-speed line to high-speed lines. Analog signals, such as television, voice, or data signals, can be frequency division multiplexed (FDM) by assigning each incoming channel to a

Table 4-2   SONET/SDH Bit Rates

Bit rate	SONET	SDH
51.84Mbps	OC-1	—
155.52Mbps	OC-3	STM-1
622.080Mbps	OC-12	STM-4
2.488Gbps	OC-48	STM-16
9.9532Gbps	OC-192	STM-64

specific frequency. Digital signals can be time division multiplexed (TDM) by positioning each incoming channel to a fixed time slot of the high-speed outgoing channel. Neither FDM nor TDM make any effort to gain bandwidth efficiency.

Multiplexors are used at network nodes aggregating traffic and moving data over lines. Each line terminates in a port. Each port tends to support one networking protocol only.

In general, networking nodes move packets from input port to output port by routing or switching. Switching requires establishing a prior path between nodes and sending a variable-length packet, a fixed-length cell, or a time slot in a multiplexed data stream. Routing does not establish a prior path but treats packets as individuals, providing destination addresses rather than node addresses.

Routers have several advantages. They do not need complicated time-consuming connection setup and tear down protocols. They are not committed to a single path but can rerout around a congested area.

Signals

Backbones are high-speed transmission channels that provide the fastest and most direct path for data to travel. Backbones are typically built around fiberoptic cables termed optical carrier (OC) and digital signal (DS) lines.

Digital signals are categorized as DS digital signals (DS0,1,2,3,4), and optical signals are categorized as OC optical channel (OC1,3,9,12,18,24,36,48,96,192,768), where the OC number represents a multiple of 672 channels at 64kbps each. Table 4-2 provides a specific breakdown of signal categories.

Dense Wavelength Division Multiplexing

The optical networks provide all the basic network requirements in the optical layer, such as capacity, scalability, reliability, survivability, and manageability. Today, the wavelength is the fundamental object of the optical network. Basic network requirements can be met through a combination of the optical transport layer that provides scalability and capacity beyond 10Gbps and the SONET/SDH transport layer. The long-term vision of an "all optical network" is of a transparent optical network in which signals are never converted into the electrical domain between network ingress and egress. The more practical implementation for the near term will be an opaque optical network that minimizes optical/electrical/optical conversions.

The natural evolution of optical transport is from a DWDM-based point-to-point transport technology to a more dynamic networking technology. Optical networking will use any of several optical multiplexing schemes to multiplex multiple channels of information onto a fiber and to the optical transport layer provided by SONET/SDH.

In the year 2000, nearly 200,000 km of new optical fiber went underground or undersea. Fiber networking companies, such as Global Crossing, use multiple OC-48 lines (2.5Gbps) with OC-192 lines (10Gbps) in high-traffic areas and through DWDM can achieve speeds of 1.28Tbps on a single fiber. This is accomplished by using state-of-the-art hyper-DWDM, which can split a single fiber into 128 separate wavelengths of light, to give one fiber a total capacity of 1.28Tbps.

How is the growth in networking bandwidth happening? Largely as a result of DWDM, which can exponentially increase the bandwidth of those fiberoptic strands.

Telecom transmissions, whether voice or data, have always been multiplexed in some way. Multiplexing simply involves combining multiple communications into a single compact transmission. Initially, digital systems used TDM, which broke different signals into pieces and sent them in alternating slots in one stream. TDM enabled a single fiber strand to carry 32,000 voice calls simultaneously.

To accommodate all the traffic at the edges, the Internet backbone will keep pace by adding fiberoptics and new WDM technologies to carry a lot more information.

Switching

Switches and routers are the essential joints of the Internet's skeleton that relay information. Switches forward information from one host to another without knowing anything about the paths between the hosts. Routers understand the Internet layer protocol used between hosts. WAN services are provided through three primary switching technologies: circuit-switched, packet-switched, and cell-switched.

Circuit-switched networks dedicate a circuit to users during a particular time, using TDM methods. The telephone industry is an example. Although circuit

Portal

Portals (corporate portals, enterprise information portals, and business intelligence portals) provide a single point of access to aggregated information. Portals have been applied for general audiences on the Web (Internet portals), for organizational Web sites (intranet portals), and for specialized online communities (vertical portals).

The goal of portals is ease of use. Besides having a single point of access, portals provide a specialized navigation structure. Portals using Web pages for their user interface will, for example, often include numerous hyperlinks on the front page.

switching for the telephony industry has been losing ground to IP switching over Ethernet, there has been a rebirth of circuit-switching technology through optical circuit switching, which is able to function complimentarily with IP packets. Applied networking systems have been finding ways to work together (see sidebar).

A telephone voice connection uses a circuit-switched connection. Circuit-switched connections provide a temporary dedicated line, or circuit, between two end points. A circuit is dedicated from the moment the caller dials a phone number and makes a connection until the caller hangs up. However, circuit-switched connections are appropriate for voice calls that tend to be long, two-way, and highly interactive. This makes circuit-switched connections appropriate for data transactions. Data is received in the order sent and is not likely to be lost, separated, or incomplete. For example, a file transfer that requires the use of a network connection for a long period would be best served by a circuit-switched connection. Circuit-switching can take time to establish, because a direct connection must be made. For example, a modem connection might take up to 40 seconds to establish, depending on modem protocols.

Packet-switched networks allow end stations to share bandwidth. Ethernet and token rings are examples. Packet-switching services do away with dedicated circuits. Data is transmitted one packet at a time through a network with each packet able to take various paths through the network. Switching is generally thought to be a layer-2 function maintaining a virtual link between two network end points. Because there are no predetermined virtual circuits, packet switching can increase effective bandwidth. They do so by tracking packet flows through a node, taking note of common destination addresses and building tables to route subsequent packets.

In contrast to circuit-switched connections, IP packet-switched connections do not use a dedicated circuit between two end points. Rather, packet-switched connections allow multiple simultaneous users access to multiple locations across a network. Packages of data (packets) are sent from source to destination using the quickest route available. Whereas circuit-switched connections operate the same as a phone call, packet-switched connections are much like sending a series of letters through the mail. Because each packet contains a source and destination address, packets that make up a single transaction can be sent out of order and along different routes. Although packets can be of any size, typical packet sizes range from 100 to 1,500 bytes.

Transmitting information in packets can result in vastly increased efficiency and reduced costs to users. All packet-switched services require a connection from the customer site to the access point of the packet-switched network or a connection via the Internet.

Whether to choose circuit switching or packet switching depends upon the type of traffic on the networks and the costs involved. Traffic such as video is sensitive to delays and needs the guaranteed bandwidth of circuited-switched service. Unfortunately, this is expensive.

Cell-switched networks move fixed-size data, termed *cells,* using statistical time division multiplexing (STDM)- and TDM-based access. ATM and SMDS are examples of cell-switched technology.

The battle between IP and ATM has been basically the battle between the data communication industry and the telephony industry. IP comes from the bottom; it is a protocol that solves a relatively local problem, multiplatform minicomputer networking, and has been scaled for larger applications.

ATM comes from the top; it is a protocol of slow evolution, far-sighted but ponderous, inflexible. ATM developed so slowly that it gave IP/Ethernet an opportunity to come up with Ethernet switching and fast 100Mbsp Ethernet transmission.

By 1999, IP and Ethernet were too firmly entrenched for the corporate marketplace to bypass them in favor of ATM. Some of the problems presented by IP/Ethernet disappear as they move to local switching paradigms. ATM multiplexing and switching will ultimately force frame relay aside for WAN networking. ATM and IP/Ethernet will continue to coexist and struggle in their continuing protocol war for some time to come.

Data can be transmitted across cellular networks using either circuit-switched or packet-switched connections. Each type of connection has unique characteristics and appropriate uses. As network technologies continue to upgrade and merge, new technologies adapt the best features of their competitors.

So far, we have reviewed the media, signals, hardware, and connectors for wired networks. In the next section, we will present the media, signals, hardware, and connectors for wireless networks. Subsequently, we will discuss how these components will merge to form a compatible interoperable Internet that can support speech recognition, mobile devices, and adaptive Web services.

◆ Wireless Networks

Table 4-1 illustrated how networks progressed from analog to digital for data, voice, and video. It presented technologies largely based on wired networks. However, the big lure to wireless is the potential for big money in implementing wireless architectures that can send packets from people with small personal devices, such as cell phones, to a company's Web and there conduct transactions. The number of wireless subscribers is expected to grow globally from the relatively small number today to many millions within just five years. Table 4-3 summarizes connection access.

Fixed wireless Internet access uses RF for two-way transmission, although the exact method of transmission, as well as the distance and efficiency of the trip, varies from one service provider to another. The various wireless service providers use different portions (or bands) of the radio spectrum to broadcast at certain frequencies. These frequencies affect transmission speed, interference, and power.

Fixed wireless connection provides Internet access that operates in both directions (uploads and downloads) between an ISP and a user in a fixed (stationary) location, without data cables or phone lines. By comparison, until now, cellular wireless access providers generally transmit e-mail and stock quotes in one direction to mobile customers.

When you access the Internet through a fixed wireless ISP, an antenna that is along the route of the network picks up your transmission and transfers it to another

Table 4-3 Connection Access

Year	Cable Modems	Wireless Broadband	Satellite
2000	1.6 million	52,000	78,000
2003 (estimate)	8.3 million	450,000	900,000

antenna, until it reaches the service provider. The request is then converted back into TCP/IP and routed to the Web's page server, thereby becoming a data packet traveling the optical-electrical components that make up the wired Internet infrastructure.

The number and height of antennas required for transmission depend upon the technology of that network. Some companies can only provide service to users located within a few miles of the sending antenna, whereas others transmit for 25 miles or more. In addition, radio waves travel through some solid objects, such as wooden buildings. To ensure continuity of transmission, wireless providers install line-of-sight antenna that transmit and amplify the signal from one point to another. Some providers get around hills and difficult terrain by offering hybrid systems that include satellite/wireless transmission.

Whereas many cellular ISPs transmit at a clumsy 14.4kbps, fixed wireless ISPs have the capability to send and receive Internet data at speeds of 128kbps to 3Mbps. One technology currently being deployed (Multipoint Microwave Distribution System [MMDS]) can reach up to 1Gbps.

Wireless transition modes include

- Radio wave
- Microwave
- IR
- Laser

Wireless LAN technology is rapidly becoming a vital component of data networks. Most wireless LANs are 802.11-compliant, allowing companies to realize applications based upon open systems. To optimize the operation of wireless systems, software options for interfacing wireless handheld appliances must emulate various systems and directly connect to databases.

Today, radio frequency LANs (RFLANs) are being installed that fully integrate with their wired Ethernet counterparts. RFLANs conforming to the IEEE 802.11 specification can connect to an Ethernet TCP/IP backbone with a simple bridge referred to as an access point and are able to make the wireless network appear as just another network segment. Mobile devices associated with an 802.11 access point can communicate with nodes on the wired network just like any stationary workstation. This lets manufacturers and systems integrators bring to their wireless customers the benefits of technology bought and paid for by the much larger wired network market.

Network technologies and radio communications were first brought together at the University of Hawaii in 1971 in the ALOHANET system. It enabled sites on seven campuses across four islands to communicate with the central computer without using unreliable telephone wires.

In the 1980s, amateur radio hobbyists kept radio networks operating by designing terminal node controllers (TNCs) to interface their computers through radio equipment. The TNCs acted much like a telephone modem in which the computer's digital signal was converted into a radio frequency sent over the airwaves by using packet-switching techniques.

In 1985, the Federal Communication Commission (FCC) made the commercial development of radio-based LANs possible by authorizing the ISM bands 902MHz to 5.85GHz.

In the late 1980s, the Institute for Electrical and Electronic Engineers (IEEE) 802 Working Group began developing wireless LAN standards. The IEEE 802.11 standard for wireless LAN medium access control and physical layer specifications was developed. These standards were approved and published in 1997.

Benefits of Wireless Networking

The emergence and growth of wireless networks has been driven by lower costs of infrastructure and application support, as well as gains in efficiency, accuracy, and lower business costs. Mobility enables users to move while using the devices. Many jobs require workers to be mobile, such as inventory clerks, healthcare workers, police officers, and emergency care specialists. Mobile applications that require wireless networking include those that depend on real-time access to data. For accurate price changes, for example, many retail stores employ wireless networks to interconnect handheld bar code readers to databases, having items listed in central databases.

Because of the lack of infrastructure to tether the user's application and server, wireless networks can offer reduced cost. Another problem faced by wired networks is downtime caused by cut or faulty cables. In fact, faulty cables are often the cause of system downtime. Wires and connectors are susceptible to weather, moisture, breakage, and accidental cutting, all of which contribute to system downtime.

In addition, when companies reorganize, the relocation of people incurs recabling costs.

Concerns

The benefits of wireless networks must be balanced against the following concerns:

▶ Radio signal interference

▶ Power management

▶ Interoperability

▶ Security

▶ Frequency availability

▶ Connection problems (for example, dealing with queuing technology that holds transactions offline and transmits when connections are available)

▶ Installation issues

▶ Health risks

The process of transmitting and receiving radio and laser signals through the air makes wireless vulnerable to noise and interference. Network security on wireless systems depends primarily on its encryption capability (see Appendix E).

Crowded Airways

Although the usable portion of the radio spectrum is from 6KHz to 300GHz, this spectrum is already reserved for specific purposes. Governments have mandated that the remaining airspace rights be auctioned off. Different frequency ranges have different physical attributes and have differing value for specific applications. For example, the 2.4GHz band is less useful for wireless Internet communications because it suffers from interference from microwave ovens and obstacles such as trees. Figure 4-3 shows a breakdown of the spectrum into various frequencies for communications.

The U.S. FCC is the primary regulator of communications policy and continues to play a key role after the Telecommunications Act of 1996, which was intended to promote deregulation of telecommunications based on a competitive, market-driven model. This is not to say that other government agencies have no role; on

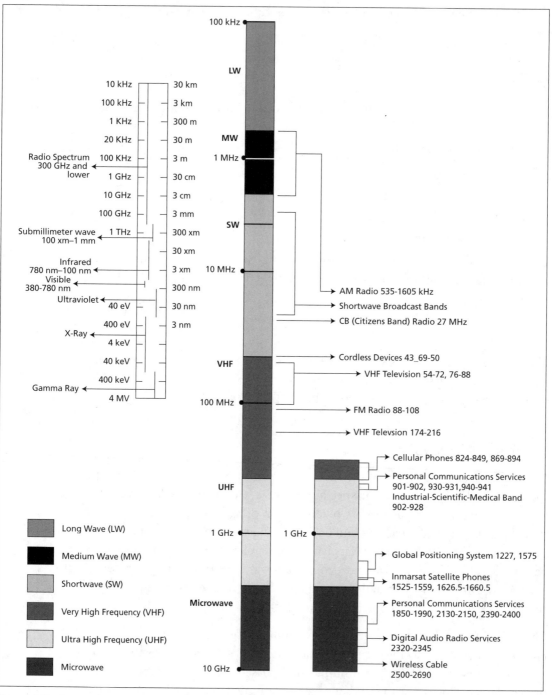

Figure 4-3 Spectrum

the contrary, the various aspects of the Internet and electronic business (e-business) applications are of potential interest to many different agencies. The Federal Trade Commission (FTC) has broad authority over the entire economy, and has an active interest in emerging wireless Internet and data technologies and the privacy, security, and consumer protection issues they raise.

Terrestrial Microwave

The most common microwave antenna is the parabolic dish of about 3 m in diameter fixed with a focused beam. The maximum distance between antennas conforms to

$$d = 7.14\sqrt{(Kh)}$$

where d is the distance between antenna in kilometers, h is the antenna height in meters, and K is the adjustment factor (usually 4/3). To achieve long-distance transmission, a series of microwave relay towers are used and point-to-point microwave links are strung together.

The primary use for terrestrial microwave systems is long-haul telecommunications services, as an alternative to coaxial cable or fiberoptics. The microwave systems require fewer amplifiers, or repeaters, than coaxial cable over the same distance but require line of sight. Another application is short point-to-point links between buildings for closed-circuit television or LAN networks.

Microwave transmission has attenuation losses, expressed as

$$L = 10\log(4\pi d/\lambda)dB$$

where d is distance and λ is wavelength in the same units. As microwave becomes more popular, frequency overlaps will cause additional interference.

A communication satellite is basically a microwave relay station in space used to link two ground microwave stations. The satellite receives transmissions on one frequency band (uplink), amplifies or repeats the signal, and transmits it on another frequency (downlink). A single satellite will operate on several frequency bands termed the *transponder channel*. However, the frequency band must be spaced to avoid interference, with a three- to four-degree separation.

For a communication satellite to function properly it must remain stationary with respect to its position over the earth. Therefore the satellite must have a period of rotation equal to earth's period of rotation. This requires a height of 35,784 km.

Communication satellites compete with fiberoptic networks in delivering broadband signals for the following:

▶ Television

▶ Long-haul telephone

▶ Private business networks

Satellites are well suited for television broadcast. The Public Broadcasting Service (PBS) distributes its television programming exclusively by satellite. Direct broadcast satellite (DBS) uses a satellite to distribute its programming directly to the home. Satellite transmission is also used for point-to-point trunks between telephone exchanges. In addition, satellite transmissions are used for business data applications over private networks.

The optimal frequency for satellite transmission is 1GHz to 10GHz, because below 1GHz there is significant background noise and above 10GHz the signal is severely attenuated by the atmosphere.

Because of the long distance of satellite transmission for satellites in high (geosynchronous) orbit, there is a time delay of a quarter of a second from earth to the satellite. The principal difference between broadcast radio and microwave is that the former is omnidirectional and the latter directional.

Wireless Local Area Network

Wireless LANs occupy an increasingly important niche in the LAN market. Wireless LAN is viewed as a viable adjunct to traditional wired LAN. It meets the requirements of mobility, relocation, ad hoc networking, and coverage of locations difficult to wire.

Early LAN products of the 1980s were marketed as substitutes for wired LANs and cost considerably more. Most wireless LANs operate over unlicensed frequencies at Ethernet speeds using carrier protocols to share a radio wave or infrared medium. A typical wireless LAN configuration includes a backbone wired LAN, such as an Ethernet, that supports several servers, workstations, and one or more bridges or routers to link to other networks. A control module interfaces to a wireless LAN that regulates access by polling or token-passing schemes. Hubs that control stations off a wired LAN may be part of the configuration. All of the wireless end systems are within range of a single control module. These devices are capable of transmitting up to 1,000 feet between computers and equipment. Most wireless LAN products use Simple Network Management Protocol (SNMP). The components of a wireless LAN consist of a Network Interface Card (NIC) and a local bridge termed an *access point*. The wireless NIC interfaces the device with the wireless network, and the access point interfaces the wireless network with the wired network.

Although computers process information in digital form, with low direct current voltages, representing data as zeros and ones, this is not optimal for transmitting data over wireless media. A wireless network interface couples the digital signal from the end user's appliance to the wireless media, air. This process includes the modulation and amplification of the digital signal to a form acceptable for propagation to the receiving location. Wireless media modulate the digital signal to frequencies that propagates well in air—radio waves and IR light.

Modulation translates the baseline digital signal used by the appliance to an analog form for transmission through the air. The wireless network interface is a wireless NIC or an external modem that facilitates the modulation and communication protocols. The interface between the user's device and the NIC includes a software driver that couples the application to the card.

The antenna radiates the modulated signal through the air to the destination. Antennas come in a vast variety but have the following electrical characteristics: propagation pattern (direct or omni), gain (degree of amplification), and transmit power and bandwidth (the effective part of the frequency spectrum that the signal propagates).

A wireless LAN must meet high-capacity, short-distance coverage, full connectivity, and broadcast capabilities. The following are important parameters for a wireless LAN: throughput, number of nodes, connection to backbone, service area, transmission robustness and security, collocated network operations, hand-off/roaming, and dynamic configuration.

Wireless LANs are generally categorized according to the transmission technique that is used. Current wireless LAN products can be categorized as

▶ Spread spectrum LAN

▶ Infrared LAN

▶ Narrowband microwave

Radio Based

To appreciate the problems and issues of merging wired and wireless technologies, it is useful to review some of the basic features of the various wireless technologies. In the next few sections, we will present a few brief comments on the key elements of each of the more important technologies.

Radio waves are the dominant wireless LAN medium. A radio wave by itself does not carry any information. For it to convey data, either frequency or amplitude is altered. The main advantage of radio waves is that they connect users without line of sight and propagate through walls. Although several walls might separate a user from the server, the user can connect to the network.

A disadvantage of radio waves is that they must be managed along with other electromagnetic propagation such as medical equipment.

Radio-based wireless LAN configurations include

- ▶ Medium access control
- ▶ Spread spectrum modulation
- ▶ Narrowband modulation
- ▶ Wireless local bridges
- ▶ Single-cell wireless LANs
- ▶ Multi-cell wireless LANs

Medium Access Control

Medium access control (MAC) is a data link layer function in a wireless radio LAN that enables multiple appliances to share a common transmission medium. The protocol that permits this also enables a group of wireless computers to share the same frequency and space.

Several people talking in a room where each person can hear when someone speaks is a reasonable analogue to communicating using the same frequency and space. To avoid having two people speak at the same time, each person should wait until the room is silent before starting. Carrier Sense Multiple Access with Collision Detection (CSMA/CD) offers this simple protocol.

Spread Spectrum Modulation

Modulation is a physical layer function; it is a process by which a radio transceiver prepares the digital signal on the NIC for transmission over the airways. Spread spectrum "spreads" the signal's power over a wider band of frequencies to gain signal-to-noise performance at the expense of bandwidth. The spread process makes the data signal much less vulnerable to noise interference. Spread spectrum modulation uses either frequency hopping or direct sequence methods to spread the signal (see sidebar).

> **Industrial, Scientific, and Medical Frequency Bands**
>
> In 1985, the FCC modified Part 15 of the radio spectrum regulations authorizing wireless network products to operate in the Industrial, Scientific, and Medical (ISM) bands (902MHz to 928MHz, 2.4GHz to 2.4835GHz, and 5.725GHz to 5.850GHz). Wireless LANs deployed in the United States operate at 902MHz, but this frequency is not available throughout the world.

- ▶ Frequency hopping takes the data signal and modulates it with a carrier signal that hops from frequency to frequency over time. A frequency could hop over the 2.4GHz frequency band between 2.4GHz and 2.483GHz, for example, according to a hopping code.

- ▶ Direct sequence spread spectrum combines data signals at the sending station with a higher data rate sequence. A high processing gain improves the signal resistance to interference.

Narrowband Modulation

Narrowband modulation is used by conventional radio systems, such as television and AM/FM radio. These systems concentrate all their transmit power within a narrow range of frequencies. This helps to conserve bandwidth.

Wireless Local Bridges

Network bridges connect multiple LANs at the MAC layer to produce a single logical network. There are two types of bridges: local and remote.

Infrared Light-based Wireless Local Area Networks

IR light is an alternative to using radio waves for wireless LANs. The wavelength of IR light is shorter (higher in frequency) than radio waves. IR LAN operates at 820-nm wavelengths and is invisible to the human eye.

An IR LAN consists of an adapter card and a transducer (similar to the antenna for a radio-based LAN).

Diffuse Infrared-Based Local Area Networks

The television remote control is an example of a diffuse IR device. When a user presses a button, the remote transmits a corresponding code in modulated IR light to the television. Diffuse IR LANs utilize infrared light at slightly higher power levels with communication protocols to transport data.

In a point-to-point IR LAN, each station interfaces with an IEEE 802.5 (token ring) interface board using token-ring protocols. The point-to-point LAN uses a directed light beam to connect token-ring–based computers.

Wireless Point-to-Point Networks

Traditionally, companies use guided media to provide connections within a location of multiple buildings. Point-to-point wireless networks are very similar to wireless LANs.

IEEE 802.11 Standard

Through most of the 1990s, wireless networks market sales remained flat because of low data rates, high prices, and especially the lack of standards. There are two main types of standards: public and official. A *public standard* is controlled by a private organization and provides common practices. An *official standard* is published and known to the public but controlled by an official organization, such as the IEEE. The IEEE is a nonprofit professional organization based in the United States with over 320,000 members located in 150 countries (see Appendix A).

In terms of LAN standards, IEEE produced some very popular and widely used standards, including IEEE 802.3 (Ethernet) and IEEE 802.5 (token ring). Before 1998, only proprietary wireless hardware and software were available; then IEEE developed the first internationally recognized wireless standard: IEEE 802.11.

Compliance with IEEE 802.11 makes interoperability between multivendor appliances and wireless networks possible. The expectation is that wireless LANs should flourish in a manner similar to 802.3 Ethernet.

The IEEE 802.11 standard provides LAN MAC and physical layer functionality for wireless connectivity of fixed, portable, and moving stations at pedestrian and vehicle speeds. The specifications include support for asynchronous and time-bonded delivery systems, continuity of service, accommodation of transmission rates of 1Mbps to 2Mbps, support for applications, multicast, networks, management, registration, and authentication services.

The IEEE 802.11 standard takes into account the following important differences between wireless and wired LANs: power management, bandwidth, security, and addressing.

A complete wireless system consists of the elements specified in IEEE 802.11 plus components necessary to depict the architecture relevant to the application requirements such as communication protocols (that is, TCP/IP), connectivity software, and network management protocols. The components specified by the system design may include the distribution system or companies may already have an existing distribution system, such as Ethernet LANs or WAN connectivity.

The IEEE 802.11 standard avoids the definition of a particular distribution system for connecting access points, to allow for system architectural variety. A network distribution system is also necessary if databases and applications on the system are accessible only from a wired network. In most cases, a wired LAN backbone may act as the distribution system. Vendors may sell access points capable of connecting to either IEEE-compliant Ethernet or token-ring LANs. In addition, WAN components may be necessary to connect LANs separated by longer distances.

Ethernet products support the following wiring: unshielded twisted-pair (UTP) wire, fiberoptical cable, and coaxial cable.

The most obvious place for 802.11 networks is in the workplace. An inordinate amount of time is already spent by IT departments all over the world trying to guess how many network drops are required and in pulling cable to those places. Replacing that with the relatively short time needed to set up a wireless hub that costs much less provides a powerful economic incentive. This spreads into the home network, as well. An attempt has been made to deploy HomeRF as a wireless network for the home, but no good reason exists to have a separate standard for the home and the office.

Intel's recent decision to abandon the HomeRF platform in favor of IEEE 802.11B may be an important step toward standards convergence. Yet, as the industry leaders coalesce around 802.11B, others are developing new standards, such as 802.11A. IEEE 802.11A employs orthogonal frequency division multiplexing (OFDM), a spread-spectrum modulation technique that enables 200MHz of spectrum to be split into 52 subchannels, each carrying a separate stream of data. 802.11A will operate in the 5GHz UNII unlicensed frequency band. Theoretically, 802.11A could increase transmission speed from 11Mbps to 54 Mbps.

◆ Wireless Wide Area Networks

The step above LANs in the hierarchy of networks are WANs. The Wireless WAN technologies include packet radio, analog cellular, cellular digital packet data, satellite communications, meteor burst communications, and combining location devices with wireless WANs. In this section, we review some of the key features of wireless WAN technologies.

Packet radio WAN uses packet switching to move data to a user with a portable computer and radio modem. Packet radio systems do not yet have worldwide coverage but are economical and efficient in transferring short bursts of data. A radio modem provides an interface between the user and radio relays. These modems typically transmit and receive radio waves omnidirectionally at rates up to 20kbps. The radio relay nodes implement routing protocol and forward packets closer to the destination. The packet radio network continuously transmits data packets and updates routing tables at the relay nodes.

Broadcast radio is traditionally used for one-way analog A/V service, but it is being reborn using digital technology to expand system capacity and allow for two-way transmission. The most popular two systems considered for two-way "wireless cable" are

▶ Multipoint multichannel distribution system (MMDS)

▶ Local multichannel distribution system (LDMS)

Wireless cable systems (MMDS/LMDS) were originally planned as a wireless broadcast alternative to cable television service, with the potential capability of two-way digital access services. Both systems planned to use digital technology to increase broadcast channel capacity and to provide for limited two-way interactive service. The FCC allocated spectrum 2.596GHz to 2.644GHz for the new wireless cable services. Thirteen video channels, termed multipoint microwave distribution service (MDS) and multichannel multipoint distribution service (MMDS), have been allocated. Additional spectrum (20 channels), using frequencies originally set aside for educational programming, has also been made available to MMDS operators.

The FCC has since set aside certain RF spectrum for "response bands" for upstream signaling for interactive video services. The FCC recently proposed allocating another 2GHz (in the 27.5GHz to 29.5GHz band) to LMDS. If allowed by the FCC, wireless cable systems could use two-way digital channels for telephony.

Other system designs for single-channel broadcast systems include

- Single master antenna television (SMATV)
- Interactive television (ITV)
- Low-power television (LPTV)

The analog cellular telephone system uses frequency modulation (FM) radio waves to transmit voice signals. To accommodate mobility, the cellular system switches the radio connection from one cell to another as the signal travels to different areas. Every cell within the network has a transmission tower that links mobile callers to a mobile telephone switching office (MTSO). The MTSO connects the privately owned cellular carrier to the public switched telephone network. As a result, the cellular caller is able to connect to landline phones.

Analog cellular WANs make use of the cell phone's mobility and employ it to transfer data, just like wired telephones. You use the cell phone to dial in to your corporate network just as with a wired telephone. This technology typically provides up to only 14.4kbps data transfer rates. The technology connects a computer to a cellular telephone via modem and then with a remote system through a dial-up connection. This provides an easy way to transfer data wirelessly via cellular telephone service, which covers most of the world.

Cellular systems are separated into geographical market areas, creating segment "cells" with their own radio base station. This allows various users to share the same frequencies and allows reuse of the same frequency spectrum in different cells across geographical coverage areas. It also allows using relatively large cells (macrocells), relatively smaller ones (microcells), or even smaller ones yet (picocells). The primary modes of operation for cellular networks are

▶ Frequency division multiple access (FDMA)

▶ Time division multiple access (TDMA)

▶ Code division multiple access (CDMA)

Digital advanced mobile phone service (AMPS-D) allows for substantial capacity gains over AMPS. In the United States, the purpose of first-generation digital cellular systems is primarily for upgrading analog AMPS systems, to expand network capacity. AMPS-D systems operate in "dual mode" with current AMPS systems. TDMA allows AMPS operators to expand capacity by sharing the same communication channel among users. TDMA offers 3 to 8 times the capacity of AMPS, without adding new cell sites or resorting to microcell deployment.

The cellular digital packet data (CDPD) standard was established to provide dedicated wireless data network for mobile users. It overlays the conventional analog cellular telephone system. The advantage of analog cellular is widespread coverage—operating in the 800MHz and 900MHz bands and offering up to 19.2kbps data rates. Because the CDPD piggybacks on this system, it provides nearly global coverage and uses digital signals to improve transmission.

Global system for mobile communications (GSM) was the earliest and most prevalent global standard for digital cellular service (TDMA). It operates in two distinct frequency bands that the FCC has allocated to cellular mobile (900MHz) and personal communication services (PCS) (1,800MHz GSM and 1,900MHz U.S.). GSM TDMA techniques can achieve considerable capacity gains over AMPS. Although the United States has adopted interim IS-54 (TDMA) standard for AMPS-D, it is still possible for U.S. wireless access network operators to adopt GSM techniques. The carrier channels in GSM have more bandwidth than in AMPS-D, but the real advantage of GSM's wider carrier channel bandwidth (200Khz) may be migration from supporting voice-to-multimedia and high-speed data services. The per-subscriber costs of GSM systems are in range of those for AMPS-D.

GSM systems turned to half-rate (8kbps) voice-coding schemes. The system capacity constraints were alleviated, and expansion costs were minimized. New

GSM enhanced full rate (EFR) voice coders operate at about 13kbps, increasing voice quality. GSM network services on the horizon will provide

- ▶ Conferencing and related group calling services
- ▶ Enhanced and intelligent network services
- ▶ Packet data
- ▶ High-speed data services

Cordless telephone (CT) technology includes the universal mobile telecommunications system (UMTS) and future public land mobile telecommunication system (FPLMTS). The CT technology features very low power, slow (or no) hand-off, and limited base station coverage area with cell sizes that are very small. There are no major players in the United States.

Most wireless WANs, such as analog cellular, packet radio, and CDPD, provide good coverage but at relatively low data rates. Satellite communications, alternatively, provide high-speed transmission, though at a higher cost. Satellite systems in 2000 supported transmission of video, voice, and data for global coverage. A satellite in geostationary orbit has a 24-hour period over the equator. This enables the antennas on earth to remain fixed rather than track the satellite.

Satellites rely on orbital satellite transmissions, and most popular systems considered for application in wireless broadband use

- ▶ Low earth orbit (LEO) satellites
- ▶ Medium earth orbit (MEO) satellites
- ▶ Geosynchronous earth orbit (GEO) satellites

Historically, the original GEO systems dominated satellite telecommunications with high orbital altitude using low orbit period (24 hours). They achieved effective global coverage with three satellites and used relatively low frequencies requiring lower operating power levels. The newer GEO systems use higher power levels and frequency bands, support very small aperture terminal (VSAT) telecommunications systems, and provide direct broadcast satellite (DBS) services.

LEO and MEO systems reduce problems of signal delay, making them more acceptable for voice service. MEOs require 10 to 15 satellites with orbit periods of 6 to 12 hours. LEOs require more than 48 satellites with orbit periods of about 1.5 hours. In 2000, there were 680 satellites in orbit, with 32 new launches scheduled in 2001.

Meteor burst communication directs a radio wave modulated with a data signal at the ionized trail of microscopic meteors in the atmosphere. Its advantage is that it reaches remote areas.

Global positioning systems (GPS) technology is based on a worldwide satellite radio navigation system, providing three-dimensional position and time information anywhere on Earth.

SMR is a wireless access technology based on the traditional model of two-way mobile radio that uses RFs located adjacent to mobile cellular service frequencies. The enhanced version of SMR (ESMR) relies on the same advances in digital signal processing that opened the future for all land-based wireless access companies. ESMR systems operate in a TDMA "cellular-like" environment and may expand the capacity of single SMR radio channel sixfold.

A WAN may be necessary when deploying a wireless system, to provide wired connections between facilities. For example, a department store chain in a large state would maintain its pricing information in a central database. Each of the 100 individual stores within the chain could retrieve pricing data from the central database each day over a frame relay WAN. The components of the WAN would consist of routers and links. The routers receive routable data packets, such as IP or Internetwork Packet Exchange (IPX), review the destination address, and direct the packet forward to the final destination.

The State of Wireless Wide Area Networks

The ultimate end point of wireless data access is to be connected to the Internet all the time, wherever a user happens to be. Unfortunately, big gaps currently exist between expectation and reality, with major parts of the globe not having access.

Wireless access business applications, such as monitoring stock prices and real-time auctions, may force the deployment of wide-area coverage. As of yet, most of the business applications of wireless data have been constrained to either internal business applications or support for specific high-end clients. The next major growth phase will be when businesses adopt wireless communications for business-to-business transactions.

Wireless Application Service Provider

Although wireless phones, PDAs, and other devices are making it possible to access corporate data from virtually anywhere, challenging obstacles exist, such as security (see Appendix E) and bandwidth. Wireless applications do not need to become obsolete as quickly as the devices they run on. Ideally, a wireless platform could implement, for example, JavaScript on the client to handle transaction tasks to alleviate network strain, but not all tools support this approach.

Over 1,000 different types of wireless devices are available today, and building applications that run properly can be challenging. For example, these devices require an alphabet soup of markup languages such as CHTML, HDML, HTML, VoiceXML, WML, and XML (see Chapter 5).

Wireless Application Service Providers (WASPs) typically provide tools for designing pages for multiple devices that include business logic and are integrated with existing Web sites and data sources, as well as the necessary servers and gateways needed to make the data accessible. Wireless platform companies are extremely young. Nevertheless, these companies are expected to be ready for the next generation of wireless devices.

WASPs are also looking to provide voice recognition features. Voice recognition application, based on VoiceXML, will let users browse through the company data or Web content by speaking into a wireless device instead of fumbling with a tiny keyboard and squinting at a small screen. In fact, from the perspective of technology maturity, today's Wireless Web is reminiscent of the wired Web in 1994.

Mobile development tools are divided into three categories: those (www.aethersystems.com, www.mshift.com, and www.2roam.com) that make existing Web sites available to wireless devices, those (www.iConverse.com) that use proprietary graphical interface to ease the development of wireless applications from scratch, and those (www.ThinAirApps.com) that require you to do all coding in a language, such as C++ or Java (see Table 4-4).

Additional WASP and mobile development tools include wireless access gateway (WAG) services, such as Air2Web and Alter Ego. There are also mobile Internet

Table 4-4   Examples of Wireless Application Service Providers

	Aether	Covigo	iConverse	MShift	ThinAirApps	2Roam
OS	Win NT	Unix, Solaris, Linux, Win NT, Win 2000	Win 2000	Win 2000	OSs that support Java VM	N/A
Time to implement	2–4 weeks	2–4 weeks	2–4 weeks	2–4 weeks	1–2 months	1–3 weeks
Interface	Text, Web-based	Visual, text	Visual, text	Text, Web-based	Other	Visual, text
Mark language support	CHTML, HTML 3.2, WML 1.1, XHTML, XML	CHTML, HDML, HTML, VoiceXML, WML	HDML, HTML, VoiceXML, WML	CHTML, HDML, HTML, MML, WML	HDML, HTML, WML	CHTML, HDML, MML, WML, XHTML, XML
JavaScript support	No	Yes	Yes	No	No	Yes
SSL encryption	Yes	Yes	Yes	Yes	Yes	Yes
Auto conversion between devices	Yes	No	Yes	Yes	No	Yes

platforms that are hosted by a vendor or third-party Application Service Provider (ASP), such as Brience, mPortal, and Veriprise.

◆ Network Integration

When two networks cross, that intersection or junction is termed an *Internet exchange* point or *network access point* (NAP). Metropolitan area exchange (MAE) is an example of a NAP in a metropolitan location. Points of presence are the points where individuals connect to the Internet. They're maintained by the ISPs.

The local-loop bottleneck occurs where LANs, which link devices within a building or a campus, join to WANs, which transmit cross-country and hold the Internet together. Advances in fiber technology have extended the capacity of WANs to trillions of bits per second. However, LANs are evolving from rates of 10Mbps to gigabits per second. The connection between these two domains has become a critical limitation.

Of the variety of technologies developed for high-speed wireless access, LMDS offers a way to break through the local-access bottleneck. Like cell phone networks, LMDS is a wireless system, but it is designed to deliver data through the air at rates of up to 155Mbps (typical cell phone voice calls use a mere 64kbps, or 8kbps in compressed digital systems). It supports voice connections, the Internet, videoconferencing, and other high-speed data applications.

A major advantage of LMDS technology is that it can be deployed quickly and relatively inexpensively. LMDS is also attractive to complement existing networks. And although cable modems are making inroads in the residential markets, the business market remains a prime target for LMDS. The higher capacity of LMDS is possible because it operates in a large, previously unallocated expanse of the electromagnetic spectrum, a total bandwidth of about 1.3GHz in the "millimeter" waveband at frequencies of about 28GHz. In other countries, depending on the local licensing regulations, broadband wireless systems operate between 2GHz and 42GHz. Regular digital cell phone systems operate at about 0.8GHz, with a typical bandwidth allocation of 30MHz or less.

LMDS uses digital signals at 28GHz, made practical by the performance of technologies such as digital signal processors, advanced modulation systems, and gallium arsenide integrated circuits, which are cheaper and function much better than silicon chips at these high frequencies.

LMDS uses wireless cells that cover an area 2 km to 5 km in radius. The transceiver of an LMDS customer has a fixed location and remains within a single cell. The LMDS cell size is limited by rain, walls, hills, and trees, which distort the signal and create significant shadow areas for a single transmitter.

LMDS provides a high-quality voice service that can run concurrently over the same data stream as Internet, data, and video applications. In summary, LMDS can be a versatile, cost-effective option for both providers and users of broadband services, with the rapid and inexpensive deployment being particularly attractive to the providers.

As we know, there are other services now in the home besides telephone, such as cable TV, and wireless local loop can incorporate a much broader concept, such as video on demand, interactive video, and data services, as well as telephony. One of the most important aspects of wireless local loop will be competition.

Fixed wireless and cellular are merging, and even though the number is small today (about 4 million fixed wireless), it is growing at an estimated annual rate of 40 percent. Fundamentally, anything that can be delivered on wire can also be delivered on wireless, including video and high bandwidth demand systems, with the advantage of mobility. About half of the demand today is still for analog, with an installed base of approximately 200 million, but it's shrinking.

The quest for the last mile may be met with a combination of fiber and wireless. In dense metropolitan areas, free-space optical networks will provide 622MB of bandwidth to buildings without digging the streets. Second-generation LMDS and MDDS fixed wireless will be deployed to buildings requiring less bandwidth.

The digitization of wireless cable signals can now allow for video compression and a dramatic increase in channel capacity and system functionality. In comparison, satellite costs have high upfront costs, although potential per-subscriber costs of satellite network systems are very competitive. For an overview see Figure 4-4.

Migrating Networks

x-DSL, fiberoptic networks, and cable networks are all wired broadband solutions. In contrast, several wireless technologies are also capable of competitive broadband access (see Table 4-5).

Over time there will be a migration of core networks to optical fiber simply because photons carry a lot more information more efficiently and at less expense than electrons. By 2003, ultra-long-haul (greater than 4,000 km), high-bandwidth optical transport will be deployed in the United States.

A wireless network can be deployed to cover a broad geographical area to achieve economies of scale. Because of this characteristic, wireless networks may have large market opportunities in rural areas and developing countries that do not have existing communication infrastructures. Wireless networks have proven technologies, including broadcast TV, cellular phones, paging, and DBSs.

Several wireless technologies for delivering broadband services either already exist or are undergoing active research. These are grouped as satellite technologies and

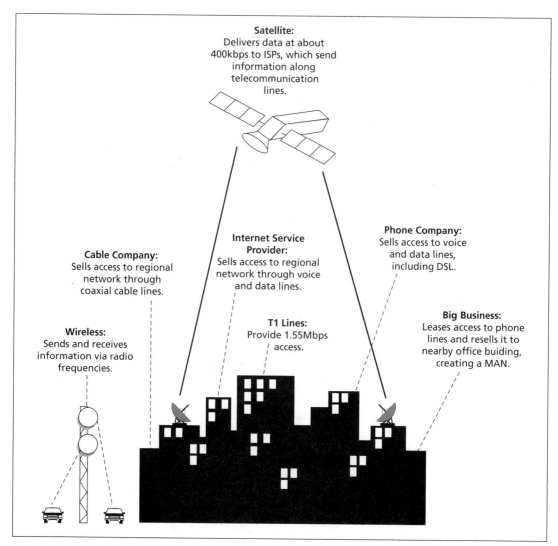

Figure 4-4   Delivering data

over-the-air technologies. Satellite wireless technologies include DBSs and LEOs; over-the-air technologies include MMDS and LMDS. Both forms of technology provide wireless local loops (WLLs).

Because all wireless technologies transmit data through the air, a major problem is transmission errors caused by interference. Transmission errors result in lost data packets, which can either reduce throughput or cause unreliable data transfer. A

Table 4-5   Comparing Broadband Technologies

Technology	Expected Baud Rate	Market Segment	Geographical Location	Consumer Connections	Carrier
x-DSL	16kbps–52Mbps	Residential, small office, home office (SOHO)	Urban areas	DSL modem, POTS splitter, and OS patch	DSL interface card
Private fiberoptics	622Mbps	Residential, SOHO, business	Urban/rural areas	Network interface card (NIC)	Fiberoptic cabling
Cable modems	1.5Mbps–27Mbps	Residential	Urban/rural areas	Cable modem	HFC upgrades, two-way upgrades, head-end equipment
Wireless networks	16kbps–45Mbps	Business, developing countries	Rural areas, developing countries	Receiver	Satellites, transmission towers

second problem is security. Data traveling through the air can be easily intercepted; therefore additional measures must be employed to guarantee the security and integrity of the data. Another problem is latency, particularly in DBS networks that use GEO satellites. Because the satellites are in orbit, transmitting data up to the satellite and back down to earth incurs large delay overheads.

◆ Broadband Access

Even after heroic effort on your part in optimizing bandwidth for your network, a significant barrier remains to delivering your content over the Web. That is the "last mile" connection to the client.

The bandwidth of Internet communication has been steadily increasing because of the overall pressure from users to improve performance. The important point is that the infrastructure provided by the Internet has become widespread and has developed sufficient performance to allow rapid transmission of large volumes of data.

The ideal vision for broadband may be an end-to-end optical fiber network with fiber direct to the home. But this expensive, long-term option may be preempted by a combination of a near-term breakthrough in compression technology and/or inexpensive wave division multiplexing. Obviously, the data compression standards will play a critical role in the form of required bandwidth reduction. This in turn will further contribute to technology convergence.

What all this fiber development means to bandwidth over GANs, WANs, MANs, and LANs is that it will soon be ubiquitous and cheap. However, efficient delivery will depend on the "last mile" connection into homes and businesses.

In contrast to the "last-mile" for residential areas, telephones companies are laying fiber cables for digital services from their switches to office buildings where the high-density client base justifies the additional expense.

High-speed consumer connections are now being implemented through cable modems and digital subscriber lines (DSL). Approximately 2.3 million homes will have cable modems by the end of 2001, compared with 600,000 DSL connections primarily to businesses. By 2006, it has been estimated that 40 million cable modems and 25 million DSL lines may be installed.

Table 4-6 shows a comparison of the five main options, including the role of wireless, for providing broadband access, along with their related technologies and problems.

Table 4-6 Summary of Broadband Access Architectures

	IDLC	HFC	FTTC/FTTH	LMDS/MMDS	DBS
Transmission	Twisted pair	Coaxial fiber	Fiber/twisted	Wireless fiber	Satellite
Technology	SONET, TMDA	MPEG-2, ATM	MPEG-2, ATM, TDM, WDM, x-DSL	MPEG-2, TDMA, CDMA, FDM, ATM, GSM	MPEG-2, FDM, TDMA, ATM
Problems	Legacy	Upgrade to two-way	Cost to deploy	Cost to deploy	One-way

IDLC, Integrated digital loop carrier; *HFC*, hybrid fiber coaxial; *FTTH*, fiber to the home; *FTTC*, fiber to the curb; *LMDS*, local multipoint distribution systems; *MMDS*, microwave multipoint distribution systems; *DBS*, direct broadcast satellite.

Computer Networking in Today's Schools

Should all elementary and secondary schools be fully networked? Schools can profit from computer networking through faster access to more information, improved communication and collaboration, and more convenient access to software tools.

Students and teachers are interested in working with network software applications such as Web browsers and e-mail clients. To support these applications, several other technologies, including computer hardware, network OSs, and network hardware, must first be put in place.

Desktop computers generally provide the most networking flexibility and computing power, but for mobility, notebook computers also may make sense. Handheld devices are a lower-cost alternative to notebooks for basic mobile data entry. Wearable devices extend the small and portable personal space one step further.

Today's handheld and wearable devices typically come bundled with their own custom OSs. These devices usually also include built-in hardware for networking functions. For desktop and laptop computers, however, network adaptors must be installed.

A fully networked school can offer several benefits, including increased speed for file sharing and added reliability. Central printers can be made accessible to students more conveniently. News and class project information can be easily disseminated to students. Students can more easily collaborate on group projects using network software applications. Teachers can carry out their day-to-day communications with each other more efficiently through e-mail and messaging.

Figure 4-5 shows the growth comparison of wired and wireless modem connection speeds over the past few decades. The trend suggests that the wireless development will follow the wired experience.

Mobility and the Wireless Web

The next generation of networking is Internet-centric but with the introduction of the mobility factor, extending to a variety of small devices, such as wireless phones or PDAs (see sidebar). Only recently, through standards and advances in computing and communications technologies, has that the convergence of wireless networks and the Internet begun to take place.

Networks' capability to route and adapt to current channel conditions and loss characteristics can be developed. This adaptability is essential for wireless channels, whose peak bandwidth and error characteristics can vary dynamically. RF channels, for example, are affected by terrain, weather, and interference from other transmitters. Instead of always using complex and costly error correction, they will use only as much as applications require.

Regardless of what economic force is compelling voice traffic onto a wireless network, some basic technological hurdles must be cleared, such as bandwidth. Traditional data transactions flowing from a handheld terminal to a logistics server require short bursts of traffic. Bandwidth, however, is rapidly opening up in the wireless world. Raw channel bandwidths of 1Mbps are common today. Frequency hopping, spread spectrum radio networks offer scalability; by overlapping the coverage of two or more access points, the bandwidth available in any location can be effectively doubled or tripled.

The second consideration for handling voice over wireless networks is network latency. Voice transmis-

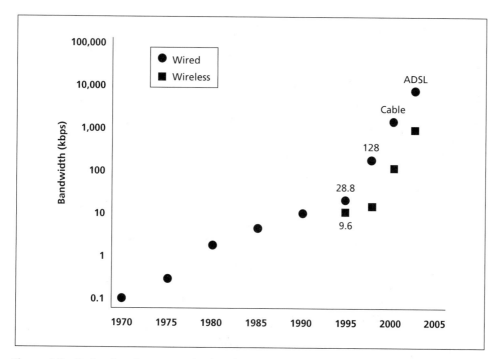

Figure 4-5 Delivering data over wired and wireless modems

sions are broken down into small packets for transmission across the network. The time required for a packet to travel from a digital phone through the network to another digital phone is termed *network latency*. If network traffic is moderate, the absolute latency is not a problem. On the other hand, for a satellite, the delay between speaking a question into a telephone in one country and hearing the reply from your colleague in across the globe can be confusing. However, your voice's total travel time through your LAN is generally undetectable.

The unpredictability and variation in latency are the factors that cause problems. Once the digital-to-analog converter in your headset begins "playing" the data stream into your ear, any disruption in that data stream will cause severe degradation in the quality of the signal. If you have no way to guarantee the maximum latency you might encounter during the transmission, you have no way to guarantee there will be no interruption. Most of the data networks used in supply chain environments, including TCP/IP networks, offer no such guaranteed quality of service.

Voice-over-data networks sometimes go beyond digital phone calls. Speech recognition is a powerful data interaction in applications such as parts inspection or single-item picking, where the user's hands and eyes are busy.

Developments in cell phone technology are leading to new applications. Imagine the applications you could deliver to clients if you could provide basic access to Web sites from millions of cell phones. With the right Web site software, these cell phones can handle most basic access tasks, including data entry, display, and calculation. Because most of the infrastructure is being installed by cell carriers, all that is needed is to write the server-side application.

Access to Web sites from digital cell phones is a specialized process, the technical challenges of which are very different from those faced by wired users. Wired users want three things from their Internet experience: bandwidth, bandwidth, and more bandwidth. Users of portable electronic devices, from cell phones to Palm Pilots, want three very different things: battery life, battery life, and more battery life. Because bandwidth drains batteries, wireless Internet access is destined to remain a low-bandwidth proposition for a while yet.

To contend with the lower bandwidth availability of wireless Net access, a new protocol has emerged. WAP conserves bandwidth by communicating in efficient tokenized binary instead of text. It assumes frequent temporary loss of connection with the host and compensates for it. It also assumes a restrained environment of low memory, slow processors, and small displays.

Developments at the high and low ends of wireless bandwidth lead to the same conclusion: Data and voice are merging into a single application. Data networks will increasingly be expected to handle voice traffic in addition to their traditional digital transactions. Now that cell phones are moving their voice payloads in digital packets, carriers, as well as customers, are more interested in exploiting their digital networks in the most profitable ways possible.

◆ MIT's Project Oxygen Network 21

At MIT's AI Laboratory Project Oxygen, networks, named N21s (for Network 21st century), are designed to be dynamic and capable of changing configurations to accommodate mobile and stationary devices. N21s integrate various wired, wireless, and satellite networks into one seamless Internet. Using algorithms and protocols, they configure topologies and adapt them to mobility and change, as well as provide secure access to networked resources and location discovery.

N21 networks integrate name resolution and routing. Intraspace routing protocols perform resolution and forwarding based on queries that express the characteristics of the desired data or resources in a collaborative region.

N21 networks allow devices to use multiple communication protocols. Vertical handoffs among these protocols allow MIT's H21 devices to provide seamlessness and connectivity over point-to-point transmissions. They also enable applications to adapt to changes in channel conditions and bandwidth. This enables end-to-end resource management based on a congestion manager. Unlike TCP, which is tuned for bulk data transfers, the congestion manager handles congestion resulting from audio, video, and other real-time streaming applications, as well as multiple short connections.

Project Oxygen is showing the way toward exciting technology based upon flexible, decentralized N21s. The N21 will dynamically change configurations for self-identifying mobile and stationary devices, offering a new level in network adaptability.

◆ Challenges and Opportunities

Today's computing infrastructure is built primarily from fixed-location resources, including servers (for example, Web servers, e-mail servers, file servers, database servers, application servers, DNS servers), clients (for example, PCs, workstations), and wired networks with cables, hubs, switches, and routers. This infrastructure supports client-server architectures, where the application's central data and logic reside in a server and the application's user interfaces reside in the client machines. Small, mobile wireless devices are now being developed as extended client devices with wireless connections.

The challenge for small, mobile wireless devices is integrating into the existing network infrastructure and client-server architectures. For example, the way current wireless instant messaging applications are designed, one cell phone can't send an instant message to another cell phone in the same room if either one is out of range of its cellular service provider. In addition, small, mobile wireless devices are constantly coming into and going out of radio range with each other as their users move about. Thus the network configuration requires constant dynamic adjusting as individuals with small devices transit a particular wireless personal area network's radius of inclusion.

In addition to traditional client-server architectures, the computing power available in small, mobile wireless devices opens up the possibility of distributed architectures involving peer-to-peer interactions among the devices themselves. In a peer-to-peer architecture, a wired network is not a necessity. Using their wireless networking capabilities, the devices could discover each other and connect to form an ad hoc network, even if there is no portal to the wired network nearby.

The low-level technology needed to make ad hoc peer-to-peer mobile distributed architectures a reality is already available. Wireless LAN technology, including IEEE 802.11 and Bluetooth, is now available. In addition, the Java programming language enables the development of platform-independent programs, which are needed to run distributed applications in an environment of heterogeneous mobile devices. The Java 2 Micro Edition (J2ME) is a version of Java designed to run in small devices with limited memory. Several J2ME-enabled cell phones, pagers, and PDAs are available, and more J2ME-enabled devices are on the way. Java APIs for Bluetooth are also under development.

However, the high-level technology needed to make ad hoc peer-to-peer mobile distributed architectures a reality is still emerging. Standard routing protocols for networks of mobile devices are also still under development. Distributed standards, including CORBA and Jini network technology, have been designed primarily for fixed-location hosts and wired networks, and software implementations of these standards are too large to use in small, mobile wireless devices. As a result, there is a lack of distributed software designed specifically for ad hoc networks of these devices.

Technological diversity may be wonderful in offering choices, but it is a daunting challenge to providing universal access. In the United States alone, there are over 400 wireless carriers and more than 6,000 operating companies. Each carrier and operating company has a unique way of communicating with devices on their network. In addition, there are multiple standards for wireless networks.

For opportunities for service providers to exist, providers must be able to reach all mobile users. This will require developing infrastructure to support any wireless carrier, any network, any device, any application, or any format. To succeed, either a uniform set of standards or complete interoperability must be developed. In Chapter 7, we will explore learning algorithms and adaptive software for enhancing network performance. In addition, Chapter 7 presents Intelligent Web Architecture innovations, including Web Services using Microsoft.NET and J2EE, and World Wide Web Consortium's (W3C) Semantic Web Architecture.

◆ Conclusion

In this chapter, we presented wired networks and wireless networks. We discussed the IEEE 802.11 standard and the background for transitioning to third-generation mobile wireless devices. In addition, we provided insights into the merging and convergence of the wired and wireless worlds. From this chapter, you may conclude that

1. Wired and wireless will continue to merge and provide a peak performance at greater than 10Tbps.

2. Intelligent networking software for routing and tracking will lead to general changes in IP networking protocols to Mobile IP (see Chapter 5).

3. Over time, core networks may migrate to optical fiber because photons carry more information more efficiently and at less expense than electrons. By 2003, ultra-long-haul (greater than 4,000 km), high-bandwidth optical transport will be used in the United States. The last mile of connection will be met with a combination of fiber and wireless technologies. In densely populated, metropolitan areas, free-space optical networks will provide 622MB of bandwidth to buildings. Second-generation LMDS and MDDS fixed wireless will bring service to buildings with less bandwidth requirement.

4. MIT's Project Oxygen is developing exciting technology based upon flexible, decentralized N21 networks that may dynamically change configurations for self-identifying mobile and stationary devices.

Merging Wireless Devices with the Web

In this chapter, we discuss how mobile wireless devices are converging with the Internet. We review the status of mobile wireless protocols and software for the current and next-generation mobile wireless technologies.
In addition, we discuss the development of IP version 6 and Mobile IP.

A s we move through a world of ever-changing technology, we realize that everything is converging. Just as we saw that wired and wireless communications networks were becoming seamlessly integrated, the Internet and mobile wireless data technologies are also converging. The distinctions between the wireless and wired ISPs have already begun to blur. And the goal of mobile wireless—"any time, anywhere" access—is the catalyst for the convergence of the entire structure.

◆ Mobile Wireless

Mobile wireless has the potential to both simplify and revolutionize communications. But the success of mobile communications lies in its ability to provide instant connectivity any time, anywhere in a practical and user-friendly manner. If the convergence of the mobile wireless and fixed information networks is to have significance, the quality and speeds available in the mobile environment must begin to match those of the fixed networks. How to build this broadband wireless network is the difficult question. Telecom companies will need to spend billions of dollars to catapult today's narrowband (9.6kbps) cell-phone infrastructure to achieve broadband capabilities.

Working against broadband access is a fundamental law of data communications. Back in 1948, Claude E. Shannon of Bell Labs found that the maximum amount of data that can be transmitted through any channel is limited by the available bandwidth (the amount of RF spectrum it occupies) and its signal-to-noise ratio (the signal to be communicated versus the background interference). The need for high-speed data services and high-quality voice transmission under roaming conditions represents significant challenges for wireless communications.

A range of reasonably successful mobile technologies already exists today in various parts of the world. The invasion of digital communications into the wireless world is already in progress. Analog cell phones were found to be useful as a tool, but digital phones have become a mainstay of wireless communications throughout the world.

Today, you can buy a book from Amazon.com, reserve tickets for a concert, or access your company's intranet right from your mobile phone. But technical limitations make it a tedious task. Wallets, such as Microsoft's Passport and Yahoo!Wallet, simplify and speed up data entry by automatically sending the pertinent information to an "e-tailer" when a transaction is complete. However, mobile-commerce (m-commerce) is more attractive when viewed from the perspective of a 5- to 10-year time horizon.

Various mobile competitors are influencing different regions of the world. The most widely used cellular network technology is the global system for mobile (GSM) communications, a time division multiple access (TDMA) system used in both Europe and Asia. Unfortunately, TDMA is less adaptable to the Internet's bursty data flows. A key alternative, code division multiple access (CDMA), faces strong opposition in many quarters. Table 5-1 presents the characteristics of worldwide wireless telecommunication standards.

In the following sections, we will discuss the mobile wireless technologies and their next-generation versions for a perspective of how they will converge with future Internet technology.

How Cellular Technology Works

Cell phones and other wireless devices send and receive data in a rather simple manner. There are only a few basic steps in the process, starting when you dial a number and press the send button (see Figure 5-1).

Table 5-1   Wireless Telecommunication Standard's Characteristics

Wireless Telecommunication	Standard	Multiple Access Method	Channel Bit Rate (kbps)
Analog cellular	AMPS*	FDMA	N/A
	TACS	FDMA	
	NMT	FDMA	
Digital cellular	IS-54/136	TDMA/FDM	48.6
	IS-95	CDMA/FDM	1.22
	GSM	TDMA/FDM	270.8
Analog cordless	CT0	FDMA	N/A
	JCT	FDMA	
	CT1/CT1+	FDMA	
Digital cordless	CT2/CT2+	TDMA/FDM	72
	DECT	TDMA/FDM	1152
	PHS	TDMA/FDM	384
Wireless data	CDPD	FDMA	19.2
	RAM-Mobitex	TDMA/FDM	8
	Ardis-RD-LAP	TDMA/FDM	19.2
	IEEE 802.11	CSMA	1000
Personal communication system	High tier	PCS/CDMA	—
	Low tier	PACS/DCT/CDMA/TDMA	

* The analog network is termed Advanced Mobile Phone Service (AMPS) and operates at 800MHz.

First, the phone seeks a nearby cellular antenna that will transmit the signal. This antenna is a base station located in a cell site. In general, the phone scans surrounding stations and locks to the base station that it is closest to or the one emitting the strongest signal. For TDMA and CDMA systems, the phone maintains a cell site location. Then the phone requests authorization to make a call. The base station checks the phone's mechanical serial number (MSN) and electronic serial number (ESN). After authorizing the call, the base station sends a channel assignment message to the phone. If the phone is analog, the voice signal is sent as a modulated radio wavelength. If the phone is digital, then the voice is sent as a binary digital language in ones and zeros. The base station connects a landline call to the mobile switching center (MSC) through Public Switch Telephone Network (PSTN), the

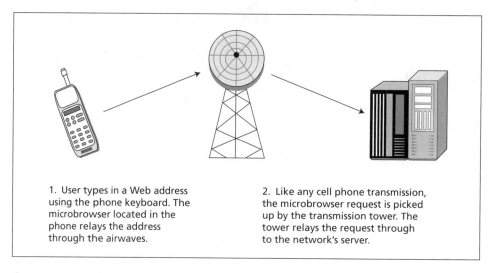

Figure 5-1 How cellular technology works

local phone network, to the number dialed, and then conversation can begin. In a call from one cell phone to another, the call skips the local phone company and sends a radio transmission to the other cell phone. When the call is received, the digital data, or radio waves, are converted back into voice (see Figure 5-2).

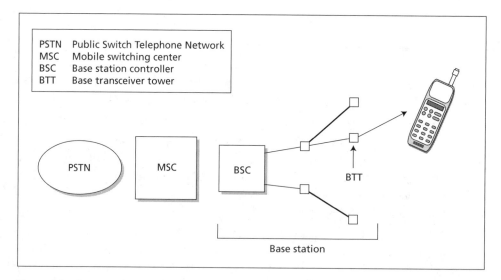

Figure 5-2 Base stations and cell sites

◆ Second-Generation Mobile Wireless Technologies

QUALCOMM founder Irwin Jacobs offered the "cocktail party" analogy to explain how the different types of cellular systems operate (see sidebar).

Consider a cocktail party with several guests paired in conversation. But for each listener, the sum total of all the other speakers' words are noise, interfering with his ability to understand the signal he wants to hear. As each speaker struggles to be heard, he talks louder, but that only increases the total noise in the room.

The hostess tries several different solutions. First, she disperses her guests into different rooms, one pair to a room. With no noise in the room except their own conversation, each pair converses unimpeded. This solution illustrates frequency division multiple access (FDMA) (the solution used by analog mobile systems) in which a pair of narrow-frequency channels are solely dedicated to one pair of users.

Unfortunately, there are not enough empty rooms (channels) for everyone. Trying to resolve the problem, the hostess now places three pairs of conversationalists in each room. All three pairs may converse, but they take turns. Every 20 seconds, one pair gets to talk and the other two pairs remain silent. Adapting to the problem, the guests find that, when it is their turn, they tend to talk faster than usual. And while waiting, they search for economical expressions, to encode more meaning in less time. This solution illustrates TDMA, made possible by digitizing the voice signals so we can send them in rapid bursts, combined with some speech compression codes to save bits; this triples the number of conversations the hostess can accommodate.

But there still are too many guests. So the hostess provides a final solution; she asks everyone to return to the main room and speak as softly as they can manage, but each pair in a different language. This represents CDMA.

CDMA spends logical million instructions per second (MIPS) to improve efficiency. The variable-rate Vocoder alone accounts for a 250 percent increase in the capacity of a CDMA cell.

Many 2G mobile technologies exist today, each having influence in specific parts of the world. The leading wireless

The Evolving Technologies of Mobile Wireless Communications

The evolution of mobile wireless technology is frequently viewed as coming about in three generations of change.

- The first generation (1G) refers to existing analog voice technology with local roaming capability.
- The second generation (2G) introduced digital voice and messaging capabilities, some international roaming, and improved quality of performance.
- The third generation (3G) will expand to include multimedia data, as well as voice, introduce global roaming, and enable Internet, e-mail, and video capabilities.

technologies include GSM digital mobile communications network (Europe and Asia), TDMA networks (North and South America), and CDMA (North America). In the following sections, we will discuss the mobile 2G standards in more technical detail.

Global System for Mobile Communication

GSM's air interface is based on narrowband TDMA technology. Available frequency bands are divided into time slots, with each user having access to one time slot at regular intervals. Narrowband TDMA allows eight simultaneous communications on a single 200KHz carrier and is designed to support 16 half-rate channels. The fundamental unit of time in this TDMA scheme is called a *burst period* and lasts approximately 0.577 ms. One physical channel is one burst period per TDMA frame. A GSM mobile can seamlessly roam nationally and internationally, which requires that registration, authentication, call routing, and location updating functions exist and be standardized in GSM networks. GSM offers a variety of data services. GSM users can send and receive data at rates up to 9,600bps to users on plain old telephone service (POTS), Integrated Services Digital Network (ISDN), packet-switched public data networks, and circuit-switched public data networks using a variety of access methods and protocols, such as X.25 or X.32. GSM also provides short message service (SMS)—a bidirectional service for short messaging.

The European version of GSM operates at the 900MHz frequency and 1,800MHz frequency. The North American version of GSM operates at the 1,900MHz frequency; thus the phones are not interoperable. Tri-band 900-1800-1900 GSM phones are expected to be manufactured in the next few years, which will allow interoperability between Europe and North America.

The GSM network voice is coded at 13kbps over the air interface. Using enhanced full-rate (EFR) coding, the voice quality approaches the landline voice quality. Recent developments such as adaptive multirate (AMR) coding, allow speech coding and channel coding to be dynamically adjusted, giving acceptable performance even in the case of bad radio conditions.

Recent developments include

- The GSM Association is working toward interstandard roaming between GSM and TDMA (ANSI-136) networks.
- The majority of European GSM operators plan to implement general packet radio system (GPRS) technology as their network evolution path to 3G communication systems.

▸ The GSM cordless telephony system will be used to provide a small home base station to work with a standard GSM mobile phone in similar mode to a cordless phone.

Time Division Multiple Access

TDMA IS-136 technology divides frequency bands available to the network into time slots, with each user having access to one time slot at regular intervals. For example, three users share a 30kHz bandwidth by splitting a 30kHz carrier into three time slots. TDMA networks transmit at a higher data rate on a relatively low bandwidth channel. As with GSM, the time slot structure allows the mobiles to conserve battery power and collect information about other channels. TDMA makes more efficient use of available bandwidth than the previous-generation analog technology. TDMA networks have increased the capacity of the analog networks by three times. Major U.S. carriers using TDMA include AT&T Wireless Services, BellSouth, and Southwestern Bell.

Code Division Multiple Access

CDMA technology (IS-95) (cdmaOne), used in North America, is based on the IS-95 protocol standard, first developed by QUALCOMM. CDMA differs from the other two technologies by its use of spread spectrum techniques for transmitting voice or data over the air. Rather than dividing RF spectrum into separate user channels by frequency slices or time slots, spread spectrum technology separates users by assigning them digital codes within the same broad spectrum. Like TDMA IS-136, CDMA operates in both the 1,900MHz band and the 800MHz band.

Work to develop CDMA as a 3G technology has also resulted in improving the current performance of CDMA as a 2G technology. The CDMA Development Group has formally adopted the cdmaOne name for all IS-95-based CDMA systems. The term represents the end-to-end wireless system and the necessary specifications that govern its operation.

The CDMA technology maximizes spectrum efficiency and enables more calls to be carried over a single 1.25MHz channel. In a CDMA system, each digitized voice is assigned a binary sequence that directs the proper response signal to the corresponding user. The receiver demodulates the signal using the appropriate code. The resulting audio signal will contain only the intended conversation, eliminating any background noise. Major U.S. carriers include Sprint PCS and Verizon Wireless.

Advantages of CDMA include frequency reuse, soft hand-offs, power control, and variable-rate Vocoders. CDMA disadvantages include the quality of reception and voice squeakiness. Advantages of the cdmaOne version are

- ► Capacity gains of eight to ten times that of AMPS analog systems
- ► Improved call quality
- ► Simplified system planning
- ► Enhanced privacy through the spreading of voice signals
- ► Improved coverage characteristics
- ► Increased talk time for portables

The 2G CDMA systems enhancements include enhanced roaming, which enables transparent roaming across cellular and PCS networks. Enhanced roaming will provide roaming between CDMA systems similar to that on GSM systems, in which registration, authentication, and credit checking are automatically carried out between the networks.

◆ Third-Generation Mobile Wireless Technologies

Third-generation wireless, or 3G, aims to provide enhanced voice, text, and data services. This will enable the provision of advanced services by seamless roaming between different networks. It also will bridge the gap between the wireless world and the Internet world. The 3G networks may support real-time video, high-speed multimedia, and enhanced mobile Internet access.

Highly evolved air interfaces, packet core networks, and increased spectrum may be used to accomplish 3G goals. The 3G high data capacities will bring the Internet closer to the mobile customer.

Higher capacities can be obtained from additional spectrum or by using new evolved air interfaces, and the data requirements can be served by overlaying 2.5G technologies on the existing networks. In many cases, higher-speed packet data can be obtained by adding a few network elements and software upgrades.

Technologies such as GPRS, high-speed circuit-switched data (HSCSD), and enhanced data rates for global evolution (EDGE) fulfill the requirements for packet data service and increased data rates in the existing GSM/TDMA networks. GPRS is actually an overlay over the existing GSM network. It provides packet data services using the same air interface by adding two network elements, the SGSN and GGSN, and a software upgrade. Although GPRS was basically designed for GSM networks, the IS-136 TDMA standard will also support GPRS.

The General Packet Radio Service

GPRS is a transition technology between 2G and 3G. It is a delivery mechanism for a range of high-band wireless services and delivers data in a series of packets, rather than in a smooth stream of bits. Theoretically, GPRS could provide data rates of up to 172kbps. Because the GPRS scheme uses bandwidth sharing, speeds for GPRS are actually around 50kbps. The second phase of GPRS, in 2002, will deploy EDGE, which offers data rates comparable to those of standard digital subscriber line (DSL) services. Typical single-user speeds are likely to be around 112kbps. The full 3G networks will be capable of offering data rates of between 384kbps and 2Mbps.

GPRS introduces two new major network nodes in the GSM architecture:

▶ Serving GPRS support node (SGSN): The SGSN tracks packet-capable mobile locations and performs security functions and access control. The SGSN is connected via frame relay.

▶ Gateway GPRS support node (GGSN): The GGSN interfaces with external packet data networks (PDNs). The GGSN is designed to provide interworking with external packet switched networks and is connected with SGSNs via an IP-based GPRS backbone network.

Theoretical speeds of up to 171kbps are achievable with GPRS, using all eight time slots at the same time. This is about three times as fast as the data transmission speeds possible over today's fixed telecommunications networks and ten times as fast as current circuit-switched data services on GSM networks.

Packet switching means that GPRS radio resources are used only when users are actually sending or receiving data. This efficient use of scarce radio resources means that large numbers of GPRS users can potentially share the same bandwidth and be served from a single cell. The actual number of users supported depends on the application being used and how much data is being transferred. Because of the spectrum efficiency of GPRS, there is less need to build in idle capacity that is only used in peak hours.

Coupled with other technologies such as WAP, GPRS can lead the convergence of cellular service providers and ISPs (see Table 5-2).

High-speed circuit-switched data (HSCSD) is the product of the evolution of circuit-switched data within the GSM environment. HSCSD will enable the transmission of data over a GSM link at 57.6kbps. This is achieved by adding together consecutive GSM time slots, each of which is capable of supporting 14.4kbps. HSCSD is circuit switched and is more suited to applications such as video conferencing and multimedia than "bursty" types of applications such as e-mail.

An advantage for HSCSD is that although GPRS is complementary for communicating with other packet-based networks such as the Internet, HSCSD could be the best way of communicating with other circuit-switched communications media.

In 2001, about 300 million wireless phones are used worldwide. By 2005, an estimated 1 billion will be in use. At the same time, full development of 3G is expected to take 3 to 5 years, thereby benefiting from the growth demand.

Standardization of 3G mobile systems is based on International Telecom Union (ITU) standards. By providing multimedia capacities and higher data rates, these 3G systems are expected to enhance the range and quality of services provided by 2G systems. The main contenders for 3G systems include wideband CDMA (W-CDMA) and cdma2000 (see Table 5-2). Infrastructure vendors, such as Nokia and Ericsson, are backing W-CDMA. cdma2000 is being backed by the North American CDMA community, led by the CDMA Development Group and including infrastructure

Table 5-2   The Technologies of Each Generation

2G Technology	2.5G Technology	3G Technology
GSM	GPRS HSCSD EDGE	W-CDMA–UTRA UMTS
cdmaOne-IS-95	1XRTT HDR	3XRTT W-CDMA–cdma2000
TDMA-IS-136	GPRS EDGE	UWC-138
PDC (Japan) IMODE (Japan)	N/A	W-CDMA–ARIB

vendors such as QUALCOMM and Lucent Technologies. Universal mobile communications system (UMTS) is the widely used European name for 3G technology.

Migration Strategies

Migration toward 3G technology will be a progression of steps as vendors move from 2G to 3G capabilities. Their progress will be based on the following technology steps:

- Network upgrades in the form of EDGE, GPRS, HSCSD, CDPD, IS-136+, HDR, and so on. Evolution to 2.5G technology basically will provide support for high-speed packet data. Though these technologies are extensions to 2G rather than precursors to 3G, they will have a major impact by either proving or disproving demand for specific services.
- Service trials to test infrastructure, handsets, and applications.
- Introduction of WAP-based services that bring the Web to the wireless phone. In the short term, WAP will provide a standard framework for accessing wireless Internet content, enabled by 2.5G technology.
- The development of mobile Web portals.
- Development of microbrowsers and operating systems (OSs).
- Wide acceptance of short-range wireless connectivity technologies such as Bluetooth, HomeRF, and so on (see Chapter 3).

Wireless Streaming Video Technologies

Nokia, the mobile handset supplier, will offer RealNetworks' RealPlayer technology on its EPOC-based communicators and smart phones. The streaming media will be delivered to mobile phones and wireless mobile computing devices. It will allow mobile phone users with suitably enabled devices to experience streaming content from Web sites worldwide.

The RealPlayer for the first Nokia EPOC products will to be available in 2002. The EPOC OS is an alliance—including Nokia, Matsushita, Motorola, Ericsson, and handheld computer maker Psion—as the OS for smart phones and other mobile communication devices.

In addition to RealNetworks, Microsoft Europe is already working to put Windows Media Player capabilities into PocketPC devices. Several smaller companies, including

ActiveSky and PacketVideo, are also providing software media players for mobile devices.

Technology Projections

The debate as to which standard is superior revolves around TDMA and CDMA. TDM systems, such as GSM, have the advantage of having very big market penetration, an easy and cheap upgrade path to packet-based data services, and almost global roaming. The proponents of TDMA claim that their networks are more rugged compared to the CDMA technology. The possible advantages of CDMA over TDMA include

▶ A CDMA system uses a combination of frequency division and code division to provide multiuser access. Although the capacity of a CDMA system is not unlimited, its range is considerably higher than those of a TDMA system.

▶ Because multiple transmissions are possible over the same bandwidth, the frequency reuse in CDMA networks can be very high.

▶ CDMA provides better signal quality.

▶ CDMA allows privacy of coded digital communications.

▶ CDMA allows for the easy addition of more users. However, additional users add more noise to the cell.

The very fact that CDMA technology is so new, however, makes it a risk for companies. Also, existing service providers who are heavily invested in TDMA networks would like to protect their investments.

In 2001, 89 percent of all cellular subscribers are using digital technology, and around 65 percent of these are GSM (including TMDA) subscribers, with CDMA and AMPS-D having around 13 to 14 percent of digital subscribers each. Some estimates indicated that the number of digital cellular subscribers is expected reach about 1 billion at the beginning of 2003. At the same time, the number of analog cellular subscriptions may fall from 80 million at the beginning of 2001 to 37 million by the beginning of 2003. As a result, the 3G technologies should not have a major impact in the market until 2003, and then they will have to coexist with 2G technologies for another 2 to 3 years before gaining prominence.

An important technology feature of successive generations of wireless technology will be the shift to expanded utilization of software (see Figure 5-3).

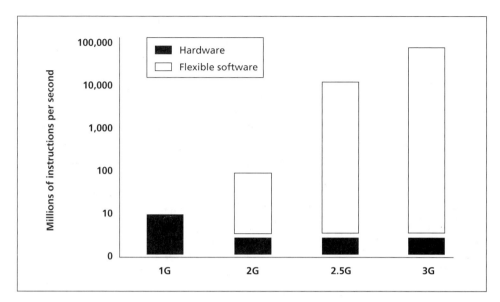

Figure 5-3   Wireless software

Wireless Handheld Devices

Nowhere is the convergence of technologies more visible than in the consumer product devices that provide individual access to information and communications networks: cell phones, pagers, portable computers, PDAs and more. Although a single integrated device for mobile phone and mobile multimedia applications may ultimately be the consumer choice, a PDA-type device with a large color touch screen linked to a handset via Bluetooth wireless technology is also a competitive possibility. But ultimately, a handheld unit, such as an H-21 with speech recognition and mobile software remains an attractive goal.

Wireless, handheld, and Internet technologies are converging to provide access to e-mail and the Internet. Today, Palm OS, Windows CE (now Pocket PC), or Psion handheld provide connection to the Internet without plugging into AC power and a phone jack. Most of the wireless PDAs must be connected to a cellular phone by cable or infrared (IR), to access a dial-up connection. But some major wireless technologies, such as Bluetooth short-range radio connection technology, let devices communicate selectively within 10 m. The PDA with a wireless Internet connection can be used for e-mail, to access special PDA-formatted Web channels, or to browse Web sites, as well as to synchronize a PDA with a host PC.

The greater utility and screen size of PDAs make it likely that these devices will be accepted by consumers. The Wireless Application Protocol (WAP), will be a boost to reading Internet content on devices with small screens. However, wireless PDA connections share several major limitations with other current mobile wireless solutions: network coverage, data throughput rate, usage costs, and screen display size.

Data rates for mobile wireless connections with current technologies range from 9,600bps to 19,200bps—significantly slower than most desktop modem connections.

It's likely that wireless service coverage will expand, data rates will improve, and costs will come down, but if you need to connect today, you already have many choices. The most common method of wireless connectivity for mobile devices is a data cable to connect an analog or digital cell phone to your PDA. Another choice is a digital phone, many of which can be used in data mode as modems, with a direct serial connection to a notebook computer or to a PDA.

For wireless PDA connectivity using a mobile phone without cables, Windows CE and Psion PDA users can use certain models of Ericsson GSM digital phones with built-in IR modems.

The wireless mobile technology with the fastest data rate used in the United States in 2001 is cellular digital packet data (CDPD), which has a top rate of 19,200bps. The downside of CDPD is that coverage is limited largely to major cities, but CDPD is available from major carriers such as AT&T and Bell Atlantic.

The Palm VII has a wireless radio that uses the BellSouth wireless network to run a service called PalmNet for connections in most U.S. metropolitan areas.

Several wireless Springboard expansion modules snap into the HandSpring Visor PDA (which uses the Palm OS). Among these expansion modules are a two-way wireless messaging module, a Bluetooth communications module, and a cell phone connector.

Technology is at the developmental stage, and no matter how revolutionary the wireless devices are, adoption is likely to come about relatively slowly. Device manufacturers have been struggling to design smart devices that incorporate enhanced features and integrate data functionality. As demand for more functionality on smart phones increases, designing simple-to-use devices will continue to be one of the greatest challenges for phone manufacturers. Low bandwidth, low battery life, and high latency also restrict device use and limit how much information can be displayed attractively on tiny screens.

Technical standards and the expense of roaming outside a carrier's territory are obstacles. Clearly, wireless devices need standards for their OS, communications protocols, applications languages, and network.

One obstacle to the Wireless Web is the coverage of services. The services that offer the most coverage today, Go.Web, OmniSky, Palm.Net, Ricochet Web-Connect!, and YadaYada are limited geographically. Instead of using the analog infrastructure, which blankets the United States, they each use one of three digital subscriber networks: CDPD, GSM, or Metricom's Ricochet Network.

Local cellular companies in over 120 cities provide CDPD over TCP/IP networks. WAP phones and Sierra Wireless AirCard300 can use this service. The CDPD antennas share space on the same cell towers that provide cellular voice service. CDPD offers data at 19.2kbps and uses cellular frequencies in the 800MHz to 900MHz range.

Ricochet[1] is a 128kbps upgrade of the 28.8 Metricom system, which has been in service since the mid 1990s. Like CDPD, Ricochet is a packet-switching technology using IP-based networking, and mobile units use the 800MHz to 900MHz frequencies, although Metricom's pole-top radios and wireless access points also use 2.3GHz and 2.4GHz frequencies.

GSM is a worldwide digital standard used primarily outside of the United States. Japan offers WAP service for low data rates.

Just like wired Internet services, the wireless world is grappling with transaction security issues. Network security on wireless systems depends primarily on its encryption capability (see Appendix E).

In the following sections, we will review the essential Internet standards and protocols necessary for merging wireless handheld devices with the Web.

◆ The Internet

The convergence of telecommunications and computing industries is becoming a reality, with IP gradually dominating over the traditional telecommunications systems. This is because IP packet-switching performance doubles every 10 months or

---

1. Ricochet is currently shutting down service in numerous locations due to financial losses.

The Internet Revolution

The explosion in the Internet Revolution can be traced to Tim Berners-Lee's 1991 creation of the graphical interface, which allowed the Internet to become a popular communication Web.

The Internet had existed for many years, with the primary users being scientific workers and the military. Its principal functions were e-mail communication and remote computing. In 1989, while working at the European Particle Physics Laboratory (CERN) in Geneva, Berners-Lee proposed a global hypertext system he called the World Wide Web. It could link more than just text. It could link graphics, sound, and video, to create an entire "hypermedia" system. Instead of a single database, the basis for his World Wide Web would be the Internet, the vast network of networks around the world.

Over the next couple of years, Berners-Lee and his collaborators laid the groundwork for the Web, inventing and refining the Hyper-Text Transfer Protocol (HTTP) to link Web documents, the Hyper-Text Markup Language (HTML) for formatting Web documents, and the universal resource locator (URL) system for addressing Web documents. These days, most of us reach the Web through commercial browsers, such as Netscape Navigator or Internet Explorer.

so, whereas telecommunication's circuit-switching equipment takes 4 times as long. Because Internet traffic doubles every 6 months, only packet switching can keep up. As a result, ever-expanding data networks are exerting dominance over voice communications circuit switching. With IP data packets increasingly dominating telephone networks, a circuit-switched infrastructure optimized for voice just doesn't make sense (see sidebar).

In addition, across the United States, efforts are underway to upgrade the network infrastructure. Universities are connecting to the next generation of the Internet, called Internet2. About 20 corporate partners are currently involved with 154 universities in establishing gigabits-per-second points of presence nationwide. In late February, 1999, Internet2 went live, with speeds up to 2.4Gbps. Colleges and universities must now upgrade campus networks to fiberoptic cabling to take advantage of the Gbps speeds promised by the high-speed network. The payoff will come when this wide bandwidth will accommodate powerful Web applications.

Internet Transfer Protocols

To exchange information over a network, computers must use a protocol, or common language. TCP/IP is the dominant one, and IP is the native language of the Internet

TCP/IP actually refers to a collection of protocols that are used for data transfer. TCP/IP was developed in 1973 and was published as a four-layer standard in 1983 for the ARPAnet WAN, which was the forerunner of the Internet. Almost every computer OS today provides support for at least part of this suite of protocols.

The International Standards Organization (ISO) developed a seven-layer reference model (Figure 5-4) called Open Systems Interconnection (OSI) in the 1980s as a network system standard. The four-layer TCP/IP model (see Figure 5-5) and the seven-layer OSI are the two most referenced network protocol models.

Layer #	Layer Name	Layer Function
7	Application	Program such as Netscape Navigator to send/receive data
6	Presentation	Formats screen data appropriately for network send or receive
5	Session	Checks arranged packets for completeness and logic
4	Transport	Error-checks packets and arranges them in order
3	Network	Data traffic cop to send packets to destination
2	Data link	Arranges data as network packets
1	Physical layer	Data stream as zeros and ones in and out of hardware

Figure 5-4   ISO/OSI seven layer model

Other network protocols include Serial Line Internet Protocol (SLIP), Point-to-Point (PPP), and Parallel Line Internet Protocol (PLIP). These protocols were designed to work efficiently over serial/parallel lines, in part by compression/decompression of data to make the most of limited bandwidth.

TCP/IP is an open standard that will run a wide range of hardware, including Ethernet, token ring, and X.25 on varying computer platforms such as UNIX, Linux, and Windows. It contains a standard method of addressing unique units on a vast network and can route data via a particular route to reduce traffic.

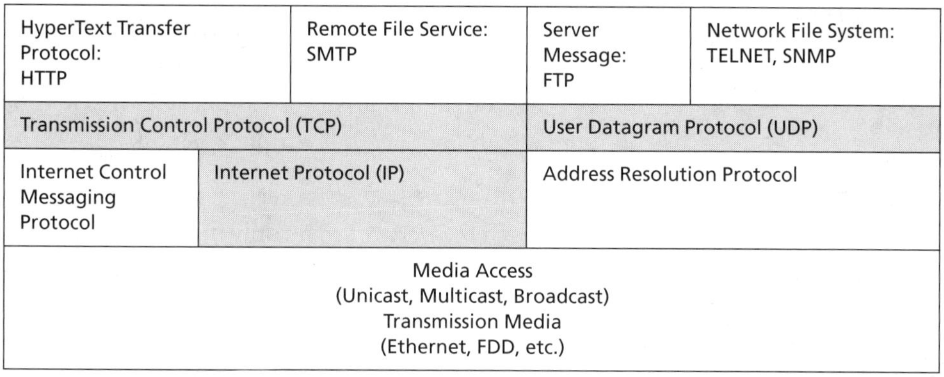

HyperText Transfer Protocol: HTTP	Remote File Service: SMTP	Server Message: FTP	Network File System: TELNET, SNMP
Transmission Control Protocol (TCP)		User Datagram Protocol (UDP)	
Internet Control Messaging Protocol	Internet Protocol (IP)	Address Resolution Protocol	
Media Access (Unicast, Multicast, Broadcast) Transmission Media (Ethernet, FDD, etc.)			

Figure 5-5   TCP/IP model

TCP/UDP Protocols

Transmission Control Protocol (TCP)

TCP is a protocol that provides for a highly reliable, connection-oriented delivery of data. TCP handles data as a stream of bytes, not frames. The unit of transfer is defined as a segment. TCP has features to ensure reliability, flow control, and connection maintenance. By using TCP, one is able to recover data that is damaged, lost, duplicated, or delivered out of sequence. In order to do this, a sequence number is assigned to each byte transmitted. The receiving host returns a response for bytes received within a specified period. If the response is not received, the data is retransmitted. Damaged data is detected by adding a checksum to each segment. If a segment is damaged by the receiving host, it discards the segment. The sender will then resend the segment since the response for the segment was not received.

User Datagram Protocol (UDP)

UDP is a "connectionless" protocol. It uses IP to send datagrams in a similar fashion to TCP, except that, like IP and unlike TCP, UDP does not care if the packets reach their destination. UDP is used in applications where it is not essential for 100 percent of the packets to arrive. It is up to program designers to choose what method is most suitable. While TCP is safer and more accurate, UDP is becoming more common. TCP is important in transferring software programming, where the loss of a single bit of information could be important. UDP is especially favored for streaming or real-time applications.

The Internet layer, IP, shields the higher levels from network architecture and establishes, maintains, and terminates connections between systems.

The packets that are passed over the network are called datagrams. Each datagram contains a header of relevant information necessary to deliver the datagram correctly. It includes the source and the destination port numbers between computers. A sequence number allows the destination computer to reconstruct the datagrams in the correct sequence.

The transmission control protocol HTTP uses TCP as the protocol for reliable document transfer. If packets are delayed or damaged, TCP will effectively stop traffic until either the original packets or backup packets arrive.

Mobile Protocols

The Web is a graphical interface represented by a browser that interprets HTML and other protocols to display images and interact with a user. The Internet is a data communication path controlled by the TCP/IP protocol stack. It does not make sense to provide Web access on some devices, but it might make a good deal of sense to provide Internet access. The difference is whether the device is displaying the data or using it internally. A smart device that can use the resources of the Internet can make itself more useful. One that has a display screen on it that simply duplicates what can be obtained from PC screen is simply wasteful.

The TCP/IP stack has done a very good job of adapting to changes in the network. The only major change that is anticipated is the change to IPv6 (IP version 6), which primarily will allow an expansion to the address space to accommodate the explosive growth of the number of devices on the Internet. However, it does not reassign addresses to devices on the fly. Unfortunately, this is necessary in a wireless world.

If you move your laptop between two different subnets via wireless links, it will become unable to communicate. This is important if it was expected to switch automatically between a local IEEE 802.11 link and a wide-area PCS link. There is a proposed standard (Mobile IP) that will allow this to happen. Mobile IP will require upgrades to the protocol stacks on portable devices, however, as well as set up servers on the networks that can support these mobile devices.

Mobile IP

The Mobile IP Working Group of the Internet Engineering Task Force (see Appendix A: IETF) has developed routing support to permit IP nodes (hosts and routers) using either IPv4 or IPv6 to seamlessly roam among IP subnetworks and media types. The Mobile IP method supports transparency above the IP layer, including the maintenance of active TCP connections and UDP port bindings.

Normally, IP routes packets from a source to a destination according to routing tables. The routing tables maintain the next-hop (outbound interface) information for each destination IP address. The network number is derived from the IP address.

To maintain existing transport-layer connections as the mobile node moves from place to place, it must keep its IP address the same. However, in TCP, the connection is indexed by a quadruplet IP address—with port numbers for both end points. Changing any of the four numbers will cause the connection to be lost. The problem is that delivering packets to the mobile node's current point depends on the network number contained within the mobile node's IP address, which changes at new points of attachment.

Mobile IP has been designed to solve this problem by allowing the mobile node to use two IP addresses. In Mobile IP, the home address is static to identify TCP connections. The care-of address changes at each new point of attachment and can be thought of as the mobile node's topologically significant address. This address shows the network number and identifies the mobile node's point of attachment.

Whenever the mobile node is not attached to its home network, the home agent gets all the packets destined for the mobile node and arranges to deliver them to the mobile node's current point of attachment.

Whenever the mobile node moves, it registers its new care-of address with its home agent. To get a packet to a mobile node from its home network, the home agent delivers the packet from the home network to the care-of address.

In addition, IPv6 includes many features for streamlining mobility support that are missing in IP version 4 (IPv4). The most pressing problem facing Mobile IP, however, is security. Firewalls cause difficulty for Mobile IP because they block classes of incoming packets that do not meet specified criteria (see Appendix E).

Mobile IP has great potential, and the IETF standardization process requires the working group to rigorously demonstrate interoperability among various independent implementations before the protocol can advance. Since both IPv6 and Mobile IP have little direct effect on the operating systems of mobile computers outside of the network layer of the protocol stack, application engineers will find it to be an acceptable programming environment. Figure 5-6 summarizes the challenges of implementing Mobile IP.

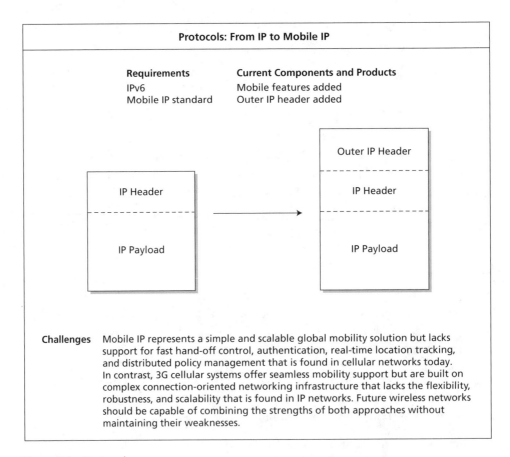

Figure 5-6   Protocols

◆ The Wireless Internet

Programmers around the world are working to bring Internet content to your cell phones and other wireless devices. The protocol to provide this service is WAP and its associated Web page language, Wireless Markup Language (WML). WAP is intended for the high-speed, 3G networks; however, WAP technology is currently available on enabled GSM, TDMA, and GPRS phones in Europe.

WAP is built on the idea that data communication and display of Web data is very difficult for small devices such as cell phones. The solution that WAP provides allows for the slow data rates, small display areas, limited keyboards, and limited computing capability of current and next-generation cell phones. This solution combines a trimmed-down protocol stack, a "deck of cards" philosophy (which we will explain later) and a heavy reliance on push technology to solve these problems. The equivalents of HTML and JavaScript under WAP are WML and WMLScript. Each of these is a subset of their full Web counterparts, with extensions added to maintain sessions and to handle transactions better.

The advantage of WAP is that it does adapt Web content to cope with the limitations of small handheld devices. Unfortunately, this involves the conversion and special handling of large amounts of data. If Wireless Web access becomes popular, the devices will have to adapt. This may make the specialized language defined in WAP obsolete.

One way to get access to your personal information while traveling is to set up a virtual private network (VPN) that will extend your local network across the Internet through a "tunnel" that connects to your home PC. This option is available to full laptops, but as yet no cell phones or PDAs support VPNs.

Consumer applications are interesting if they can be deployed through widespread wireless access. One strong indication has been the use of SMS. E-mail in general will be a very strong consumer application because the low data rates of current wireless service are not a particular problem for text-based e-mail.

One of the interesting problems is that of middleware, software that glues together applications and OSs. This category includes communication software, as well as database systems and other operating environments. This software is complicated by the fact that at least half of it must run on small devices that generally do not have hard drives or large amounts of memory and that must be as efficient as possible because they run on batteries. They also are characterized by small display screens

WAP and Speech Recognition

The key differences between WAP and traditional Internet applications are that it uses less memory and is more adaptable to the slow data rates currently found in wireless environments. These characteristics make it a good choice as an applications platform for the next generation of cell phones and for the lower end of the PDA market, but they also limit its capability for growth.

But what happens to WAP when the next generation of these devices leaves these limitations behind? Certainly the prospects for speech recognition, understanding, and synthesis becoming available will greatly affect the use of small, handheld devices, even if they only act as intermediate transmission devices to off-load the computational demands of processing to a nearby, or embedded, computer server.

and inadequate or completely absent keyboards. These are very different devices from the PC that is on your desk—something that software has to take into account. There are already database systems that interface Structured Query Language (SQL) databases to wireless devices and form packages that are adapted to the small displays.

WAP is both a communications protocol and an application environment. It is a standardized technology for cross-platform, distributed computing. WAP is similar to the combination of HTML and HTTP optimized for low-bandwidth, low-memory, and low-display capability environments. These types of environments include PDAs, wireless phones, pagers, and other handheld communication devices. It can be built on any OS (including PalmOS, EPOC, Windows CE, FLEXOS, OS/9, and JavaOS). It provides service interoperability, even between different device families. WAP will also be accessible to

▶ CDMA IS-95

▶ TDMA IS-136

▶ GSM-900, GSM-1800, GSM-1900

▶ 3G systems—IMT-2000, UMTS, W-CDMA, Wideband IS-95

The WAP approach to content distribution is similar to the Web approach in concept. Both distribute content to remote devices using standardized client software. Both rely on back-end servers for user authentication, database queries, and intensive processing. Both use markup languages derived from SGML for delivering content.

How WAP Works

WAP client applications make requests very similar in concept to the URL concept in use on the Web. A WAP request is routed through a WAP gateway, which acts as an intermediary between the client (GSM, CDMA, TDMA, etc.) and the computing WAP gateway. The gateway then processes the request, retrieves contents or calls CGI scripts or Java servlets, then formats data for return to the client. This data is formatted as WML, a markup language that is an application of Extensible Markup

Language (XML). Once the WML has been prepared (known as a deck), the gateway then sends the completed request back to the client for display or processing. The client retrieves the first card off of the deck and displays it on the monitor.

The deck of cards metaphor is designed to take advantage of small display areas on handheld devices. Instead of continually requesting and retrieving cards (the WAP equivalent of HTML pages), each client request results in the retrieval of a deck of one or more cards. The client device can also use the logic of embedded WML-Script (the WAP equivalent of client-side JavaScript).

In summary, the client makes a request and this request is received by a WAP gateway that then processes the request and formulates a reply using WML. The WML is sent back to the client for display in a very similar way to the standard HTTP transaction involving client Web browsers.

Communication Between Client and Server

The WAP Protocol Stack is implemented by a layered approach similar to the OSI network model (see Figure 5-7). WSP capabilities include

▶ Provide HTTP/1.1 functionality

▶ Exchange client and server session headers

▶ Interrupt transactions

▶ Push content from server to client

▶ Negotiate support for multiple, simultaneous asynchronous transactions

Wireless Application Environment (WAE)	Other Services and Applications
Wireless Session Protocol (WSP)	
Wireless Transaction Protocol (WTP)	
Wireless Transport Layer Security (WTLS)	
Wireless Datagram Protocol (WDP)	
Bearers (GSM, IS-136, CDMA, GPRS, CDPD, PHS, IDEN, etc.)	

Figure 5-7　Wireless application protocol architecture

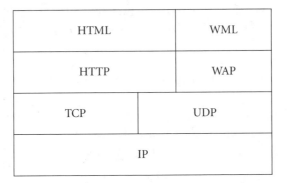

HTML	WML
HTTP	WAP
TCP	UDP
IP	

Figure 5-8 Wireless application protocol layer

WTP allows interactive (request/response) browsing applications and defines the transaction environment in which clients and servers exchange data.

The Wireless Datagram Protocol (WDP) layer operates above the bearer layer used by the communications provider. This layer allows applications to operate transparently over varying bearer services. While WDP uses IP as the routing protocol, it does not use TCP. Instead, it uses User Datagram Protocol (UDP), which does not require messages to be split into multiple packets. Due to the nature of wireless communications, the mobile application must talk directly to a WAP gateway, which reduces the overhead required by TCP (see Figure 5-8).

◆ Wireless Markup Language

WML is an XML document type defined by a standard XML Document Type Definition. WMLScript is a case-sensitive language that supports standard variable declarations, functions, and other common constructs such as IF-THEN statements, and for/while loops.

The first two lines in a WMLScript are required. They give the XML version number and the public document identifier, respectively. From there, all WML decks (one WML file equals one deck) begin and end with the <wml></wml> tags. For example

```
<?xml version="1.0"? >
<!DOCTYPE wml PUBLIC "-//WAPFORUM//DTD WML 1.1//EN"
"http://www.wapforum.org/DTD/wml_1.1.xml">
```

```
<wml>
  <card id="First_Card" title="First Card">
    <p>
     Hello World!
    </p>
  </card>
</wml>
```

Individuals cards are arranged with the <card></card> tags. Included in the WML specification are elements that fall into the following categories: decks/cards, events, tasks, variables, user input, anchors/images/timers, and text formatting.

The purpose of WMLScript is to provide additional intelligence through client-side procedural logic. It is based on ECMAScript (which is based on JavaScript), modified to support low-bandwidth communications and thin clients. WMLScript allows code to be built into files transferred to mobile clients.

WMLScript is a weakly typed language, and no type checking is done at compile or runtime and no variable types are explicitly declared. Internally, the following data types are supported: Boolean, integer, floating-point, string, and invalid.

The programmer does not need to specify the type of any variable; WMLScript will automatically attempt to convert between the different types as needed. The operators and expressions supported by WMLScript are virtually identical to those of the JavaScript programming language.

While WMLScript does not support the creation of new objects via object-oriented programming, it does provide six "prebuilt" libraries that aid in the handling of many common tasks.

Alternatives to WML

Ironically, U.S. companies have been looking to Japan for alternatives, especially since WAP has been heavily criticized recently. Japan has three competing standards—HDML, compact HTML (cHTML), and MML—none of which is compatible with WML as it's used in American and European WAP systems.

I-mode is a wireless technology developed by the Japanese company NTT DoCoMo that enables users to access Internet services via their wireless phones. I-mode (the *i* stands for information) is based on packet data transmission technology. This means that i-mode is always online, and therefore users are charged only for how much information they retrieve, not how many minutes they are using the service. I-mode can be used to exchange e-mail with computers, handheld devices, and other i-mode cellular phones. DoCoMo has approximately 60 percent of market share in Japan. The most common complaints are about unstable connections and that the i-mode service runs at only 9.6kbps.

The i-mode service lets users access Web sites in compact HTML (cHTML) format. Because cHMTL format is a subset of HTML 3.2, content providers and application developers can build sites without learning new methods of programming or relying on restricted WAP gateways.

The cHTML specification can be thought of as a stripped-down version of HTML with the new ACCESSKEY attribute that can be used in ANCHOR and INPUT tags. The language doesn't have fancy HTML 4.0 positioning features such as layers or style sheets. The DIV support is limited, with only left, right, and center formatting and no JavaScript support.

Reformatting engines will have challenges with any DHTML, scripting, or frames features on existing pages. And for a site to operate nicely on a mobile phone, developers will need to recode pages while thinking of the small screen and small buffer size on most handheld devices.

J-Phone's SkyWeb service requires sites to use the Mobile Markup Language (MML) to be viewed on its phones. MML is a superset of cHTML in that it has all the features of cHTML plus support for TABLE tags.

The Handheld Device Markup Language (HDML) was developed by Phone.com. Phone.com is one of the developers of WAP-enabled browsers, so it's not surprising that WML, the common markup language for WAP, grew out of the HDML standard. HDML was developed for small-format devices, with a transaction-oriented model.

◆ Comparing Wireless Web Services

The Wireless Web is already becoming a business tool as PDA and cell phone Web access is expanding. Although there is still a conglomerate of incompatible standards, eventually access to corporate servers from virtually anywhere will become commonplace. However, for now, the Wireless Web is not the Web we are accustomed to, but rather a small, select subset of information. The browsers on digital phones and PDAs require sites to be especially coded with WML or HDML. Hence many sites are not yet accessible to wireless users. Even worse, connections are still too slow while we wait for 3G technology.

With all this effort, wireless devices are improving quickly to prepare for full access to the Wireless Web. And the number of users is growing. As standards take hold, providing wireless services will become financially viable for banks, retailers, and airlines. For example, almost every bank plans to offer the ability to check balances, pay bills, and trade stocks wirelessly via phone or PDA. Table 5-3 compares some of today's services.

Web Services Description Language

In 2001 the Web Services Description Language (WSDL) supported by Microsoft, IBM, Oracle and others, requested acceptance as a standard protocol from the World Wide Web Consortium (W3C). WSDL is an XML-based grammar for describing network services as collections of communication points cable of exchanging messages. WSDL supports Microsoft's .NET implementations as well as Simple Object Access Protocol (SOAP: see Chapter 7).
(See msdn.Microsoft.com.)

Table 5-3　Wireless Web Services in 2001

Type of Service	Company	U.S. Coverage	Connection Speed	Internet Browsing	E-mail
Palm OS services	Go.Web	–	o	o	+
	OmniSky	–	o	o	o
	Palm.net	o	o	o	+
	SkyWriter	o	–	–	–
	YadaYada	–	–	+	o
Pocket PC services	Go.Web	–	+	+	+
	OmniSky	–	o	+	o
Internet phone service	AT&T Digital PocketNet Service	o	o	o	o
	Nextel Online	–	o	o	o

–, Less than average; o, average; +, better than average.

Table continued on next page.

Table 5-3 Wireless Web Services in 2001 (*continued*)

Type of Service	Company	U.S. Coverage	Connection Speed	Internet Browsing	E-mail
Internet phone service, (*continued*)	Sprint PCS Wireless Web	+	+	o	o
	Verizon Wireless Mobile Web	o	+	o	+
Two-way paging service	Go.Web	o	o	–	o
	SkyTel eLink	+	o	–	o

–, Less than average; o, average; +, better than average.

◆ Challenges and Opportunities

The cellular phone industry has been unsuccessfully trying to market wireless packet data services to consumers since 1994. At that time, the industry offered packet data overlay AMPS analog cellular service. But because of bandwidth limitations (that is, maximum data throughput with CDPD), wireless data failed to catch on with U.S. consumers.

More recent technologies, such as HDML, WAP, HTML, and J2ME, have helped solve part of the bandwidth issue by reducing the amount of information sent over wireless, and new wireless packet data technologies (for example GPRS, IEEE 802.11) are increasing bandwidth. The problem remains, however, of what to do when the mobile subscriber unit roams to a different IP subnetwork.

Mobile IP offers a solution to this problem by having the router on the home subnetwork tunnel IP packets to the mobile at a care-of address on the new IP subnetwork.[2] Some technical issues, such as firewalls, remain to be worked out with Mobile IP.

---

2. The main difference between Mobile IP for IPv4 and IPv6 is that in IPv6 there is no foreign agent. IPv6 implements a colocated care-of address and registers directly with the home agent.

Mobile IP represents a simple and scalable global mobility solution, but lacks support for fast hand-off control, authentication, real-time location tracking, and distributed policy management that is found in cellular networks today. In contrast, 3G cellular systems offer seamless mobility support but are built on complex connection-oriented networking infrastructure that lacks the flexibility, robustness, and scalability that is found in IP networks. Future wireless networks should be capable of combining the strengths of both approaches without inheriting their weaknesses.

◆ Conclusion

In this chapter, we presented the convergence of mobile wireless phone and other small handheld devices with the Internet. We reviewed the growth of mobile wireless and the development and requirements of the Internet. Then we presented standards, protocols, and technology of the current and future mobile technologies.

From this chapter, you may conclude that

▶ Mobile wireless convergence with the Internet is happening now and Wireless Web services will soon become broadly available.

▶ WAP may prove to be only an intermediate solution.

▶ The 2G and 2.5G market will continue to increase.

▶ CDMA could have a growing influence through 3G technologies in the next 5 to 10 years.

▶ IPv6 should develop along with Mobile IP support.

PART III

Connecting Devices to People

In Part III, we discuss communication between devices and people and how increasingly intelligent ways are being developed for interactions from devices to people.

We start in Chapter 6, by presenting the topic of artificial intelligence and developing a thesis of growing intelligence for the Web. In Chapter 7, we explore Web Services and the transition of Web architecture toward a Semantic Web with a logic layer. Then, in Chapter 8, we present speech synthesis and translation.

We digress in Chapter 9 to discuss the economic basis for rapid progress of an Intelligent Wireless Web. Finally, in Chapter 10, we weave the "Big Picture" of the likely progress over the next decade in actually "building" the Intelligent Wireless Web.

6

Artificial Intelligence

In this chapter, we address the questions

- What is intelligence?
- How is artificial intelligence different?
- What types of methods are used to develop and apply AI?
- What is the role of learning, neural networks, and adaptation?
- Could Web protocols support AI?
- What is distributed artificial intelligence?
- How can Semantic Web architecture be used to improve Web intelligence?

In 1947, shortly after the end of World War II, English mathematician Alan Turing first started to seriously explore intelligent machines. By 1956, John McCarthy of MIT contributed the term artificial intelligence (AI). By the late 1950s, many researchers were working in the field of AI, most basing their work on programming computers. Eventually, AI became more than a branch of science—it expanded far beyond mathematics and computer science into such fields as philosophy, psychology, and biology.

AI means different things to different people. Some confusion arises because the word "intelligence" is so ill-defined; so it is important to discuss what we mean by intelligence, both natural and artificial. AI is sometimes described in two ways: strong AI and weak AI. Strong AI asserts that computers can be made to think on a level (at least) equal to that of humans. Weak AI simply holds that some "thinking-like" features can be added to computers to make them more useful tools. Examples of Weak AI abound: expert systems, drive-by-wire cars, smart browsers, and speech recognition software. These weak AI components may, when combined, begin to approach the expectations of strong AI.

◆ Intelligence

Before discussing AI or "thinking machines," it is appropriate to consider what we mean by real, as opposed to artificial, intelligence. The Greek philosopher Aristotle considered intelligence to be the main distinguishing feature of humans: he described man as a "rational animal." He established many precedents in the study of logic and began the process of codifying syllogisms, a process later extended by the mathematician Leibnitz. In addition to his work in developing the mathematics of calculus, Leibnitz initiated an effort to represent human logic and reasoning as a series of mechanical and symbolic tasks. Later, George Boole developed Boolean logic and algebra, paving the way for the use of mechanical rules to carry out logical deductions.

Unfortunately, the definition of "real" or "human" intelligence is itself the subject of great controversy and disagreement. Many different definitions are offered in dictionaries and textbooks, and different connotations are attached to the concept of intelligence. Included among these are the ability to learn and understand; mental alertness and responsiveness; speed of understanding; the capacity to understand complex concepts; the resourcefulness to derive new insights from existing information; and the ability to assimilate, process, and remember large amounts of information (see sidebar). No one of these descriptors adequately characterizes the concept of intelligence, and no particular combination of them would be universally accepted by experts as a definitive characterization.

Attributes of Intelligence

Some attributes related to intelligence include

1. Problem-solving ability
   - Speed
   - Complexity
   - Creativity
1. Memory capacity
   - Quantity
   - Information organization and retrieval
1. Ability to learn
   - Facts
   - Concepts
   - Processes
1. Self-awareness

One perspective on intelligence holds that human intelligence is whatever intelligence tests measure. Early intelligence testing measured parameters such as reaction time and processing speed on perceptual tasks. The methods of Binet and Simon, introduced in the early 1900s, used tests of practical knowledge, memory, reasoning, vocabulary, and problem solving to predict academic success in school. Subsequent tests of the so-called "intelligence quotient" (IQ) attempted to relate test performance to the "mental age" of the subject; an IQ result of 100 indicating that the subject performed at the average level for individuals in that age group. Most recently, standardized tests such as the Scholastic Aptitude Test have been criticized by many as being tests of cultural knowledge rather than intelligence.

Although it is not possible to resolve controversial differences of opinion over the nature of human intelligence, it is possible to recognize certain attributes that most would agree reflect the concept. These include such elements as the ability to learn; the ability to assimilate, organize, and process information; and the ability to apply knowledge to solve complex problems. Many of these attributes can be traced into the various areas of research in the field of AI, which address the basic questions of what it means for a machine to have intelligence (see sidebar).

In Turing's seminal work more than 50 years ago, he determined that a computer could be called intelligent if it could deceive a human into believing that it was human. His test, referred to as the Turing Test, consists of a person asking a series of questions to both a human subject and a machine. The questioning is done via a keyboard so that the questioner has no direct interaction between subjects, man or machine. A machine with true intelligence will pass the Turing Test by providing responses that are sufficiently human-like that the questioner cannot determine which responder is human and which is not. A scaled-down version of the Turing Test, known as the Loebner Prize, requires that machines "converse" with testers only on a limited topic, to demonstrate their intelligence.

How far is AI from reaching human-level intelligence? Some have suggested that human-level intelligence can be achieved by writing large numbers of programs and assembling vast databases of facts in the languages used for expressing knowledge. However, most AI researchers believe that new fundamental ideas are required before true intelligence can be approached.

Two main lines of research are being conducted. One is biological, based on the idea that because humans are intelligent, AI should study humans and imitate the psychology or physiology of human intelligence. The other is phenomenological, based on studying and formalizing common-sense facts about the world and the problems that the world presents to the achievement of goals, thereby providing functionality that, in humans, would be considered intelligent behavior, even if the approach used is quite different from what would be found in a human.

Artificial Intelligence

AI can be defined as the study of the ways in which computers can be made to perform cognitive tasks. Examples of such tasks include

- Understanding natural language statements
- Recognizing visual patterns or scenes
- Diagnosing diseases or illnesses
- Solving mathematical problems
- Performing financial analyses
- Learning new procedures for problem solving
- Playing complex games, such as chess

Computational Complexity Theory

Computational complexity theory is the study of how much of a resource (such as time, space, parallelism, or randomness) is required to perform certain classes of computations. Problems are classified according to how difficult they are to solve. Among the many different classifications, the following are some of the most commonly encountered:

- **P**: Problems that can be solved in polynomial time. An example problem in *P* is the task of sorting a list of numbers. Because by systematically swapping any disordered pair, the task can be accomplished within quadratic time, the problem is considered to be in *P*.
- **NP**: Problems that are "nondeterministic in polynomial time." A problem is in *NP* if a selected (or guessed) trial solution can be quickly (in polynomial time) tested to determine if it is correct.
- **PSPACE**: Problems that can be solved using an amount of memory that is limited as a polynomial in the input size, regardless of how much time the solution takes.
- **EXPTIME**: Problems that can be solved in exponential time. This class contains most problems likely to be encountered, including everything in the previous three classes.
- **Undecidable**: For some problems, it can be proved that there is no algorithm that always solves them, no matter how much time is allowed.

In the 1930s, the mathematical logician, Kurt Gödel, along with Alan Turing, established that, in certain important mathematical domains, problems exist that cannot be solved or propositions are made that cannot be proved or disproved and are therefore undecidable. Whether a certain statement of first-order logic is provable as a theorem is one example, and whether a polynomial equation in several variables has integer solutions is another. Although humans solve problems in these domains all the time, it is not certain that arbitrary problems in these domains can always be solved. This is relevant for AI because it is important to establish the boundaries for problem solution (see sidebar).

In the 1960s, computer scientists Steve Cook and Richard Karp developed the theory of NP-complete problem domains. Problems in these domains are solvable, but they take an exponential amount of time in proportion to their size. Humans often solve problems in NP-complete domains in times much shorter than is guaranteed by the general algorithms but can't solve them quickly in general.

The theory of the difficulty of general classes of problems is called computational complexity. Algorithmic complexity theory was developed by Solomonoff, Kolmogorov, and Chaitin. It defines the complexity of a symbolic object as the length of the shortest program that will generate it.

NP-complete problems are encountered frequently in AI. Alternatives to addressing them include

▶ Use a heuristic. If the problem cannot be quickly solved deterministically in a reasonable time, a heuristic method may be used certain cases.

▶ Accept an approximate instead of an exact solution. In some cases, a provably fast algorithm exists that doesn't solve the problem exactly but comes up with an acceptable approximate solution.

▶ Use an exponential time solution anyway. If an exact solution is necessary, an exponential time algorithm may be the best approach.

▶ Redefine the problem. Normally, the NP-complete problem is based on an abstraction of the real world. Revising the abstraction to eliminate unnecessary details may make the difference between a P and NP problem.

In the following sections, we review some important aspects of AI by considering the methods of AI, intelligent software, and the application of those in the Web.

◆ Artificial Intelligence Methods

AI is a broad field with different meanings and methods, depending on the application. It is primarily concerned with getting computers to do tasks that would normally require human intelligence. However, there are tasks, such as solving complex mathematics problems, that computers do well already. The field of AI is the science and engineering of making intelligent machines and intelligent computer programs.

AI is not only a scientific discipline but also an engineering field. Its depth and breadth have provided a large amount of room for researchers to address problems of great diversity and range, and a tremendous amount of research has been conducted over the past 40 years. Traditionally, the specific problem areas that have been the subject of AI have included

▶ *Planning:* The evaluation and selection of optimal sequences of actions to achieve goals

▶ *Communicating:* The ability to communicate with others in human language

▶ *Sensing:* The ability to sense and understand the environment

▶ *Robotics:* The ability to move and act

The application of AI appropriate for the Web, however, involve a subset of these traditional AI problems because it deals primarily with the areas of planning and communications and much less with the fields of sensing and robotics.

The methods and techniques of AI have centered on the following (somewhat overlapping) set of primary topics: problem solving through search, knowledge representation and inference, expert systems, learning, neural networks and adaptation, and natural language processing and agents.

Problem Solving Through Search

The basic technique of search (or state space search) refers to a broad class of methods that are encountered in many different AI applications; the technique is sometimes considered a universal problem-solving mechanism in AI. To solve a search problem, it is necessary to prescribe a set of possible or allowable states, a set of operators to change from one state to another, an initial state, a set of goal states, and additional information to help distinguish states according to their likeliness to lead to a target or goal state. The problem then becomes one of finding a sequence of operators leading from the initial state to one of the goal states.

Search algorithms can range from brute force methods (which use no prior knowledge of the problem domain and are sometimes referred to as blind searches) to knowledge-intensive heuristic searches that use knowledge to guide the search toward a more efficient path to the goal state.

Search Techniques

Search techniques include

1. Brute force
   - Breadth-first
   - Depth-first
   - Depth-first iterative-deepening
   - Bidirectional

2. Heuristic
   - Hill-climbing
   - Best-first
   - A*
   - Beam
   - Iterative-deepening-A*

Brute force searches entail the systematic and complete search of the state space to identify and evaluate all possible paths from the initial state to the goal states (see sidebar). These searches can be breadth-first or depth-first. In a breadth-first search, each branch at each node in a search tree is evaluated, and the search works its way from the initial state to the final state, considering all possibilities at each branch, one level at a time. In the depth-first search, a particular branch is followed all the way to a dead end (or to a successful goal state). Upon reaching the end of a path, the algorithm backs up and tries the next alternative path in a process called backtracking.

The depth-first, iterative-deepening algorithm is a variation of the depth-first technique, in which the depth-first method is implemented with a gradually increasing limit on the depth. This allows a search to be completed with a reduced memory requirement and improves the performance where the objective is to find the shortest path to the target state.

The bidirectional search starts from both the initial and target states and performs a breadth-first search in both directions, until a common state is found in the middle. The solution is found by combining the path from the initial state with the inverse of the path from the target state.

These brute force methods are useful for relatively simple problems, but as the complexity of the problem rises, the number of states to be considered can become prohibitive. For this reason, heuristic approaches are more appropriate in complex search problems where prior knowledge can be used to direct the search.

Heuristic approaches use knowledge of the domain to guide the choice of which nodes to expand next and thus avoid the need for a blind search of all possible states. The hill-climbing approach is the simplest heuristic search; this method works by always moving in the direction of the locally steepest ascent toward the goal state. The biggest drawback of this approach is that the local maximum is not always the global maximum, and the algorithm can get stuck at a local maximum.

To overcome this drawback, the best-first approach maintains an open list of nodes that have been identified but not expanded. If a local maximum is encountered, the algorithm moves to the next best node from the open list for expansion. This approach, however, evaluates the next best node purely on the basis of its evaluation of ascent toward the goal, without regard for the distance it lies from the initial state.

The A* technique goes one step further by evaluating the overall path from the initial state to the goal, using the path to the present node combined with the ascent rates to the potential successor nodes. This technique tries to find the optimal path to the goal. A variation on this approach is the beam search, in which the open list of nodes is limited to retain only the best nodes and thereby reduce the memory requirement for the search. The iterative-deepening-A* approach is a further variation, in which depth-first searches are completed a branch at a time, until some threshold measure is exceeded for the branch, at which time it is truncated, and the search backtracks to the most recently generated node.

A classic example of an AI search application is computer chess. Over the years, computer chess-playing software has received considerable attention, and such programs are a commercial success for home PCs. In addition, most are aware of the highly visible contest between IBM's Deep Blue supercomputer and the reigning world chess champion, Garry Kasparov, in May, 1997. Millions of chess and computing fans observed this event in real time, when, in a dramatic sixth-game victory, Deep Blue beat Kasparov. This was the first time a computer had won a match with a current world champion under tournament conditions.

Computer chess programs generally make use of standardized opening sequences and end-game databases as a knowledge base to simplify these phases of the game.

For the middle game, they examine large trees and perform deep searches, with pruning to eliminate branches that are evaluated as clearly inferior, and select the most highly evaluated move.

We will return to search techniques in Chapter 7, when we examine data searches across the Web. This chapter will include how a database schema for the Web will become an important stepping-stone toward improving Web intelligence.

Knowledge Representation and Inference

An important element of AI is the principle that intelligent behavior can be achieved through processing of symbol structures representing increments of knowledge. This has given rise to the development of knowledge-representation languages that permit the representation of knowledge and allow for its manipulation to deduce new facts from the existing knowledge. Thus knowledge-representation languages must have a well-defined syntax and semantics system and, at the same time, must support inference.

Three techniques have been used for knowledge-representation and inference: frames and semantic networks, logic-based approaches, and rule-based systems.

Frames and semantic networks, also referred to as slot and filler structures, capture declarative information about related objects and concepts where there is a clear class hierarchy and where the principle of inheritance can be used to infer the characteristics of members of a subclass from those of the higher-level class. The two forms of reasoning in this technique are matching (that is, identification of objects having common properties) and property inheritance, in which properties are inferred for a subclass. Because of these limitations, frames and semantic networks are generally limited to representation and inference of relatively simple systems.

Logic-based approaches use logical formulas to represent more complex relationships among objects and attributes. Such approaches have a well-defined syntax, semantics, and proof theory. When knowledge is represented with logic formulas, as in this approach, the formal power of a logical theorem prover can be applied to the knowledge to derive new knowledge. However, the approach is inflexible and requires great precision in stating the logical relationships. In some cases, common-sense inferences and conclusions cannot be derived and the approach may be inefficient, especially when dealing with issues that result in large combinations of objects or concepts.

Rule-based approaches are more flexible. They allow the representation of knowledge using sets of IF-THEN or other condition action rules. This approach is more procedural and less formal in its logic. Reasoning can be controlled in a forward or backward chaining interpreter.

In each of these approaches, the knowledge representation component (that is, problem-specific rules and facts) is separate from the problem-solving and inference procedures.

Knowledge-based systems contain knowledge as well as information and data. The information and data can be modeled and implemented as a database. Knowledge engineering methodology addresses design and maintenance of the knowledge, data, and information.

Logic is used as the formalism for programming languages and databases. It can also be used as a formalism to implement knowledge methodology. Any formalism that admits a declarative semantics and can be interpreted both as a programming language and a database language is a knowledge language.

Let's define what we mean by the fundamental terms *data*, *information*, and *knowledge*. An item of data is a fundamental element of an application. Data can be represented by population and labels. Information is an explicit association between data things. Associations are often functional in that they represent a function relating one set of things to another set of things. A rule is an explicit functional association from a set of information things or data things, called a *body*, to a single data or information thing, called a *head*. So, in this sense, a rule is knowledge.

Expert Systems

The term *expert system* can be considered to be a particular type of knowledge-based system. An expert system is a system in which the knowledge is deliberately represented

Expert Systems Tools

Many tools are available to develop expert systems. One such tool is the C-Language Integrated Production System (CLIPS).

- CLIPS is an expert system tool that provides a complete environment for the construction of rule- or object-based expert systems. It uses a forward-chaining production system written in ANSI C by the National Aeronautics and Space Administration (NASA).
- The CLIPS inference engine includes truth maintenance, dynamic rule addition, and customizable conflict-resolution strategies.
- Knowledge representation: CLIPS provides a cohesive tool for handling a wide variety of knowledge, with support for three different programming paradigms: rule-based, object-oriented, and procedural.
- Portability: CLIPS is written in C for portability and speed and has been installed on many different computers.
- Integration/Extensibility: CLIPS can be embedded within procedural code, called as a subroutine, and integrated with languages such as C, FORTRAN, and ADA.
- See http://www.ghg.net/clips/clips.html.

"as it is." Expert systems are applications that make decisions in real-life situations, that would otherwise be performed by a human expert (see sidebar on page 177).

Expert systems can be of many different forms. In general, they are programs designed to mimic human performance at specialized, constrained problem-solving tasks. Frequently they are constructed as a collection of IF-THEN production rules combined with a reasoning engine that applies those rules, either in a forward or backward direction, to specific problems (see Figure 6-1).

A key element of an expert system is the acquisition of the body of knowledge that is contained within the system. Such information is normally extracted from a human expert or experts, and is frequently in the form of rules of thumb or heuristic information, rather than statements of absolute fact.[1]

We will discuss examples of Web knowledge bases and inference engines in Chapter 7.

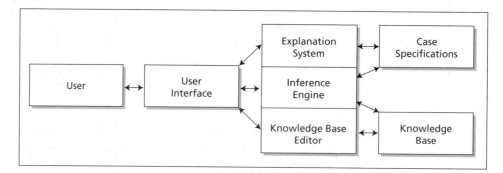

Figure 6-1 Expert system architecture

Learning, Neural Net, and Adaptation

One of the most significant aspects of human intelligence, and therefore a proper and important subject for AI, is the ability to learn. But learning is not just the accumulation of facts, although rote learning is an important piece of the puzzle. As computer memory (internal and external) has become cheaper and faster, the capacity of computers, even low-end computers, to accumulate information has been tremendous. Learning, as part of AI, is much more than this simple capacity to store and retrieve data.

---

1. A fuzzy expert system is an expert system that uses a collection of fuzzy membership functions and rules, instead of Boolean logic, to reason about data.

Learning entails the ability to realize new procedures, approaches, or algorithms to address new problems and achieve adaptability in a changing environment. This is clearly a far more challenging task than the accumulation of large amounts of data (see Figure 6-2).

One way to view the problem of learning is in the context of state space search. A learning program could search a state space of programs or knowledge to find a new program, algorithm, or body of knowledge that enables the solution of a new problem. Because of the large state space of programs, this requires a highly informed heuristic approach to consider only programs with a reasonable likelihood of providing a solution and avoiding the much larger number of ineffective possibilities. Some relevant topics to consider include neural networks, adaptive software, and data mining. We will discuss Web examples of Learning Algorithms in Chapter 7.

Neural Networks

Neural networks are systems that simulate intelligence by reproducing the types of physical connections found in brains. Because of the current technology limitations, the number of these connections is small (in terms of the billions of connections found in the human brain) but still capable of reproducing some very interesting

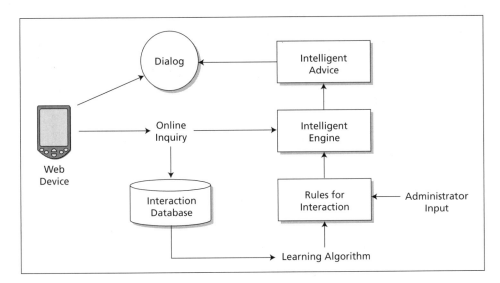

Figure 6-2 Learning Algorithms

behavior in disciplines such as voice or optical character recognition and natural-language processing.

Nevertheless, artificial neural networks (ANNs) (and the related approach of parallel distributed processing) are based on the model of the densely interconnected parallel structure of the human brain. ANNs comprise collections of mathematical models that emulate some of the observed properties of the brain and draw on the analogies of adaptive biological learning. An essential aspect of ANN is the novel structure of the information processing system that is used in its implementation. Such systems are composed of a large number of highly interconnected processing elements, analogous to neurons, tied together with weighted connections, analogous to synapses.

Learning in biological systems involves, among other things, adjustments to the synaptic connections that exist between the neurons. ANNs mimic this principle as well. Learning typically occurs by example through training or by exposure to connected sets of input/output data, and the training process iteratively adjusts the connection weights (synapses). These connection weights store the knowledge necessary to solve specific problems. Some interesting applications for ANNs may be found on the Web through Distributed AI.

Adaptive Software

As businesses shift from resource-based products to knowledge-based products, software development will help determine which companies prosper in increasingly complex environments. Software development will need to migrate toward an adaptive viewpoint to meet the demands of this unstable, complex, messy new world in which high speed, high change, and uncertainty are key characteristics. Adaptive software is one such approach that is receiving significant attention.

In the 1970s, structured programming made it feasible to build larger-scale software systems based on an existing specification. A typical application was a database program that read an input file and produced an output file.

In the 1980s, object-oriented programming made it easier to reorganize for changes, because functionality was split into separate classes. A typical application was a desktop publishing system using user-initiated events (mouse clicks or menus).

Problems with existing software, however, are that it takes too much time and money to develop and is brittle when used in situations for which it was not explicitly designed. Various software design methodologies can alleviate this problem.

A growing percentage of software product development projects are becoming so complex that their outcomes are inherently unpredictable. And yet, successful products emerge from such environments all the time. So what is happening? One of the most difficult mental model changes in the development of adaptive software is that although the direct linkage between cause and effect is broken, there is an equally strong replacement. The replacement is emergence.[2] Although emergence is only a part of complex adaptive systems, it may be the most important.

A primary element in adaptive software is to realize that optimization of structured programs is not the only solution to increasingly complex problems. The optimization approach is based on maintaining control to impose order on uncertainty. Imposed order is the product of rigorous engineering discipline and deterministic, cause-and-effect–driven processes. The alternative idea is one of an adaptive mindset, of viewing organizations as complex adaptive systems, and of creating emergent order out of a web of interconnected components

Complexity has more to do with the number of interacting agents and the speed with which those agents interact. For software products, the need for adaptive development arises when there are a great many independent agents—developers, customers, vendors, competitors, stockholders—interacting with each other, fast enough that linear cause-and-effect rules are no longer sufficient for success. Size and technological complexity are less important factors.

One part of the vision for the future of an Intelligent Wireless Web is very simple—it will be a network that learns. The Web needs to develop user control over what networks provide. It needs a significantly higher degree of dynamism and mobility, as well as a robust network infrastructure and protocols. To achieve this, the Web will need innovations in new approaches, such as self-organizing software, adaptive protocols, and object-oriented dynamic languages.

▶ Self-organizing software means the ability of networks to organize and configure themselves.

▶ Adaptation means the ability of protocols and applications to learn and adapt to the changing conditions in the network, such as levels of congestion and errors. The next-generation programming languages will support intelligent, adaptive, complex software systems. "Reflection" or reasoning will be built

---

2. Highsmith, James A. III. *Adaptive Software Development: A Collaborative Approach to Managing Complex Systems,* Dorset House, 2000.

into the language's own structure, performance, and environment, along with support for dynamic modification of behavior. Adaptive software will use information from the environment to improve its behavior over time.

▶ Object-oriented dynamic languages form a higher level of abstraction, semantics, automatic memory management, incremental development, and reflection.

Although several efforts, such as Jini and Universal Plug and Play, have goals for integrating device networks, they don't begin, as yet, to have the scalable and flexible self-organization support that is required to address adaptive requirements.

Today, adaptive programming is aimed at the problem of producing applications that can adapt to changing user needs and environments. This makes it possible for the user to change goals without a need to rewrite the program. A typical application is an information filter.

Traditional software development was based on principles such as exact specifications, complex maintenance, and high levels of abstraction. Today, software is expected to do more for us because of our increasingly complex environments—users, systems, devices, and goals. Programmers who were accustomed to trading time versus space now have to worry about bandwidth, security, quality of information, resolution of images, and other factors.

Adaptive software changes this by adding a feedback loop that provides information based on performance. The design criteria themselves become a part of the program, and the program reconfigures itself as the environment changes.

Significant adaptive software research challenges lie ahead. The first is the problem of scaling to large networks and to large numbers of applications. The second issue is an end-to-end adaptation framework with underlying layers of the protocol stack to applications. This will allow learning about what's going on in the network and enable new algorithms and new protocols to react.

Challenges include deployable intelligence mechanisms for pattern recognition algorithms and data mining algorithms, so that different applications can reuse the same algorithm-level software. It is important to be able to guide the automation process and override decisions.

Data Mining

The hope of e-commerce's targeted marketing and the bane of privacy advocates, data mining is still more of a potential than an actual Web technology. Data mining consists of three main components: clustering or classification, association rules, and sequence analysis.

Classification/clustering analyzes a set of data and generates a set of grouping rules, which can be used to classify future data. One of the important problems in data mining is the classification rule for learning that involves finding rules that partition given data into predefined classes. In data mining in which millions of records and a large number of attributes are involved, the execution time of existing algorithms can become prohibitive, particularly in interactive applications.

An association rule implies relationships among a set of objects in a database. Finding association rules in databases may show patterns for decision support, financial forecast, and other applications.

Sequential analysis searches for patterns with data that appear in separate transactions. Examples of the variety of algorithms are

- Statistical algorithms
- Neural networks: Artificial neural networks mimic the pattern-finding capacity of the human brain.
- Genetic algorithms: Optimization techniques that use genetic combination, mutation, and natural selection.
- Nearest neighbor method: A technique that classifies each record in a dataset based on a combination of the classes of the k record(s) most similar to it in a historical dataset.
- Rule induction: Extracts of useful IF-THEN rules from data based on statistical significance.
- Data visualization: Visual interpretation of complex relationships in multidimensional data.

Most of the traditional data-mining techniques fail because of the sheer size of the data. New techniques will have to be developed to handle the volume of data.

Agents

An intelligent agent is a computer software system that is situated in some environment and capable of autonomous action and learning in its environment to meet its design objectives. Intelligent agents have the following characteristics: reactive—they perceive their environment and respond; proactive—they exhibit goal-directed behavior; and social—they interact with other agents.

Real-time intelligent agent technology offers a powerful Web tool. Agents are able to act without the intervention of humans or other systems: they have control both over their own internal state and over their behavior. In complexity domains, agents must be prepared for the possibility of failure. This situation is called nondeterministic. Normally, an agent will have a repertoire of actions available to it. This set of possible actions represents the agent's capability to modify its environments. Similarly, the action "purchase a house" will fail if insufficient funds are available to do so. Actions therefore have preconditions associated with them that define the possible situations in which they can be applied.

The key problem facing an agent is that of deciding which of its actions it should perform to satisfy its design objectives. Agent architectures are really software architectures for decision-making systems that are embedded in an environment. The complexity of the decision-making process can be affected by various environmental properties.

- ▶ Accessible versus inaccessible
- ▶ Deterministic versus nondeterministic
- ▶ Episodic versus nonepisodic
- ▶ Static versus dynamic
- ▶ Discrete versus continuous

The most complex general class of environments are those that are inaccessible, nondeterministic, nonepisodic, dynamic, and continuous.

◆ Distributed Artificial Intelligence

Distributed artificial intelligence (DAI) is concerned with coordinated intelligent behavior: intelligent agents coordinating their knowledge, skills, and plans to act or solve problems, working toward a single goal or toward separate, individual goals that interact. DAI provides intellectual insights about organization, interaction, and problem solving among intelligent agents.

Several research labs are working on a concept of a "computing grid," developing services and software that can manage complex physical systems of disparate, geographically separated resources. They are laying foundation for a new class of applications that need vast computing power: undoubtedly quite a few AI-related projects will benefit greatly from this concept. Tomorrow's computing grids will offer a reliable source of computing power, similar to the modern electrical power grid. Among the metacomputing platforms leading this peer-to-peer computing boom are the following:

▶ The Distance and Distributed Computing and Communication (DisCom2) program is intended to deliver key computing and communications technologies to efficiently integrate distributed resources with high-end computing resources at a distance (see http://www.llnl.gov/asci/sc99fliers/DISCOM.html).

▶ The goals of MetaNEOS are to design metacomputing environments suitable for solving large optimization problems and develop tools that can be used to solve computing problems of unprecedented size and complexity. The metacomputing platforms used in metaNEOS are inexpensive, focusing on utilization of idle time on collections of workstations, which is essentially free (see http://www-unix.mcs.anl.gov/metaneos/project/index.html).

▶ MILAN (Metacomputing in Large Asynchronous Networks) is a research project aiming to build a software environment emulating a collection of virtual machines on a nondedicated, distributed platform. It is a joint effort between New York University and Arizona State University (see http://www.cs.nyu.edu/milan/milan/index.html).

▶ NAS Systems Division is designing an information power grid, a 20-year project that aims to seamlessly integrate computing systems, data storage, specialized networks, and sophisticated analysis software. Its scheduling software will dynamically and intelligently allocate resources among dispersed computing centers as they are needed (see http://www.nas.nasa.gov/About/IPG/ipg.html).

In building the Intelligent Wireless Web, we can envision the use of parallel PC clusters coordinated by AI service providers to carry out complex tasks utilizing the principles of DAI. Adaptive configurations of such clusters will enable the task assignments (and associated software) to be distributed by AI servers to PCs within the cluster having needed capabilities that may be highly specialized. Figure 6-3

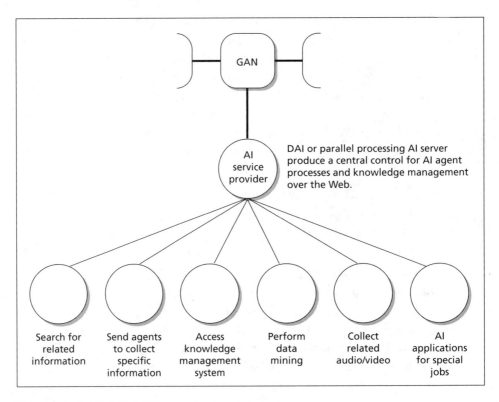

Figure 6-3   Artificial intelligence server architecture

provides a graphical representation of this process, in which a master assigns tasks and distributes software to members of the cluster that perform tasks such as

▶ Search for related information

▶ Assign agents to collect specific information

▶ Access knowledge management system

▶ Perform data mining

▶ Collect related multimedia information

▶ Perform AI applications for specific job

The basic assumption of DAI is that, in general, a single isolated intelligent agent does not possess enough knowledge or resources to complete a problem-solving task. On the contrary, it is envisioned that complex problem solving in real-world domains will be performed by communities of specialized intelligent agents, able to collaborate with each other toward the accomplishment of a given common goal and to negotiate the use of resources in the most effective way. The ability to communicate with other agents is therefore considered essential for an agent to exhibit intelligent behaviors.

An AI service provider is used as the development environment for DAI systems, using an extension to HTTP designed to support server-to-server communication. In particular, new methods enable a client agent to invoke a specific service on a server.

The implementation of a specialized HTTP server would be able to deliver DAI applications over the Web. In addition to implementing standard HTTP, the AI server would offer a library of high-level functions to dynamically generate HTML pages and a server-to-server communication method.

It would be intended to act as the front end of a network of intelligent agents that communicate with each other using an extension to HTTP. The dynamic generation of HTML pages allows complex AI applications to be delivered to end users without the need for specialized hardware and software support and using a simple and homogeneous interface model.

The most sophisticated implementation of an HTTP server written in Common Lisp is currently the CL-HTTP system developed at the MIT AI Laboratory by John Mallery, which could be implemented as a hypermedia server, but could form the basis of an AI server.

Lisp Server Pages (LSP) is an open-source project. LSP is a Common Lisp–based technology for dynamic HTML generation that transforms LSP documents embedded with Common Lisp into executable HTML generation functions. Unlike many other dynamic content packages, LSP succeeds in simultaneously providing the author with SGML and Lisp semantics while composing an LSP document. It loads `start.lisp` (after loading AllegroServe or CL-HTTP).

A Common Lisp HTTP server makes Lisp applications accessible over the Web. It offers a chance to overcome the traditional limitations of AI systems through Web technology and provides tools for developing powerful Web-based applications (see Figure 6-3).

◆ Conclusion

From this chapter, you may conclude that

▶ AI may play a role in bringing intelligence into future Web applications.

▶ As AI agents, services, and applications are introduced into individual Web applications, these applications become increasingly user friendly and productive.

▶ DAI through AI service providers offers the framework for even higher levels of AI to be introduced to the Web.

7

Merging Artificial Intelligence with the Web

In this chapter, we discuss some perplexing questions involved with merging intelligent applications as well as AI programs with the Web, including

- How smart are Web applications today?
- What is Web intelligence?
- How does the Web learn?
- Where does Web intelligence reside?

Intelligence usually refers to the ability to reason, solve problems, remember information, or learn new ideas. So, as we begin to add more intelligent agents, smart applications, and AI programs to Web sites, could we ask, "Does the Web have an IQ?"

The simple answer is, "No, at least not explicitly." The IQ measure for humans was developed based on the rates at which intelligence develops in children. Its original definition is that IQ is a measure of intellectual development determined as the ratio of a child's mental age to chronological age, multiplied by 100. The scale is extended to adults, in whom an IQ of 100 relates to the performance of an average adult on a suitable standardized test. For humans, IQ is a good predictor of various measures of success or failure in life, but making computers that can score high on IQ tests would be only weakly correlated with their usefulness. Consider the ability of a child to repeat a long sequence of digits. This correlates well with other intellectual abilities of the child because it measures how much information the child can remember and use for computation. However, repeating a lengthy information string is a trivial task for even extremely limited computers. Nevertheless, some of the problems on IQ tests present useful challenges for AI programs.

So, how will adding intelligent agents, smart applications, and AI programs to Web sites contribute to the development of the Intelligent Wireless Web? Will they support the development of a network that learns? To begin to address these questions, we will have to explore some uncharted territory and examine some probing and provocative questions, such as

▶ How smart are Web applications today?

▶ What is Web intelligence?

▶ How does the Web learn?

▶ Where does Web intelligence reside?

In the following sections, we will begin the discussion of how to introduce intelligence to enlighten the optical pathways that inhabit the Web.

◆ How Smart Are Web Applications Today?

For the most part, the Web can be considered to be a massive information system with interconnected databases and remote applications providing various services. Although these services are becoming more and more user oriented, the concept of smart applications on the Web is still in its infancy.

One of the most sophisticated applications on the Web today is the Enterprise Information Portal (EIP), operating with the state-of-the-art markup languages to search, retrieve, and repackage data. The EIP is in the process developing into an even more powerful center based on component-based applications called Web Services. In this section, we will describe EIPs and the Extensible Markup Language (XML) standards, frameworks, and schema that make up today's most sophisticated and intelligent Web tools and applications. We will also discuss the tools and competitors developing Web Services. We will consider just how smart Web Services are likely to be.

Enterprise Information Portals

During 1998, the first wave of Internet portals became very popular. They provided consumers with personalized points of entry (or gateways) to a wide variety of information on the Internet. Examples include MyYahoo (Yahoo), NetCenter (Netscape), MSN (Microsoft), and AOL.

Subsequently, EIPs, also called corporate portals or enterprise portals, provide ready access to information over intranets and the Internet (see sidebars). Corporate portals have moved beyond the delivery of information; they also provide a way to integrate the many disparate systems and processes that are typically used within an enterprise. Corporate portals are able to use XML to integrate previously separate legacy systems and provide a single point of entry, or gateway, to these processes. EIPs now act as access centers that tie together people and data by linking e-mail, groupware, workflow, collaboration, and other mission-critical applications to portals.

Does the availability of vast amounts of data, readily searched, sorted, and retrieved, constitute an intelligent application? We should also include consideration of some of the other ways intelligence may be seeping onto the Internet (see the sidebar on page 192) in the form of tools and services, such as

▶ Document analysis systems for cataloging and summarizing Web pages

▶ Profiling systems for placing selective Web advertising

▶ Data mining and analysis tools

▶ Intelligent tools for searching databases supported by Web browsers

▶ Machine translation tools that convert to and from human languages

▶ Statistical software for network caching, routing, and tracking

▶ Knowledge-based systems for automated e-mail reading

▶ Smart agents for Internet-based product and service marketing

▶ Video object recognition and searching

IBM Enterprise Information Portal

The IBM EIP provides information integration for enterprise portals, relational databases, business intelligence, and enterprise content management applications. IBM Content Manager stores, manages, and distributes all types of digital content, including text, XML and HTML files, document images, electronic office documents, computer output, audio, and video. IBM Content Manager provides a subset of EIP, including search technologies, content repository connectors, Java Server Pages (JSP), and server-based transforms. (See www-4.ibm.com/software/data/eip.)

Convera's RetrievalWare

Convera's RetrievalWare is an enterprise-wide knowledge-retrieval system (enterprise portal), which is flexible and scalable across enterprise networks, intranets, and the World Wide Web. Convera RetrievalWare enables users to index and search a wide range of distributed information resources, including text files, SGML, XML, HTML, paper documents, relational database tables, over 200 proprietary document formats (such as word processors and publishing systems), and groupware repositories. Advanced search capabilities include concept and keyword searching, pattern searching, and query-by-example. (See case study in Appendix G.) (See www.convera.com.)

OpenCyc

Cyc, named after enCYClopedia, was developed over 17 years at Stanford University under the leadership of Doug Lenat. Cyc is a knowledge base containing assertions and inferences that responds to natural language. Developed with $50 million and over 500 man-years of effort through the Department of Defense and others, the system today encompasses 1.4 million assertions.

As an experimental project, Cyc emerged as a response to ongoing controversy in the AI field. Lenat understood the problem that expert systems were "not servants, but idiot savants." What was missing was "common sense."

Within the contentious AI community Cyc is drawing criticism. Cyc is seen to focus on sorting facts and observations into logical categories, and even its ability to make inferences is considered too restrictive.

The release of OpenCyc onto the Web will allow access to a limited portion of the Cyc knowledge base for free. OpenCyc incorporates applications, such as speech recognition software, database searches, and natural-language queries. The full knowledge base (about 20 times the size of the public portion) will be licensed to commercial users. (See www.opencyc.org.)

EIPs and Cyc represent today's "smartest" Web applications, but would you categorize any of them as intelligent? Just what will it take for us to see Web applications and services as intelligent? In the next section, we will identify the key tools for developing intelligent applications on the Web. We will follow this by describing the latest Web innovation and Web Services, and we will ask how intelligent applications could reach users as services.

Extensible Markup Language Standards, Frameworks, and Schema

The tools needed to continue evolving advanced Web capabilities are based mostly on XML standards, frameworks, and schema. XML is a language that defines other languages. Like HTML, it is based on the Standard Generalized Markup Language (SGML). SGML documents were originally structured using Document Type Declaration (DTD), a mature standard now used in several thousand applications. However, the DTD limitations include the fact that it is not written in XML, does not support namespaces, and has limited data typing. As a result of DTD's limitations, schemas were developed that

▶ Were built in XML and therefore can be used in the Document Object Model (DOM) and in Visual Basic

▶ Provided data types such as float, currencies, and so on

▶ Enabled creation of user-defined data types

▶ Provided better relationships between elements

▶ Allowed a form of inheritance

▶ Offered namespaces support

XML schemas offer an externalized, extensible representation of metadata for business entities. Just as in object-oriented languages such as Java and C++ classes allow users to specify objects. The XML Schema Language from the World Wide Web Consortium (W3C) plays a similar role for XML instance documents. There are other XML Schema Languages, such as, Schema for Object-Oriented XML

(SOX) from Commerce-One and XML Data-Reduced (XDR) by Microsoft. Although schemas will definitely prove useful in the future, the current implementations are expected to undergo significant changes.

The proliferation of XML-related tools is illustrated in Table 7-1 by the variety of XML standards, frameworks, and schema.

Research and development efforts into exploiting the potential of XML are ongoing in many locations. One example is the Semantic Web Community Portal (www.semanticweb.org). Another is Fourthought (www.fourthought.com), which has been developing standards-based tools for content and presentation management, Web application metadata, next-generation hyperlinking, XML/database integration, and integrated XML servers. Also, Answerthink, Inc. (see www.answerthink.com) is a leading provider of business transformation mobile solutions.

One of the more important standards listed in Table 7-1 is the Extensible Hypertext Markup Language (XHTML). It is a reformulation of HTML in XML. XHTML is a working document endorsed by the W3C and may be the next markup language of the Web. XHTML extends the document set for the expanding variety of new devices and applications. XHTML also modularizes HTML documents that are read by a variety of new devices and applications.

Another key framework is the Extensible Stylesheet Language (XSL) W3C specification that allows separation of data from presentation for XML documents. XSL is itself an XML DTD that defines the presentation of XML (and HTML) content. XSL allows developers to prescribe on-screen display for PCs, handheld devices, cell phones, and emerging devices. EIPs that are XML-based use XSL in the application layer to format data in the data layer for end users. Extensible Stylesheet Language Transform (XSLT) transforms XML documents into XML-to-XML documents or to other document formats, such as HTML and rich text format (RTF).

The Wireless Application Protocol is an XML application that allows access to information via personal digital assistants (PDAs) and other handheld devices. Handheld devices are permeating the corporate enterprise as a means to compute, telephone, fax, and network and thereby are extending the reach of corporate information tentacles. Input is typically performed using a stylus pen or through speech, and interpreted using handwriting and speech recognition technologies, respectively. Wireless Markup Language (WML), formerly known as the Handheld Device Markup Language (HDML), is the standard language used to render text on PDAs

Table 7-1 Examples of XML Standards, Frameworks, and Schema

Designation	Description	See
XML	Extensible Markup Language	www.w3.org/XML
WebDAV	Web-based Distributed Authoring and Versioning	www.webdav.org
XHTML	Extensible HyperText Markup Language	www.w3.org/TR/xhtml1
MathML	Math Markup Language	www.w3.org/Math
DSML	Directory Services Markup Language	www.dsml.org
EDI	Electronic Data Interchange	www.xmledi.com
MCF	Meta Content Framework	www.w3.org/TR/NOTE-MCF-XML/MCF-tutorial.html
XSL	Extensible Stylesheet Language	www.w3.org/Style/XSL/
BizTalk XML	Framework for application integration and electronic commerce	www.biztalk.org
CML	Chemical Markup Language	www.xml-cml.org
XPointer XML	Pointer Language	www.w3.org/TR/xptr
RDF	Resource Description Framework	www.w3.org/RDF
XML-MP	XML Mortgage Partners Framework	www.xml.coverpages.org/xmlMortgagePartners.html
WML	Wireless Markup Language	www.oasis-open.org/cover/wap-wml.html
SVG	Scalable Vector Graphics	www.w3.org/Graphics/SVG/Overview.htm8
XPath	XML Path Language	www.w3.org/TR/xpath
SOAP	Simple Object Access Protocol	www.w3.org/TR/SOAP/
WDSL	Web Services Description Language	www.xml.coverpages.org/wsdl.html
WIDL	Web Interface Definition Language	www.w3.org/TR/NOTE-widl.html

and cellular phones via wireless access (see Chapter 5). EIP currently requires a WML presentation layer to accommodate PDAs. Through the use of EIPs the enterprise can connect any collaboration tools into the portal. Privileges to use the collaboration tools or enter "forums" can be granted to communities and individuals. Threaded discussion, chat, videoconferencing, e-mail, and newsgroups are examples of such collaboration tools.

The variety and power of these XML tools demonstrates the potential for Web development. In the next section, we will present the components and tools for delivering intelligent applications and AI capabilities over the Web through Web Services.

Web Services

Since 1994, distributed objects have been developed by several organizations under different names. NeXT called them Portable Distributed Objects, Microsoft called them Component Object Model (COM), IBM called them System Object Model (SOM), and Apple called them OpenDoc. These companies (with the exception of Microsoft) formed the Object Management Group and converged on a standard called Common Object Request Broker Architecture (CORBA). The concept was to develop an architecture that lets applications plug into an "application bus" and call a service. Based on object-oriented units, it called on specialized software components. For the most part, component software developers have been unable to achieve the desired interoperability. This has been because of the lack of universal acceptance. As a result, components' capabilities were never fully realized. To actually succeed in developing component technology standards, it will be necessary to find a minimal common ground. XML and HTTP may offer just the right minimal technology. And Microsoft's Simple Object Access Protocol (SOAP) defines the use of XML and HTTP to access services, objects, and servers in a platform-independent manner. As a result, SOAP offers a potentially bridging technology.

Today, interoperable objects, supported by IBM and Microsoft, are being called Web Services and are being coupled with a complementary technology called Universal Discovery, Description, and Integration (UDDI). Web Services allow companies to publish components and services in a directory (UDDI) that other Web applications can search and implement a call to the service.

For Web Services to work, everyone must agree on a means of communication methodology, including identifying, accessing, and involving services. SOAP describes

Microsoft.NET

Microsoft's new .NET strategy is a transition from a small to midsize department technology provider of enterprise software.

.NET Enterprise Servers include the following packages: Application Center, BizTalk Server, Commerce Server, Exchange Server, Mobile Information Server, SharePoint Portal Server, and SQL Server.

commands and parameters that can be passed between browsers and Web Services. Microsoft's current approach to Web Services is to build them into the next generation of Microsoft's .NET framework (see sidebar).

Electronic Business XML (ebXML), a joint initiative of OASIS and the United Nations, takes the Web Services model and defines a standard for applying those technologies to meet real business world demands. Its goal is to enable a global marketplace through the exchange of XML-based messages.

Although Phone.com and Nokia make many of the phone-based Web microbrowsers found on mobile phones today, Microsoft's release of the .NET Mobile Web SDK Beta 1 signals its entry into the area of mobile tools. The .NET framework, in general, jettisoned some creaky legacy technologies in favor of a new, radical approach to desktop and Web application development. The .NET framework uses XML throughout and introduces XML-based remote procedure calls using SOAP that may offer a cross-platform alternative to Distributed Component Object Model (DCOM) and an easier-to-implement alternative to Internet Inter-ORB Protocol (IIOP). In addition, it introduces a new language, C# (pronounced "C Sharp"), that presents full, object-oriented Application Programming Interfaces (APIs).

SOAP for describing commands and parameters that can be passed between browsers and Web Services is part of the .NET strategy. SOAP is an implementation of XML that represents one common set of rules about how data and commands will be represented and extended. SOAP consists of three parts: an envelope (a framework for describing what is in a message and how to process it), a set of encoding rules (for expressing instances of application-defined data types), and a convention for representing remote procedure calls and responses. SOAP messages are fundamentally one-way transmissions from a sender to a receiver using HTTP binding.

An essential part of the Microsoft.NET strategy is Web Services Description Language (WDSL), which is a new specification to describe networked XML-based services. It provides a way for service providers to describe the format of requests to their systems, regardless of the underlying protocol (such as SOAP or XML) or encoding. WSDL is a part of the effort of the UDDI initiative to provide directories and descriptions of such online services for electronic business.

In competition with Microsoft's .NET approach (which currently supports primarily Windows) are architectures based on platform independence, such as J2EE. In

1995, Sun unveiled the Java platform as a way to create applications that would run on any computer, regardless of the underlying operating system. Java technology has progressed from a tool to animate Web sites to the end-to-end Java 2 platform that spans applications from small consumer devices to enterprise data center servers. The Java programming language is now an important environment used for developing platform-independent EIPs. Java is cross-platform because of the Java Virtual Machine, a device that serves up distributed software on recognized networks; it works independent of the computer's instruction set and architecture. The three editions of the Java 2 platform are

▶ Java 2, Micro Edition (J2ME) for small devices and smartcards

▶ Java 2, Standard Edition (J2SE) for desktops

▶ Java 2, Enterprise Edition (J2EE) for creating server-based applications and services

Java technology has been broadly applied, including, automated transaction machines (ATMs), two-way pagers, mobile phones, personal organizers, game machines, cameras, industrial controllers, point-of-sale terminals, and servers. Java technology and XML can be combined to deliver Web services using J2EE as a foundation (see Figure 7-1).

Adding the strength of XML technologies to enterprise systems such as J2EE and CORBA, provides the environment for building highly scalable, secure, fault-tolerant systems. XML-based technologies SOAP and WSDL could provide the means of building a Web Services model in which business services can be catalogued via UDDI and invoked over the Web via SOAP requests. These services could be implemented in terms of CORBA, J2EE, or .NET.

Comparing J2EE and .NET

The .NET platform has an array of technology products under the Microsoft umbrella as an alternative to the standards, J2EE and CORBA. Table 7-2 lists the various characteristics, computer codes, and features of J2EE and .NET and comments on their differences.

Even with the J2EE and .NET differences, Web Services still provide the advantages of ease of integration. We can illustrate this by considering a business-to-business scenario. Before Web Services, consider a Company A that was built with Microsoft technology and wished to connect to Company B, which was built with Java

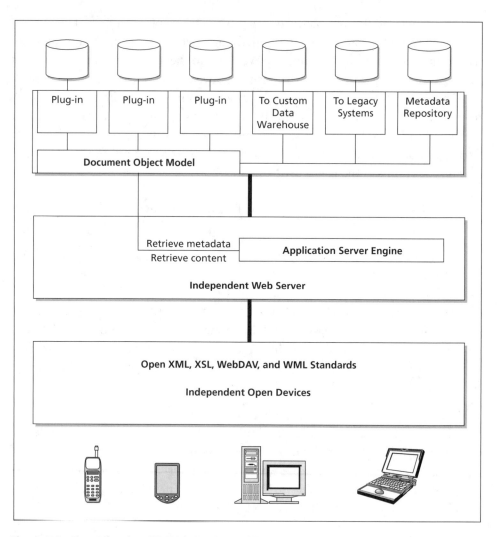

Figure 7-1 Example of an EIP Web Service architecture

servlets. The integration process would be difficult and further complicated when Company A subsequently wants to connect to Company C, which was built on CORBA/C++. The second connection would require a whole new lengthy integration effort.

With Web Services using SOAP, the process of integrating Companies A, B, and C could be reduced by an order of magnitude. SOAP is an XML technology that

Table 7-2 Comparing J2EE and .NET

J2EE	Microsoft.NET	Comments

Java	C# programming language VisualBasic.NET	J2EE is a standard while Microsoft.NET is a product.
		    C# and Java both derive from C and C++. C# borrows some of the component concepts from JavaBeans (properties/ attributes, events, etc.), adds some of its own (for example, metadata tags).
		    Java runs on any platform with a Java Virtual Machine (JVM). C# only runs in Windows for now.

Java core API	.NET common components	High-level .NET components will include support for distributed access using XML and SOAP.
Java Virtual Machine and CORBA IDL and ORB	IL common language runtime	.NET common language runtime allows code in multiple languages to use a shared set of components on Windows. JVM specs allow Java bytecodes to run on any platform with a compliant JVM.
Java ServerPages (JSP)	Active Server Pages.NET (ASP)	ASP uses Visual Basic, C#, for code snippets, compiled into native code through the common language runtime. JSPs use Java code (snippets, or JavaBean references), compiled into Java bytecodes.
JDBC, EJB, JMS, and Java XML Libraries (SOAP, UDDI, WSDL)	ADO.NET and SOAP, UDDI, WSDL	ADO is built on XML data interchange on top of HTTP (SOAP). .NET's Web services assume SOAP messaging models. EJB, JDBC leave the data interchange protocol at the developer's discretion, and operate on top of HTTP, RMI/JRMP, or IIOP.

describes remote procedure calls (RPC) similarly to Java Remote Method Invocation (RMI) but is platform and language independent. Thus a C++ program can execute methods from a Java platform, running on the other side of the world.

As a result, the potential of Web Services presents countless possibilities. For example, consider adding validated standardized AI methods and procedures available from AI servers or knowledge engine portals (such as Cyc, see page 192), as Web Services. Remote application programs could call these validated successful AI methods and procedures for their own application's execution.

Prolog

Prolog is a logic language that is well suited to problems that involve symbolic or nonnumeric computation. The name itself is short for PROgramming in LOGic. Prolog was developed in association with the research on theorem provers and other automated deduction systems developed in the 1960s and 1970s. It is a declarative, as opposed to procedural, computer programming language with several distinguishing characteristics:

- Prolog represents facts, or information about objects in the real world, together with rules or relations between these objects.
- Programming execution is directed by the information needs for the particular problem rather than by the sequential order of the commands in the program.
- A Prolog program starts with a query, which states the primary need for information. The program is run by presenting a query and seeing if it can be proved against the known rules and facts.

Because of its unique characteristics, it is a powerful language for AI applications in which manipulation of symbols and inference about them are important considerations. (See Appendix F.)

All vendors of EIP capabilities describe their services as intelligent, but this is currently met with skepticism because the level of training to install, implement, maintain, and operate the varied services is so extensive. What AI applications could be included through Web Services to improve intelligent services? If we remain reluctant to speak of today's most powerful Web applications as intelligent, what will it take to change that?

◆ What Is Web Intelligence?

Some AI applications using the Prolog computer language (see sidebar) are already being used for Web online questionnaires (see www.pdc.dk/vipexamples/pdcindex.htm). New applications are being vigorously pursued in many fields, and it shouldn't be long before Web Services include a variety of AI applications.

But whether AI programs actually think is considered to be a relatively unimportant question, because whether or not "smart" programs "think," they are already becoming useful.

Consider, for example, IBM's Deep Blue. In May, 1997, IBM's Deep Blue supercomputer played a defining match with the reigning world chess champion, Garry Kasparov. This was the first time a computer had won a complete match against the world's best human chess player. For almost 50 years, researchers in the field of AI had pursued just this milestone.

Playing chess has long been considered an intellectual activity, requiring skill and intelligence of a specialized form. As a result, chess attracted AI researchers.

The basic mechanism of Deep Blue is that the computer decides on a chess move by assessing all possible moves and responses. It can identify up to a depth of about 14 moves and value-rank the resulting game positions using an algorithm prepared in advance by a team of grandmasters.

Did Deep Blue demonstrate intelligence or was it merely an example of computational brute force? Our understanding of how the mind of a brilliant player such as Kasparov works is limited. But, indubitably, his "thought" process was something very different than Deep Blue's. Arguably, Kasparov's brain works through the operation of each of its billions of neurons carrying out hundreds of tiny operations per second, none of which, in isolation, demonstrates intelligence.

One approach to AI is to implement methods using ideas of computer science and logic algebras. The algebra would establish the rules between functional relationships and sets of data structures. A fundamental set of instructions would allow operations, including sequencing, branching, and recursion, within an accepted hierarchy. The preference of computer science has been to develop hierarchies that resolve recursive looping through logical methods. One of the great computer science controversies of the past five decades has been the role of GOTO-like statements. This has risen again in the context of hyperlinking. Hyperlinking, like GOTO statements, can lead to unresolved conflict loops. Nevertheless, logic structures have always appealed to AI researchers as a natural entry point to demonstrate machine intelligence.

An alternative to logic methods is to use introspection methods, which observe and mimic human brains and behavior. In particular, pattern recognition seems intimately related to a sequence of unique images with a special linkage relationship. Although introspection, or heuristics, is an unreliable way of determining how humans think, when they work, introspective methods can form effective and useful AI.

The success of Deep Blue and chess programming is important because it employs both logic and introspection AI methods.

When the opinion is expressed that human grandmasters do not examine 200,000,000 move sequences per second, we should ask, "How does anyone know?" The response is usually that human grandmasters are not aware of searching this number of positions or that they are aware of searching a smaller number of sequences. But then again, as individuals, we are generally unaware of what actually does go on in our minds.

Much of the mental computation done by a chess player is invisible to both the player and outside observers. Patterns in the position suggest what lines of play to consider, and the pattern recognition processes in the human mind seem to be invisible to that mind. However, the parts of the move tree that are examined are consciously accessible.

Suppose most of the chess player's skill actually comes from an ability to compare the current position against images of 10,000 positions already studied. (There is some evidence that this is at least partly true.) We would call selecting the best position (or image) among the 10,000, insightful. Still, if the unconscious human version yields intelligent results, and the explicit algorithmic Deep Blue version yields essentially the same results, couldn't the computer and its programming be called intelligent too?

For now the Web consists primarily of a huge number of data nodes (containing text, images, movies, and sounds). The data nodes are connected through hyperlinks to form "hyper-networks" that collectively can represent complex ideas and concepts above the level of the individual data. However, the Web does not currently perform many sophisticated tasks with this data. The Web merely stores and retrieves information, even considering some of the "intelligent applications" in use today (including intelligent agents, EIPs, and Web Services). So far, the Web does not have some of the vital ingredients it needs, such as a global database schema, a global error-correcting feedback mechanism, a logic layer protocol, a method of adopting Learning Algorithms systematically throughout its architecture, or universally accepted knowledge bases with inference engines. As a result, we may say that the Web continues to grow and evolve, but it does not adapt—and adaptation is an essential ingredient of learning.

If the jury is still out on defining the Web as intelligent (and may be for some time), we can still consider ways to change the Web to give it the ability to adapt and therefore to learn.

◆ How Does the Web Learn?

The various 15 billion worldwide devices available today produce about 30 percent of all data communications. The Web may be the nexus of much of this information flow, but you must admit it is not overly smart. In the future, however, the Web will need to do much more than pass raw data between people via search engines.

Facilities to put device-understandable data on the Web are becoming a high priority for many communities. Tomorrow's programs should be able to share and process data even when different applications and data sources are developed independently. The Semantic Web, as advocated by the W3C (see sidebar on the following page) is a vision of having data on the Web defined and linked in a way that it can be used by devices not just for display purposes but for automation, integration, and reuse of data.

Ideally, the wireless communication process should start by talking to a personal or embedded device that recognizes the user's words and commands. It will connect seamlessly to the correct transmission device, drawing on whatever resources are required from around the Web. Perhaps only database search, sorting, and retrieval are required. Or perhaps a specialized application program will be needed. In any case, the information will be evaluated and the content of the message with the appropriate supporting data to fill in the "blanks" will be provided. If there is appropriate supplementary audio or video, it will be included for reference. Finally, the results will be delivered to the appropriate parties in their own language through their own different and varied connection devices.

So, just how will the Web scale up to provide the infrastructure to meet this ideal process? The Web will require fundamental upgrades in its physical and intellectual components to perform intelligent tasks, including

Physical (hardware)

1. Personal and embedded devices
2. Wireless networking infrastructure
3. Processing chips

Intellectual (software)

1. Speech recognition, understanding, synthesis, and translation
2. Mobile Internet Protocols
3. Semantic Web architecture
   a. XML and schema
   b. RDF and schema layer (with Topic Maps)
   c. Ontology layer
   d. Logic layer (universal language for logic)

The World Wide Web Consortium (W3C)

The W3C (see www.w3.org/) was created in 1994 and has grown to more than 500 member organizations from around the world. The objective of W3C is to lead the World Wide Web to its full potential by developing common protocols that promote its evolution and ensure its interoperability.

The Semantic Web

The Semantic Web can be considered to be the realization of a vision of the future in which data on the Web will be defined and linked in such a way that it can be readily used by machines, not just for display but for direct use in various applications.

The technology now exists to realize the Semantic Web. We know how to build the terminologies and how to use metadata. The future vision depends on agreeing on common standards that can be used and extended everywhere.

Work is going on to realize tools and techniques, which will help to create the Semantic Web. For further information on the approaches being explored, visit: www.semanticweb.org/.

4. Adaptive software languages and Learning Algorithms

5. Parallel processing AI application over clustered networks, perhaps as Web Services

These physical and software components are necessary to implement the Intelligent Wireless Web. They require changing software applications from dumb and static to intelligent and dynamic.

In the next sections, we will highlight the innovative processes underway in these technology areas. For example, consider software agents that root around behind the scenes to complete an assigned task. Among the first bots in this category could be context-aware applications that seek to ease information overload from e-mails, pagers, and phone calls. Future agent classes could employ procedures based upon statistical reasoning to draw inferences from user behavior. As an example, Microsoft's Adaptive Systems and Interaction Group's Open Agent Architecture (OAA) take a user's request as spoken into a microphone. A speech recognition agent hears the spoken request and passes the recognized words along to the natural language agent, which translates the word strings into a logical representation of English. Then another agent, called a Digital Companion, understands the request and relays orders to agents capable of carrying out the order based upon known user preferences.

Databases and Machine Learning

Some estimates hold that the amount of information in the world doubles every 20 years. Undoubtedly, the volume of computer data increases at a much faster rate. In 1989, the total number of databases in the world was estimated at 5 million, most of which were small dBase files. Today, the automation of business transactions produces a deluge of data because even simple transactions such as telephone calls, shopping trips, medical tests, and consumer product warranty registrations are recorded in a computer. Scientific databases are also growing rapidly. NASA, for example, has more data than it can currently analyze.

In database management, discovering new knowledge is the nontrivial extraction of implicit, previously unknown, and potentially useful information from raw data. Given a set of data, and a language L, then if a pattern is found within the data, it represents a statement S in L that describes a new relationship. We often call a new pattern that is interesting to us, knowledge. The output of a program that monitors the set of facts in a database and produces patterns in this sense is called *discovered knowledge.* As a result, database researchers rank data mining among the most promising research topics.

Whereas a database management system is simply a collection of procedures for retrieving, storing, and manipulating data, we can define a *Learning Algorithm* as a process that takes a data set from a database as input and, after performing its algorithmic operation, returns an output statement representing learning. This is a critical element of exploring Web intelligence. As a growing percentage of the Web incorporates Learning Algorithms, we will look for more intelligent performance. Knowledge discovery through Learning Algorithms in databases exhibits four main characteristics:

▸ *High-level language:* Discovered knowledge is represented in a high-level language.

▸ *Accuracy:* Discoveries accurately portray the contents of the database. The extent to which this portrayal is imperfect is expressed by measures of uncertainty.

▸ *Interesting results:* Discovered knowledge being interesting implies that patterns are novel and potentially useful and the process is nontrivial.

▸ *Efficiency:* The discovery process uses run times for large-size databases that are predictable and acceptable.

Learning Algorithms are procedures designed to extract knowledge from data through two processes: identifying interesting patterns and describing them in a meaningful manner. The identification process categorizes or clusters records into subclasses that reflect patterns inherent in the data. The descriptive process summarizes relevant qualities of the identified classes. In machine learning, these two processes are referred to as unsupervised and supervised learning.

One way to look at a pattern is as a class of records sharing something in common. Pattern classes are the result of pattern identification or clustering. The two basic approaches to this problem are traditional and empirical. Discovering knowledge in large, complex databases requires both empirical methods to detect the statistical regularity of patterns and knowledge-based approaches to incorporate available knowledge.

Learning Algorithms for large databases must deal with the issue of computational complexity (see Chapter 6). Algorithms with computational requirements that grow faster than a small polynomial in the number of records and fields are too inefficient for large databases.

The Web's content is presently expanding at an enormous pace, but the quality of its structure is not improving (see Appendix C for a graph of the Web). The only mechanism for network restructuring at present is the contributions of individual Web-designer subnetworks. This results in a Web that is weakly organized. Any system capable of dynamically adapting network structure and content must use information that is locally available to HTTP servers.

WordNet

WordNet is an online lexical reference system. It is designed based upon current psycholinguistic theories of human lexical memory. English nouns, verbs, adjectives, and adverbs are organized into synonym sets, each representing one underlying lexical concept. Various relations link the synonym sets. WordNet was developed by the Cognitive Science Lab at Princeton University (see www.cogsci.princeton.edu/~wn/).

But the Web has limited control above individual HTTP servers. Many of the existing systems for flexible hypertext depend on extensive information being stored and managed (see sidebar). As a result, the control for the automatic adaptation of structure for the Web is limited to local networks.

As the Web matures, the IT community seems to be leaning toward defining the Web in terms of a database with knowledge representation. AI-based solutions for capturing and indexing vast amounts of Web information are already available. AI-related technologies are at the heart of all Internet search engine services. However, nearly 7 million pages are being added to the Web each day, making it even harder to search through the already existing 2 billion pages. Top-down, crawler-based solutions cannot keep up. As a result, only a portion of Web content is actually captured and indexed by individual services.

In addition, the limited ability of search engine spiders to extract information from a variety of database-driven sites causes problems. Such systems form a large portion of the Web, commonly referred to as the "invisible Web," and may be 500 times larger than the "visible Web."

We are currently seeing AI algorithms buried inside client-side tools that perform monitoring, content building, content streaming, and content sharing functions—especially in business and finance.

We can highlight a few of the many innovative companies in this area. For example, at the server-based end of "intelligent" search services, natural language processing (NLP) and linguistic analysis techniques are used to summarize content and identify relevant entities. Ask Jeeves and Albert were two of the first search engines to use NLP.

For intelligent content summarization and recognition, Autonomy's Bayesian Inference technology provides an automated infrastructure for user profiling, aggregation, categorization, hyperlinking, context-based searching, and personalization of large volumes of unstructured information. LexiQuest solutions analyze text to understand the meaning of each word, the structure of each sentence, and their overall concepts. LexiQuest has developed a technology leveraging a 60,000-word dictionary and 500,000 links between more than 150,000 semantic concepts.

For the Web to learn, it requires the capabilities of knowledge discovery, Learning Algorithms, and self-organization. Then the Web will autonomously change its structure and organize the knowledge it contains by "learning" the ideas and preferences of its users.

Supplementary to adding AI algorithms and agents to Web Services, the W3C suggests the use of better semantic information as part of Web documents and the use of next-generation Web languages such as XML and RDF.

The Semantic Web carries the vision of having data on the Web defined and linked in a way that it can be used by devices not just for display purposes but for automation, integration, and reuse of data across various applications. To make this vision a reality for the Web, supporting standards and technologies must enable devices to make more sense of information on the Web. For the Web to scale, programs must be able to share and process data, even when these programs have been designed totally independently.

Web-enabled languages and technologies are being developed (for example, RDF-schema), schema and ontology integration techniques are being examined, and Web Services integration standards are being defined (for example, Jini). The success of the Semantic Web will depend on a widespread adoption of these technologies.

In the next few sections, we will describe the XML, RDF (and Topic Maps), and logic layer that form the building blocks for the Semantic Web.

Extensible Markup Language

XML (see www.w3.org/XML/) is a language that defines other languages. Like HTML, it is based on SGML. It describes schematic entities and relationships between these entities. XML documents are compiled to HTML documents before they are visible on the Web. XML is a promising way for managing semistructured data and providing better schematic information for information retrieval.

XML is designed to make information self-describing. This simple-sounding change in how computers communicate has the potential to extend the Internet beyond information delivery to many other kinds of activities. The hope is that XML will solve two of the Web's biggest problems—speed and searching.

Both problems arise in large part from the nature of the Web's main language, HTML. Although HTML is the electronic publishing language, it is superficial. It only describes how a Web browser should arrange text, images, and pushbuttons on a page. People and companies want Web sites that take orders, transmit medical records, and run scientific instruments from half a world away. HTML was never designed for such tasks.

So, although your doctor may be able to pull up your drug reaction history on his Web browser, he cannot then easily e-mail it to a specialist and expect him to be able to paste the records directly into his hospital's database. His computer would not know exactly what to make of the information. HTML knows about words and their arrangement, but not what the words mean or how they are related.

HTML has no tag (angle-bracketed labels) for a drug reaction, which highlights another of its limitations: it is inflexible. Adding a new tag involves a bureaucratic process that can take so long that few attempt it. And yet every application, not just the interchange of medical records, needs its own tags.

The solution, in theory, is very simple: use tags that identify the information. For example, label the parts of an order for a book not as boldface, paragraph, row, and column   what HTML offers—but as price, size, quantity, and color. A program can then recognize this document as a customer order and do whatever it needs to do: display it one way or display it a different way, put it through a bookkeeping system or make a new book show up on your doorstep tomorrow.

SGML describes other languages and has proved useful in many large publishing applications. Indeed, HTML was defined using SGML. The only problem with SGML is that it is too complex for Web browsers.

XML was created by removing SGML's frills, producing a streamlined metalanguage. XML consists of rules to create a markup language from scratch. The rules ensure that a single compact program, often referred to as a parser, can process all these new languages. XML changes the Web by introducing the concept of metadata (that is, data about data). In XML, each piece of data includes not only the data itself but also a description of the data. For example, your database can have a list of names (the data) and a tag on the data saying that these are customers names (the metadata). XML therefore describes data, not pages. It is about the actual information content, but says nothing about the layout. The power of XML then is that it makes applications aware of what they are about. Once a spreadsheet is expressed in XML, it can link across the Web into other spreadsheets and into server-based applications. The ultimate result of adding XML to the Web will be a change of Web infrastructure (see sidebar).

> **XML and Language Translation**
>
> XML documents begin with an XML declaration that specifies the version of XML being used.
>
> For example, the following is a complete XML document:
>
> ```
> <?xml version="1.0"?> <greeting>Hello,
>     world!</greeting>
> ```
>
> How will language translation will play a role on the Web? Consider that in document processing it is often useful to identify the natural language in which the content is written. A special attribute named `xml:lang` may be inserted in documents to specify the language used in the contents.
>
> For example,
>
> ```
> <p xml:lang="en">The quick brown fox jumps over
>     the lazy dog.</p>
> <p xml:lang="en-GB">What colour is it?</p>
> <p xml:lang="en-US">What color is it?</p>
> ```

Just as HTML created a way for every computer user to read Internet documents, XML markup makes sense to humans because it consists of nothing more than ordinary text.

The unifying power of XML arises from a few well-chosen rules. One is that tags almost always come in pairs. Like parentheses, they surround the text to which they apply. And like quotation marks, tag pairs can be nested inside one another to multiple levels. The nesting rule automatically forces simplicity on every XML document.

In HTML, a document is generally in one particular language, whether that be English or Japanese. XML enables exchange of information not only between different computer systems, but also across national and cultural boundaries. The structural and semantic information that can be added with XML allows these devices to do a great deal of processing on the spot. That not only will take a big load off Web servers but also should reduce network traffic dramatically.

The latest versions of several Web browsers can read an XML document, fetch the appropriate stylesheet, and use it to sort and format the information on the screen.

The reader might never know that he is looking at XML rather than HTML, except that XML-based sites run faster and are easier to use.

XML-based semantic messaging is already revolutionizing distributed system development. Their main advantages include

▶ *More flexible data transfer:* XML-based semantic messaging lets you deal with data semantics, rather than with data position and type.

▶ *Simplified interface management:* XML-based semantics messaging expresses parameters in terms of XML documents, which are more generic and more resilient to changes of the parameters.

▶ *Simplified remote invocation:* XML-based semantics messaging minimizes processes.

Microsoft is currently pursuing XML initiatives throughout its programming and applications software and servers via its .NET efforts. Going toe-to-toe with Microsoft, Sun Microsystems has developed Sun ONE, an XML platform. Others, including IBM, Oracle, and BEA Systems, are pursuing their own technology for running Web Services.

Resource Description Framework and Topic Map Convergence

In the next few sections, we will discuss RDF and Topic Maps and the possibility of their converging to a composite standard.

Resource Description Framework RDF (see www.w3.org/RDF) is a framework for representing metadata. The goal of RDF is to enable the automation of many Web-related activities, such as resource discovery. RDF is a model for metadata, and XML can be used to represent this model. The goal of RDF is to define a mechanism for describing resources that makes no assumptions about a particular application domain, nor defines the semantics of any application. Such models are used

▶ To address reuse and components (software engineering)
▶ To handle problems of schema evolution (database)
▶ To represent knowledge representation (AI)

However, modeling metadata in a completely domain-independent fashion is difficult to handle. How successful RDF will be in automating activities over the Web is an open question. However, if RDF could provide a standardized framework for most major Web sites and applications, it could bring significant improvements in automating Web-related activities.

If some of the major sites on the Web incorporate semantic modeling support through RDF, it could provide more sophisticated searching capabilities over these sites (see sidebar). However, it is still debatable whether one could develop a global search engine that could seamlessly search through all sites that have incorporated semantic information by means of RDF. The same may be true even for the task of trying to build an algebraic structure depicting the Web contents.

> **RDF Example**
>
> The example sentence
>
> ```
> John Smith is the creator of http://
>     www.Home.com/Smith
> ```
>
> is represented in RDF/XML as
>
> ```
> <rdf:RDF>
>   <rdf:Description about="http://
>       www.Home.com/Smith">
>     <s:Creator>John Smith</s:Creator>
>   </rdf:Description>
> </rdf:RDF>
> ```

Formal Model for Resource Description Framework The RDF data model is defined formally as follows:

1. There is a set called Resources.
2. There is a set called Literals.
3. There is a subset of Resources called Properties.
4. There is a set called Statements, each element of which is a triple of the form {pred, sub, obj}, where pred is a property (member of Properties), sub is a resource (member of Resources), and obj is either a resource or a literal (member of Literals).

We can view a set of statements (members of Statements) as a directed labeled graph: Each resource and literal is a vertex; a triple {p, s, o} is an arc from s to o, labeled by p. This is illustrated in Figure 7-2.

Topic Maps A strong interest has always been expressed in knowledge organization within knowledge management research, particularly for knowledge-intensive industries (for example, healthcare, pharmaceutics, technical documentation, Web virtual libraries). The foundations of knowledge organization and applied knowledge

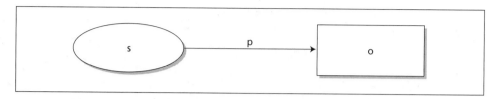

Figure 7-2 Simple statement graph template

management of large, digitized, heterogeneous resources are currently evaluating Topic Maps (TMs) in combination with ontological tools as a central resource.

TMs are an International Standards Organization/International Electratechnical Committee (ISO/IEC) 13250 standard. TMs provide a standardized notation for interchangeably representing information about the structure of information resources used to define topics and the relationships between topics. The structural information conveyed by TMs includes (1) groupings of addressable information objects around topics and (2) relationships between topics.

TMs are the online equivalent to printed back-of-the-book indexes. The knowledge is organized according to semantic categories and aids in navigation. This metadata is a structured view over a set of information resources. The structuring explicitly models an access structure to the knowledge contained in a collection.

Converging Resource Description Framework and Topic Maps Within the Semantic Web community there is a sense that a synergy exists between the work of ISO and TopicMaps.org on TMs (see www.topicmaps.org) and that of the W3C on RDF. Progress has been made in the search for a way RDF can be used to model TMs and vice versa. In addition, proposals have been made for changes to XTM to enable semantic interchange of the two standards.

Bringing these models together can provide a harmonious platform on which to build the Semantic Web. The reasoning behind bringing together these two standards is in the fact that both models are intent on describing relationships between entities with identity.[1]

---

1. The ontological and conceptual tools and languages (such as ODE, Ontolingua, Ontosaurus, WebOnto, Ontology Markup Language [OML], or Conceptual Knowledge Markup Language [CKML], or WONDEL) are used to model metadata structures (see, for example, www.swi.psy.uva.nl/wondertools and www.gca.org).

Semantic Web Road Map

The road map for achieving a set of connected applications for data on the Web in the form of a logical web of data is called the Semantic Web. An underlying idea of semantic networks is the ability to resolve the semantics of a particular node by following an arc until a node is found with which the agent is familiar. The Semantic Web, in competition with AI Web Services, forms a basic element of the Intelligent Wireless Web.

The Web was originally designed as an information space, with the goal that it should be useful not only for human–human communication but also for interactions between devices. One of the major obstacles to this has been the fact that most information on the Web is designed for human consumption, and even if it was derived from a database with meanings for its database elements, the structure of the data is not evident to an autonomous agent browsing the Web. Leaving aside the AI problem of training devices to behave like people, the Semantic Web approach instead develops languages for expressing information in a form that a device can process.

The general model is the RDF. The basic model contains only the concepts of an assertion and quotation, making assertions about assertions. RDF applications are for data about data (metadata) in which assertions about assertions are basic, even before logic.

As far as mathematics goes, the language at this point has no negation or implication. RDF documents at this level do not have great power.

Meta-assertions make it possible to do rudimentary checks on a document. In SGML, a process allows checking of whether elements have been used in appropriate positions. Likewise, in RDF, a schema allows checking, for example, whether a driver's license has the name of a person, not a model of car, as its "name."

The schema language typically makes simple assertions about allowable combinations. The constraints expressed in the schema language are easily expanded into a more powerful logical layer (the next layer).

We may want to make inferences that can only be made by understanding the semantics of the schema language in logical terms. A requirement of common RDF is the ability to follow rules for converting a document in one RDF schema into another one.

The Logic Layer

The logic layer provides documents with rules that distinguish one type of document from a document of another type; the checking of a document against a set of rules of self-consistency; and the resolution of a query by conversion from unknown terms to known terms. The layer incorporates a predicate logic (not, and, or) and the next layer quantification (for all x, $y(x)$). Figure 7-3 illustrates function flow within a RDF structure.

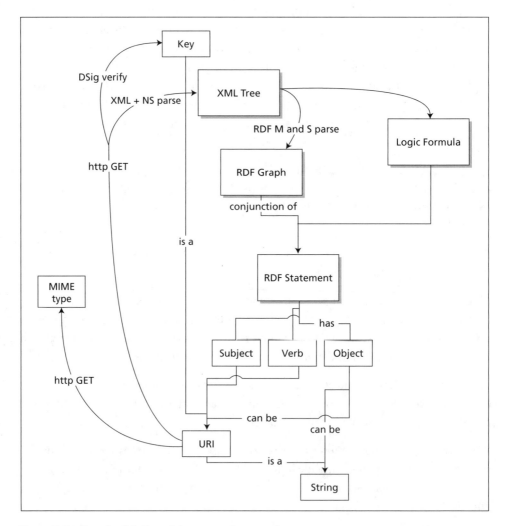

Figure 7-3   Proof validation: A language for proof

The RDF model does not say anything about the form of the reasoning engine. The proof will be a chain of assertions and reasoning rules, with pointers to all the supporting material. RDF at the logical level already has the power to express inference rules.

RDF, at the logical level, is a query engine of specific algorithms and indexes. Although search engines that index HTML pages find many answers to searches and cover a huge part of the Web, they return many inappropriate answers. There is no notion of "correctness" to such searches. By contrast, logical engines have typically been able to restrict their output to provably correct answers, but have suffered from the inability to go through the mass of connected data to construct valid answers. The combinatorial explosion of possibilities to be traced has been quite intractable.

If an engine of the future combines a reasoning engine with a search engine, it may actually be able to construct proofs. It will be able to reach out to indexes that contain very complete lists of all occurrences of a given term, and then use logic to weed out all but those which can be of use in solving the given problem.

> **Inference Engines for the Semantic Web**
>
> An inference engine processes the knowledge on the Semantic Web and deduces new knowledge from already specified knowledge. Two different approaches are used: general logic-based inference engines and problem-solving methods (PSMs) (specialized algorithms).
>
> Predicate calculus is one example of a logic in which syntax and semantics are both first order. There are logics that have a higher-order syntax but a first-order semantics. Applications for higher-order syntax are statements expressing trust about other statements.
>
> PSMs are small algorithms in the fields of knowledge-based systems and knowledge acquisition. They perform inferences within expert systems. A PSM specifies which inferences actions must be performed for a task and defines the data and flow between subtasks.

Self-Organizing Software and Adaptive Protocols

To give the Web a significantly higher degree of dynamism and mobility, as well as integration of devices and sensors embedded in the real world, the Web may benefit from self-organizing software, adaptive protocols, and object-oriented dynamic languages. Self-organizing network software refers to the ability of a network to organize and configure itself.

The problem with existing software, however, is that it takes too much time and money to develop, and it is inflexible when used in situations for which it was not explicitly designed. Various software design methodologies can alleviate this problem.

Adaptation means the ability of protocols and applications to learn and adapt to the changing conditions in the network, such as levels of congestion and errors. The next-generation programming languages may also support intelligent, adaptive, complex software systems. "Reflection" or reasoning may become part of the language's own structure and will support dynamic modification. Adaptive software may use information from the environment to improve its behavior over time. Object-oriented dynamic languages form a higher level of abstraction, semantics, development, and reflection.

Although efforts such as Jini and Universal Plug and Play have similar goals for device networks, they don't have the necessary scalable and flexible self-organization support. We can understand these limitations better if we first briefly review the foundations of computer languages.

In the 1970s, structured programming made it feasible to build larger-scale software systems based on existing specifications. A typical application was a database program that read an input file and produced an output file.

In the 1980s, object-oriented programming made it easier to reorganize for changes because functionality was divided into separate classes. A typical application was a desktop publishing system using user-initiated events such as mouse clicks or menus.

Today, adaptive programming is aimed at the problem of producing applications that can readily adapt in the face of changing user needs and environments. Adaptive software explicitly represents the goals the user is trying to achieve. This makes it possible for the user to change goals without requiring a rewrite of the program. A typical application is an information filter.

Hundreds of programming languages have developed since 1952; some of the more significant languages include FORTRAN, ALGOL, LISP, COBOL, APL, SIMULA, BASIC, PL/I, ISWIM, Prolog, C, Pascal, Scheme, OPS5, CSP, FP, dBASE II, Smalltalk-80, Ada, Parlog, Standard ML, C++, CLP(R), Eiffel, CLOS, Mathematica, Oberon, Haskell, and Java. These computer languages can be divided into the following general categories:

▶ *Imperative languages:* Operate by a sequence of commands that change the value of data elements. They are typified by assignments and iteration.

▶ *Declarative languages:* Operate by making descriptive statements about data and relations between data. The algorithm is hidden in the semantics of the language. This category encompasses both applicative and logic languages. Examples of declarative features are set comprehensions and pattern-matching statements.

▸ *Procedural languages:* State how to compute the result of a given problem. They encompass both imperative and functional languages.

▸ *Applicative languages:* Operate by application of functions to values. These are functional languages in the broad sense.

▸ *Functional languages:* In the narrow sense, a functional language is one that operates by use of higher-order functions, building operators that manipulate functions directly without ever appearing to manipulate data. An example is FP.

▸ *Definitional languages:* An applicative language containing assignments interpreted as definitions. An example is Lucid.

▸ *Single-assignment languages:* An applicative language using assignments with the convention that a variable may appear on the left side of an assignment only once within the portion of the program in which it is active.

▸ *Dataflow languages:* A language suitable for use on dataflow architecture. Necessary properties include freedom from side effects and the equivalence of scheduling constraints with data dependencies. Examples are Val, Id, and SISAL.

▸ *Logic languages:* Deal with predicates or relationships.

▸ *Constraint languages*: A problem is specified and solved by a series of constraining relationships.

▸ *Object-oriented languages:* Data and functions are treated as a unit.

▸ *Concurrent languages*: Describe programs that may be executed in parallel. This may be either multiprogramming (sharing one processor) or multiprocessing (separate processors sharing one memory).

▸ *Distributed concurrent languages:* Differ in the way that processes are created: coroutines—control is explicitly transferred.

▸ *Fourth-generation languages:* Very-high-level language using natural English or visual constructs. Algorithms or data structures may be chosen by the compiler.

▸ *Query languages:* An interface to a database.

▸ *Specification languages:* Formalism for expressing a hardware or software design.

▸ *Assembly languages:* Symbolic representation of the machine language of a specific computer.

▸ *Intermediate languages:* Used as an intermediate stage in compilation. They may be either text or binary.

▸ *Metalanguages:* Used for formal description of another language.

Despite this diversity of language types, traditional software development with these tools has always been based on principles requiring exact specification, complex maintenance, and high levels of abstraction.

Today, software is expected to do more for us because of our increasingly complex environments. The complexity comes from users, systems, devices, and goals. Programmers were accustomed to trading CPU time versus RAM space; now they have to worry about bandwidth, security, quality of information, resolution of images, and other factors.

Adaptive software may offer to change this by adding a feedback loop that provides information based on performance. The design criteria itself becomes a part of the program, and the program reconfigures itself as the environment changes.

Genetic Algorithms

Today, software engineers work to equip their Web applications to ensure survival through an exhaustive list of IF-THEN statements or extensive exception handling, all of which must be conceptualized in order to code. As Web applications become increasingly complex, the task of identifying all possible scenarios to encode becomes daunting as the requirements of new features, bugs, and virus patches produces overload. Concepts borrowed from biology, such as natural selection, are being introduced into AI to solve complex and highly nonlinear optimization problems. One such tool is genetic algorithms.

A genetic algorithm is a model for machine learning in which a population of randomly created units goes through a selection process of evolution—a digital survival of the fittest in which each unit represents a point in a problem's solution search space. Individual units are referred to as chromosomes and consist of genes or parameters of the problem being optimized. A collection of chromosomes on which a genetic algorithm operates is called a *population*. Through fitness functions, chromosomes are evaluated and ranked according to their relative strength within the population. The fitter are chosen to reproduce, and the remainder fail to survive succeeding generations. After several generations, the algorithm should converge on the chromosomes, representing an optimal solution. It is worth noting the implicit parallelism of genetic algorithms.

Although genetic algorithms exist mostly as research activities at academic institutions and commercial applications are still largely in developmental stages, they do offer Web applications the potential ability to adapt to their environment.

In the digital world, genetic algorithms that are capable of adapting to their environment faster than their competition can obtain a significant advantage for survival. Already, software engineers are introducing genetic algorithms for the Web using Java, but progress in this area would most likely benefit from the development of a language with specific qualifications for these types of applications.

Static languages, such as C and its derivatives, such as Java, require the programmer to make a lot of decisions about structure and the data. Dynamic languages such as MIT's Dylan (see Appendix D) and Common Lisp Object System (CLOS) and their progeny allow these decisions to be delayed and thus provide more responsive programming.

So, how will the Web learn? We suggest a composition of the Semantic Web with its logic layer utilizing components of AI agents, Learning Algorithms, and AI applications, including adaptive software available through Web Services (see Figure 7-4).

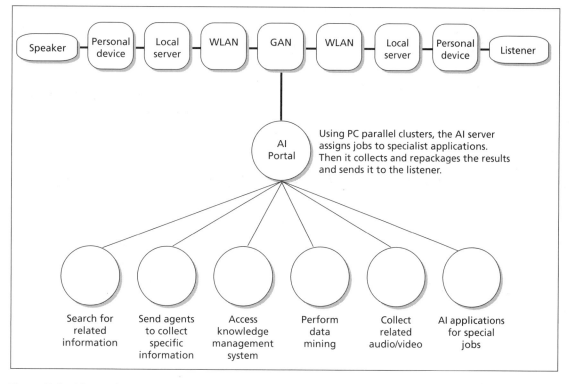

Figure 7-4   AI portals

◆ Where Does Web Intelligence Reside?

For humans, we can say that intelligence resides in the brain rather than in the appendages. But even then we must struggle to express where in the brain a particular capability resides and whether or not there exists a capability for redundancy and replacement.

So, where on the Web does, or will, intelligence reside? Is intelligence a local (centralized) or global (distributed) phenomenon? (To explore some graphical features and characteristics of the Web see Appendix C).

Two basic options exist for locating Web intelligence. Web intelligence could be globally distributed throughout the Web as a layer of the infrastructure over Web protocols. Elements of this approach are being pursued by Tim Berners-Lee of the W3C in conjunction with MIT's Project Oxygen, as well as others. Although the Semantic Web architecture is *not* actually an artificial intelligence application in itself, it is a foundation for possible AI applications that could be added to its logic layer.

An alternative approach is locating Web intelligence locally, centralized on an AI portal (providing Web Services) that is joined to its own cluster of Web computers. PC parallel clusters are now experimenting with PC clusters in projects such as the Search for Extraterrestrial Intelligence (SETI).

Each approach has a serious flaw. The AI portal approach limits uniformity and access, while the global Semantic Web approach faces combinatory complexity limitations.

Distributed Computing and Distributed Artificial Intelligence

In 2001, IBM's $100 million ASCI White was the world's largest supercomputer, rated at 12.3 teraflops (a teraflop is 1 trillion floating-point operations per second). It is the size of two basketball courts and uses enough electricity to power a small town. Few organizations today can afford to pursue computational analyses requiring the capacity of such a supercomputer. Some of these organizations are seeking to harness computers connected to the Internet to do their calculations through distributed computing instead.

Distributed computing is a model of data processing consisting of many small computers on a network working to do the same amount of processing as one supercomputer. The Internet, the world's largest network, provides vastly more computer power than ASCI White's 8,192 processors. By finding ways to allow many different computers to process smaller chunks of data, scientists hope to turn the Internet into the world's largest supercomputer.

Over the last decade, organizations such as SETI and RSA Data Security have successfully used distributed computing to analyze data. They were able to harness the idle CPU cycles of volunteer computers. A computer can process 1000 million instructions per second, but just like time, you can never recover the lost cycles of an idle computer (see sidebar).

Experiments with distributed computing began in the early 1970s over ARPAnet. In the mid-1970s, Xerox PARC (Palo Alto Research Center) created the first Ethernet network and the first worm that patrolled the network of 100 computers to use spare cycles.

More than 20 years later, parallel processing, concurrent processing, and optimized distributed computing offer a vast saving in computational time for applications of wide variety. The problem in deploying parallel processing on the Web has been software limitations. Until recently, parallel programming techniques have been highly hardware specific. For example operating systems such as Windows NT can support multiple processors, but desktop PC applications have yet to fully exploit its internal multithreading capability.

Locating Web intelligence on central AI servers, each of which is joined to its own cluster of Web computers, provides a powerful component for local centralized Web intelligence.

SETI

The Search for Extraterrestrial Intelligence (SETI) is a scientific effort to discover intelligent life in the universe. The SETI@home project is one way to harness the power of the Internet as a distributed network to analyze the noise picked up by radio telescopes. SETI@home distributes chunks of data to volunteers' computers all over the world. Using small software applications developed by SETI these volunteers analyze raw data for anomalies and send the results back to SETI.

For example, the radio telescope at Arecibo Observatory in Puerto Rico scans the radio spectrum frequencies and records it on high-density tapes—about 1GB per day. Then the observatory mails the tapes (because of limited bandwidth) to UC Berkley, where the data is divided into 250Kb chunks. Individual remote computers—over 2.5 million—in over 200 countries connect to the Internet and download a single chunk to work on. The SETI@home software crunches the data during idle-period processor times. When the chunk is completely analyzed, it is sent back to SETI@home servers, where it is merged into a database, and the process begins again (see www.setiathome.ssl.berkley.edu).

Today, hardware innovations are moving toward high-speed switched interconnections. These interconnections can make distributed-memory massively parallel processing (MPP) appear to programmers like shared memory symmetrical multiprocessing (SMP) machines. The key to future success is to get the right balance between CPU power and communications bandwidth.

Large-Scale Parallel Databases

T. Tamura and associates combined PCs and ATM switches, allowing the construction of a large-scale, inexpensive parallel platform. They used the most complex query of the standard benchmark on a 100GB database to evaluate the system compared with commercial parallel systems. Their PC cluster exhibited much higher performance compared with those in current benchmark reports. Second, they parallelized association rule mining and ran large-scale data mining on the PC cluster. Sufficiently high linearity was obtained such that commodity-based PC clusters will play a very important role in large scale database processing.

The trend toward clustering, where groups of workstations, or PCs, employ a middle-ware layer to make them behave like a single parallel computer, means that companies can leverage their existing hardware by using networks as virtual supercomputers. You can implement such a cluster using software alone. Parallel applications have been successfully implemented in single-instruction, multiple-data (SIMD) and multi-instruction, multidata (MIMD) architectures (see sidebar).[2]

The advent of multiple distributed computer software packages, such as Parallel Virtual Machine (PVM), allows workstations, mainframes, and SIMD computers to work together on a single job as a virtual supercomputer. This virtual supercomputer relies on relatively slow networks to pass information back and forth between processors, but many application codes rely on relatively little communication compared with computation. It is important to realize there are no algorithmic differences between applications on MIMD computers and on distributed computers. PVM, a message-passing environment, is currently implemented on UNIX and Windows. Forward-looking approaches today seek to leverage the rapid advances in processor design, Internet connectivity, and the implementation of distributed computing embodied in languages such as Java.

In an MPP, every processor is like every other in capability, resource, software, and communication speed. This is not true on the Internet. Message-passing packages developed for heterogeneous environments must make sure all the computers understand the exchanged data. The result is that the effective computational power across heterogeneous networks still offers significant value. The advantages of heterogeneous network computing include using existing idle computers—performance is optimized by assigning each task to the most appropriate architecture, and it provides access to different databases or special processors for those parts of the application that can run only on a certain platform.

---

2. Tamura, T., Oguchi, M., and Kitsuregawa, M. "Parallel Database Processing on a 100 Node PC Cluster: Cases for Decision Support Query Processing and Data Mining," SC97 Technical Paper, Institute of Industrial Science. The University of Tokyo, 1997.

The PVM software provides the unified framework within which parallel programs can be developed using existing hardware. PVM transparency handles all message routing, data conversion, and task scheduling across a network of incompatible computer architectures.

The programmer writes an application as a collection of tasks. Tasks access PVM resources through a library of standard interface routines. These routines allow the initiation and termination of tasks across the network and synchronize tasks.

DAI is concerned with coordinated intelligent behavior: intelligent agents coordinating their knowledge, skills, and plans to act or solve problems, working toward a single goal, or toward separate, individual goals that interact. DAI provides intellectual insights about organization, interaction, and problem solving among intelligent agents.

Implementing DAI over distributed computers through the use of local AI server nodes is a centralized form of implementing Web intelligence, possible as Web Services (see Figure 7-5).

◆ Challenges and Opportunities

AI has always been controversial because it challenges the uniqueness of human thought. Nevertheless, the boundaries of AI continue to expand. AI first demonstrated that intellectual tasks could be achieved through selective heuristic search (for example, GPS). Then AI explored knowledge through expert thinking, producing DENDRAL.[3] A third line of AI research has been on learning, for example, Siklossy's ZBIE program, which learned natural language by comparing sentences with pictures.

Central to human intelligence is the process of learning or adapting. Likewise, machine learning may be the most important aspect of AI, including behavior, cognition, symbolic manipulation, and goals. This suggests that AI software should be concerned with being changeable or adaptable. The challenge for AI is to learn capabilities for helping people derive specifically targeted knowledge from diverse information sources such as the Web. Subsequently, one of the challenges facing Web

---

3.   Lindsay, R. K., et al. *Applications of Artificial Intelligence for Chemical Inference: The DENDRAL Project.* McGraw-Hill, 1980.

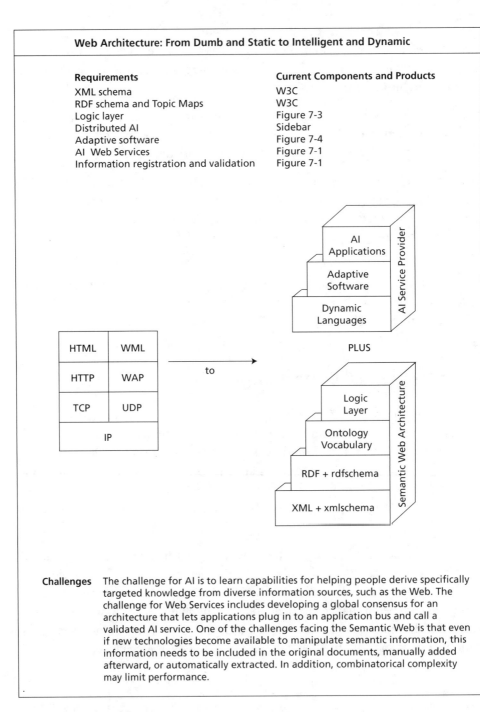

Web Architecture: From Dumb and Static to Intelligent and Dynamic

Requirements	Current Components and Products
XML schema	W3C
RDF schema and Topic Maps	W3C
Logic layer	Figure 7-3
Distributed AI	Sidebar
Adaptive software	Figure 7-4
AI Web Services	Figure 7-1
Information registration and validation	Figure 7-1

Challenges   The challenge for AI is to learn capabilities for helping people derive specifically targeted knowledge from diverse information sources, such as the Web. The challenge for Web Services includes developing a global consensus for an architecture that lets applications plug in to an application bus and call a validated AI service. One of the challenges facing the Semantic Web is that even if new technologies become available to manipulate semantic information, this information needs to be included in the original documents, manually added afterward, or automatically extracted. In addition, combinatorical complexity may limit performance.

Figure 7-5   Web architecture

Services is developing a global consensus for an architecture that lets applications (using object-oriented specialized software components) plug in to an "application bus" and call an AI service. Alternatively, one of the challenges facing the Semantic Web is that even if new technologies (RDF/Topic Maps) become available to manipulate semantic information, this information needs to be included in the original documents, manually added afterward, or automatically extracted.

Regardless of how AI applications are processed on the Web, a vital challenge will be the establishment of trusted information. The process must build trust of information and will include a form of information registration and validation. This will remain a issue for some time to come.

Finally, whether learning is achievable from AI service providers through Web Services, or through changes in Web architecture, such as the Semantic Web, or if machine learning is achievable at all, remains extremely controversial. But it is often in response to challenges mired in controversy from competing paradigms that some latent capabilities may be uncovered. The virtue of controversies is that they motivate experts into uncovering dormant capabilities in response to the challenge.

◆ Conclusion

In this chapter, we explored several possible variations of merging intelligent agents, intelligent applications, and AI capabilities with the Web. From this chapter, you may conclude that

▶ AI is already being introduced to the Web, but the jury is still out on whether the Web is, or will ever become, intelligent.

▶ Learning Algorithm is a process that takes a data set from a database as input and after performing its algorithmic operation returns an output statement representing learning. As the Web increases the percentage of applications and protocols with Learning Algorithms, we can expect improvements in performance in both quality and type.

▶ The Web may become a learning network through a combination of Semantic Web architecture and components of AI agents and AI applications built with adaptive software languages and connected to the Web via its logic layer.

▶ Web intelligence could be located globally—distributed throughout the Web as a layer over the infrastructure of Web protocols, as well as locally (for example, Cyc) on AI service providers, each of which is joined to its own cluster of specialized AI-application computers (such as a specialized Web Service).

8

Speech Synthesis and Translation

In Chapter 2, we discussed speech recognition and understanding as part of the human-to-device interface. In Chapter 7, we presented ways for devices and their distributed resources to evaluate the content of the communication and to repackage appropriate intelligent information as a response. Now, in this chapter, we present speech synthesis and translation as part of the device-to-human interface that completes the communication cycle.

We discuss current efforts to develop text-to-speech (TTS) generators and the SSML for the Web in conjunction with XML translation capabilities.

The final element in the desired communication process for the Intelligent Wireless Web is delivering recognizable speech output to the recipient through speech synthesis. Speech synthesis is the automatic generation of speech from text data or from other nontext applications. Text-to-speech (TTS) refers to audible responses from the computer. The actual voice responses can use recorded human speech phrases or audio generators that produce a natural human sound. However, a large amount of memory is needed to store the recorded voice vocabulary.

◆ Text-to-Speech Generators

Man-machine interaction applications will require a virtually unlimited vocabulary of speech output and a wide-ranging sound analysis and generation capability from TTS systems to produce ever more human-sounding speech. At the same time, current applications place practical constraints on TTS system parameters, with limitations on factors such as memory size, software flexibility, and processor performance.

For example, many embedded systems require small (and therefore limited) TTS systems for slower processors; some wireless applications require small speech generation components on the wireless client coupled with low data transmission rates. An increasing number of applications (for example, dialog systems, aids for disabled individuals, and Web page readers) will benefit from control over voice, pitch, and other aspects of the speech output.

TTS systems today do not yet meet the fundamental goal of producing speech indistinguishable from that of a human. A system that is natural-sounding in one area, such as overall voice quality or the quality of individual speech sounds, may not be natural-sounding in another, such as prosody (pitch patterns and timing); or a system that is generally more natural-sounding may be less intelligible. In some cases, a system that excels in overall voice quality may require an unacceptable amount of memory or execution time. The ultimate goal, then, is a system that not only faithfully replicates human speech but also meets the needs of applications in terms of flexibility, memory usage, and performance. Thus the most significant issue related to speech synthesis is the production of high-quality speech while minimizing the hardware and software requirements, including memory, algorithmic complexity, and speed of computation.

TTS systems typically have two main components: a text analysis component and a speech generation component. The text analysis component analyzes the input text and generates a symbolic representation containing linguistic information, such as phonemes. Phonemes are the fundamental elements of pronunciation and speech. Phonemes provide the building blocks for voice and they are combined to form syllables and words. Many applications use a combination of speech recognition and speech synthesis to create a natural interactive environment (see Figure 8-1).

To produce high-quality speech output, a speech generation component must produce acoustic values, durations, and pitch patterns that sound human. This task is highly dependent on context.

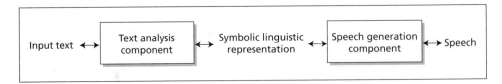

Figure 8-1   Text-to-speech architecture

The development of a speech generation application originated from one of two approaches: concatenation or rule-based. In a concatenation approach, stored speech units originally extracted from natural speech are pieced together. A separate set of units must be stored for every voice in each language. The speech units may be stored either as raw waveforms or as sets of parameters derived from the waveforms. Speech waveform is constructed from the parameter values with a signal processing component called a synthesizer.

In rule-based synthesis, all of the acoustic parameter values are generated by a set of context-sensitive rules. The primary challenge of a rule-based approach is to capture the perceptually relevant rules to produce appropriate values for high-quality synthesis. Acoustic rules are derived on the basis of knowledge of speech patterns and experimentation.

Voice quality refers to the basic sound of the voice. Currently, the better waveform concatenation schemes provide voice quality superior to parametric schemes. Another significant factor in the perception of naturalness is prosody. Prosody conveys a variety of syntactic, semantic, and discourse information. Natural-sounding synthetic speech requires appropriate prosody and natural-sounding acoustic values. In a concatenation scheme, discontinuities can be severe because waveform fragments may be difficult to concatenate smoothly.

In a rule-based system, intelligibility problems may result from incorrect generalizations concerning spectral and timing patterns. A rule-based approach has an advantage in the customization options for controlling speech output, such as voice characteristics, speaking rate, and pitch.

An important consideration is that a high-quality, rule-based system requires dramatically less memory than a high-quality concatenation. Despite the relatively natural voice quality generated by some concatenation systems, they suffer from prosodic control and segmental quality. In contrast, a rule-based system has important advantages in memory usage and performance.

Synthesizers can be categorized by the methods they use to store and generate the speech sounds. Four such categories are waveform synthesizers, terminal analog synthesizers, articulatory synthesizers, and formant synthesizers.

Waveform synthesizers store basic speech units (for example, phonemes, syllables, and words) and concatenate the basic units to create the speech. This approach is generally memory intensive, but it can yield good speech quality.

More on Linear Predictive Coding (LPC)

LPC synthesis incorporates vocal tract parameters as a set of LPC coefficients. The coefficients are determined automatically from natural language speech signals. The LPC synthesis filter is excited by either a periodic or noise source, depending on whether or not the analyzed speech is voiced. Speech units are divided into short frames of 10 to 30 ms in duration. The speech signal is analyzed to provide a spectral representation of the speech unit. Successive frames can be adequately represented by parameters if the durations of the frames are short compared with the changes in the vocal signal.

Terminal analog synthesizers produce speech by directly modeling the output of the human vocal tract without taking into account the articulatory impacts of the lips or tongue. This method produces somewhat lower-quality speech but is more efficient than the waveform analyzer approach. An example of this approach uses the linear predictive coding (LPC: see sidebar) Vocoder, discussed in Chapter 2.

Articulatory synthesizers directly model the vocal tract, including the vocal cords, lips, and tongue. This method is more complex and has generally yielded poor results due to lower quality.

Formant synthesizers use a buzz generator to simulate the vocal cords and individual formant resonators to represent the acoustic resonances of the vocal tract.

◆ Speech Synthesis Markup Language

The Speech Interface Framework working group of the W3C is developing standards to enable access to the Web using spoken language. The SSML specification is part of a set of new markup specifications for voice browsers. It is an XML-based markup language for assisting the generation of synthetic speech on the Web. It provides authors content to synthesize in a standard way and allows control of aspects of speech such as pronunciation, volume, pitch, and rate across different synthesis-capable platforms.

A voice browser is a device that interprets a (voice) markup language and is capable of generating voice output and/or interpreting voice input. A TTS system that supports SSML will render a document as spoken output.

The markup language is designed to be sufficiently rich as to allow control over each of the steps described below so that the document author (human or machine) can control the final voice output.

An XML parser is used to extract the document tree and content from the incoming text document. The structure of a document influences the way in which a document should be read. For example, there are common speaking patterns associated with paragraphs and sentences.

Once the system has determined the set of words to be spoken, it must convert those words to a string of phonemes. A phoneme is the basic unit of sound in a language. Each language (and sometimes each national or dialect variant of a language) has a specific phoneme set; for example, most U.S. English dialects have around 45 phonemes. In many languages, this conversion is ambiguous because the same written word may have many spoken forms. For example, in English, "read" may be spoken as "reed."

Prosody is the set of features of speech output that includes the pitch, timing, pausing, speaking rate, and the emphasis on words (see sidebar). The phonemes and prosodic information are used by the TTS system in the production of the audio waveform.

We will now look at some sample XML code snippets to illustrate first translation and then speech synthesis using SSML. First, the XML example code separates the body with commands by using the `<speak>` delimiter. For example,

```
<?xml version="1.0">
  <speak>
    …the body…
  </speak>
```

Next the body contains specific language commands by using the `xml:lang` attribute that defines language codes. To illustrate, translating English to Japanese requires setting the language attribute to `ja`. For example,

```
<speak xml:lang="en-US">
  <paragraph>I don't speak Japanese.</paragraph>
  <pagraph xml:lang="ja">Nihongo-ga wakarimasen.</paragraph>
</speak>
```

Prosodic Modeling

Speech synthesis produced by simply concatenating segments of speech generally has good intelligibility, but may be lacking in naturalness. Prosodic components of speech, including management of segment duration (timing), intonation (dynamics of pitch), and energy contribute to improved naturalness of the speech. Therefore prosodic modeling improves the naturalness of speech synthesized by adjusting for duration and intonation.

A duration model assigns the duration of a speech segment according to the actual accent; the position of the sound unit in the word, phrase, or sentence; and the context of the sound.

An intonation model superimposes declining or increasing pitch to represent tonal changes in natural speech. This may be done linearly to capture simple tonal changes such as would be encountered when asking a question, or more complex accentuation can be superimposed on the sound string.

The "voice" element is a production element in SSML that requests a change in speaking voice. Some of the attributes are

▶ *Gender:* Indicates the preferred gender of the voice to speak. Enumerated values are male, female, neutral.

▶ *Age:* Indicates the preferred age of the voice to speak. Values are expressed in integers.

▶ *Category:* Indicates the preferred age category of the voice to speak. Enumerated values are child, teenager, adult, elder.

We can illustrate the voice element as follows:

```
<voice gender="female" category="child">Mary had a little lamb.
</voice>
```

Then we now request a different female child's voice.

```
<voice gender="female" category="child" variant="2">Its fleece was
    white as snow.</voice>
```

ATT has a TTS demonstration Web site that is available today. It allows visitors to type in words and have their Web browser start a Windows media player that plays the audible speech. (See http://www.research.att.com/projects/tts/ or http://www.bell-labs.com/project/tts/.) Other demonstration Web pages can be found at

▶ http://www-gth.die.upm.es/research/synthesis/synth-form-concat.html
▶ http://www.oki.co.jp/OKI/DBG/english/ml2110.htm#elandemo
▶ http://babel.fpms.ac.be/French/
▶ http://www.essex.ac.uk/speech/research/spruce/demo-1/demo-1.html
▶ http://www.cs.bris.ac.uk/~eric/spruce/

The SSML specification is largely based on the Java Speech Markup Language (JSML), but also incorporates elements and concepts from SABLE, a previously published text markup standard, and from VoiceXML (see http://www.voicexml.org/), which itself is based on JSML and SABLE.

A VoiceXML application can provide a user with access to listed personnel and associated phone numbers. Typically, the system greets the user with a prompt for appropriate input. The system waits for keywords from the user's input. The application uses TTS to present a system-generated voice message about a user, then transfer the call to the appropriate phone number.

The following conversation illustrates the interaction between a user and a VoiceXML-based application.

- User dials number: 1-800-xxx-xxx
- System: "Welcome to Company Employee Directory. What can I do for you?"
- User: "Please call John Smith on his mobile phone."
- System: "Calling John Smith on his mobile phone (xxx) xxx-xxxx."
- Systems dials (xxx) xxx-xxxx and connects the user.

◆ Translation

Up to this point, we have discussed the mechanics of speech synthesis and topics such as the SSML specification for voice browsers, an XML-based markup language for assisting the generation of synthetic speech on the Web. Consideration of speech generation would not be complete without addressing the problem of automatic translation. Although a significant part of any vision for a future speech-enabled Web system could be considered without getting into the messy complexity of language translation, the inclusion of this capability would significantly enhance the global potential of such a future vision.

Substantial effort has been committed over many decades to the problem of automatic language translation. In part, this was driven by the need of government intelligence and diplomatic services to improve the access to translated documents and speech. Most recently, a large number of commercial software and service products aimed at the issue of language translation have become available. Table 8-1 provides a sample of some of the currently available products and services related to language translation.

From the products and services shown in Table 8-1, it is clear that language translation is a technology area of significant commercial interest. Many of the tools and services are devoted to translation of written documents (that is, text and Web pages). In most cases, the output of such tools is a rough or initial draft of the translated document. In cases in which the language is simple and direct, the draft

Table 8-1 Examples of Language Translation Software Tools

Supplier	Product	Description
AltaVista	Babelfish Translation Service	AltaVista's free translation service provides instantaneous translation between selected language pairs of submitted text or Web page content.
		http://www.babelfish.altavista.com/
IBM	alphaWorks	Machine translation of human language. The user can type in a sentence in one language and it is automatically translated to another.
		http://alphaworks.ibm.com/aw.nsf/html/mt
Language Force	Go Translate	*Go Translate* translates words within Web sites from one language to another.
	Universal Translator	*Universal Translator* is a translation consumer product to translate Web pages, e-mail, and instant messages. It provides omnidirectional translation with 600 language pairs and provides TTS capability.
		http://www.languageforce.com/
Lernout & Hauspie (L&H is currently under bankruptcy protection)	Power Translator	L&H's *Power Translator* software provides translation of correspondence, reports, foreign-language news, and Web sites.
	TranSphere	L&H's *TranSphere* machine translation system has been developed as an industrial and commercial system for large-scale documentation translation. The system utilizes a parser to obtain correct meanings for words, depending on context.
	iTranslator	L&H's *iTranslator* online translator provides a free text and Web page translation service.
		http://www.lhsl.com/mt/
PROMT	PROMT	*PROMT* is an English/Russian machine translation system for Windows that considers syntactic, morphological, and semantic links. It uses various modes of translation (for example, dialogue, batch etc.), has embedded technical dictionaries on different fields of knowledge, and uses advanced algorithms to update dictionaries.
		http://www.translate.ru/eng

Table 8-1   Examples of Language Translation Software Tools (*continued*)

Supplier	Product	Description
SDL International	Transend	*Transcend* is a natural language translation software package that enables translations of documents, e-mail, and Web pages.
	SDLWebflow	*SDLWebflow* provides real-time translation from the company's Enterprise Translation Server.
	SDLX	*SDLX* is a computer-aided translation tool that allows the reuse of previously translated phrases and terms.
	FreeTranslation.com	SDL also offers a free online text and Web page translation service at its *FreeTranslation.com* Web site. http://www.sdlintl.com/ http://www.freetranslation.com/
Systran	SystranPro	*Systran Professional* is a natural language document translation tool designed for corporate use.
	Systran Enterprise	Systran Enterprise is a client/server translation product tailored for use on an intranet, extranet, or LAN. http://www.systransoft.com/
Translation Experts Ltd.	Word Translator and other products	*Word Translator* allows you to translate Web pages written in a foreign language; translate e-mail messages to/from a foreign language; translate letters, facsimiles, reports and memos; and translate manuals and books to/from a foreign language. http://www.tranexp.com/

may be very close to the desired end product. In many cases, however, the initial translation requires significant additional effort to correct errors and retain nuances of meaning through the translation process. Direct word-for-word translation may give an initial clue to the nature of the source document, but is usually inadequate in retaining the richness of language meanings. Going beyond word-based translation is clearly the next step, but this has proved to be very difficult.

The problems of obtaining automated translation are closely related to the problems of speech understanding, discussed in Chapter 2. Speech recognition to the point of reconstructing an intended string of words in an utterance is a difficult task, but it is one in which great strides have been made to the point that this element of speech recognition is relatively well developed. Extending to the next step of speech understanding (that is, interpreting the meaning or intent of the string of words) is a much more difficult task. The problem of language translation, if it is to be carried out beyond the level of literal word-for-word translation, also depends on an understanding of the meaning of the word string or utterance. Language understanding is the critical step in the process.

◆ Challenges and Opportunities

Speech synthesis has come a long way in the past 20 years. Systems exist to generate reasonable, natural-sounding, human-like speech from text. The translation of speech from one language to another, however, presents serious and far-reaching challenges. Although literal, word-based translation can readily be accomplished, this produces results that are rarely satisfactory and frequently completely unreasonable. The key lies in speech understanding, and, in this sense, translation is closely linked to the topic of speech recognition.

The challenges and opportunities involved in effective automatic speech translation are centered on deriving the meaning from the speech input so that the translated speech can be properly expressed in the target language using the appropriate vocabulary, grammar, and semantic context.

◆ Conclusion

In this chapter, we presented speech synthesis and translation. We discussed current efforts to develop TTS generators and SSML for the Web in conjunction with XML language translation capabilities, and we reviewed the status of language translation as a key need for global access to the Intelligent Wireless Web. From this chapter, you may conclude that

▶ The ability to synthesize human speech is currently available, although the quality of performance leaves much to be desired. Though continuing advances, the quality, flexibility, and efficiency of future speech synthesis applications will improve.

▸ Language translation is a key element to the vision of a global system of the future and is the subject of considerable commercial interest. Although tools now exist to aid in language translation, much more needs to be done to deliver the capabilities needed in the future. Speech understanding is a key element both for speech recognition and speech translation.

9

Technological Revolution

In this chapter, we discuss the forces behind the information revolution that is transforming the world's economic system and producing the demand for the Intelligent Wireless Web and we address the questions:

1. How does revolutionary change occur?
2. Why does the Information Age save time?
3. Why do Intelligent Wireless Devices improve productivity?

Historically few individual inventions have transformed the world in an actually revolutionary way. Revolutionary change has only occurred when a dramatic improvement in the efficiency of human activities was involved. Only change, producing orders of magnitude improvement in efficiency, can produce a true revolution.

◆ How Does Revolutionary Change Occur?

Is the Information Age a force for revolutionary change? To place the Information Age in historical perspective, consider two great transformational events: the agricultural revolution (beginning around 8000 B.C. and continuing through around A.D. 1700) and the industrial revolution (beginning around A.D. 1700 and still spreading across the world today).

Ten thousand years ago, humans lived in migratory groups and fed themselves by hunting, herding, fishing, and foraging. The rise of agriculture at that time was a major, dramatic turning point in human social development.

Farmers were able to use a single acre of land to produce the equivalent food supply that a hunter-gather produced from 100 acres. The 100-fold improvement in land utilization fueled the agricultural revolution. It not only enabled far more efficient food production but also provided food above the needs of subsistence. This excess resulted in a new era built on trade.

The agricultural revolution crept slowly across villages and settlements, introducing cultivated land and a new way of life. During the long millennia that this revolution progressed, the world population could be divided into two categories: primitive and civilized. The primitives lived in tribes, and the civilized communities worked the soil. They produced foodstuffs primarily for their own use, with a sufficient amount of surplus to allow for trade, leisure time, and wealth accumulation.

This agricultural transition was still incomplete when, by the end of the seventeenth century, the industrial revolution unleashed a new global revolutionary transition. Societies, up until this period, used human and animal muscle to provide the energy necessary to run the economy. As late as the French revolution, 14 million horses and 24 million oxen provided the physical force that supported the European economy.

During the industrial revolution, factory workers were able to use machines to produce 100 times the horsepower of a farmer with his horse. The industrial revolution was a result of placing this 100-fold increase in power into the hands of the laborer. In this case, the falling cost of labor fueled the economic growth of the period.

The new industrialization process moved rapidly over Europe and across continents. It utilized flowing water, coal, oil, and gas to generate the energy that produced an abundance of food and material goods.

In agricultural societies, the population had learned the cyclic nature of planting crops. And because they consumed what they produced directly and traded their surplus locally, there was a close relationship between production and consumption.

In contrast, the industrial societies following the linear timing of machines and enabled consumers to be far removed from the producer. The industrialization process, therefore, broke down the close relationship between production and consumption. The result was a stockpiling of resources at strategic locations along a distribution path. The industrial revolution was characterized by the following six basic rules:

1. *Standardization:* Mass production of identical parts.
2. *Concentration:* Work and energy were maintained locally available. But supplies and products were stockpiled at strategic locations and maintained with complex inventory controls.

3. *Centralization:* Authoritative leadership.

4. *Specialization:* Division of labor.

5. *Synchronization:* Work at the pace of machine capabilities.

6. *Maximization:* Macro planning.

Now let's shift to the latest historic turning point, the Information Age, which may have begun in the 1950s—the decade that introduced the widespread use of the computer. However, it did not approach its full potential until the computer was specially prepared for communications. This began in the 1990s with the growth of the Internet.

The Information Age is already establishing a new set of rules. For example, "standardization of parts" is being replaced by parts "designed and manufactured to custom specifications." And "concentration of workers" is being replaced by "distant telecommuting." And, most importantly, "concentration of stockpiles" is being replaced by just-in-time inventory and reductions in planning uncertainty.

In addition, production and consumption are moving even further apart. For many years the falling cost of information has driven change as it shifted power from the hands of the producers into the hands of the consumer. Even so, the cost of information has generally changed very slowly. The evolution of information distribution from early writing to the printing press took many years. However, once moveable type was developed, the transition rapidly accelerated. When significant drops in the cost of information occurred, such as with the development of the printing press, certain types of organizations flourished, such as the newspaper. From the ancient empires to the world's industrial giants, leaders have recognized that information is power. And controlling information means keeping power.

In fact, it was the high cost of information that made early civilizations most vulnerable. If a temple was sacked, the resulting loss of that building meant the loss of all locally available knowledge—from when to plant crops to how to construct buildings. Information was expensive to collect and maintain. Even as empires rose and fell, the cost of information remained high. Empires in China, India, and Europe used large bureaucracies to control information costs and dissemination.

The Roman Empire set the pace of communications by constructing 53,000 miles of roads, thereby eliminating the traditional dependence on water transportation. The Roman Empire lasted for centuries and spread its administration across Europe, Western Asia, and North Africa. Couriers of the Imperial Post traveled over Roman roads from Rome to London.

Rome also removed the management of knowledge from the temples to libraries for civil administration and learning. But because people had to go to the libraries, information distribution remained limited.

With the invention of the printing press, common people gained access to scientific knowledge and political ideas. As a result, by the sixteenth century, information moved into the hands of the people and out of the strict control of the state. In a similar dramatic effect, the invention of the telegraph produced widespread instant information, thereby liberating the stock markets. So while there has been continuous improvement in information flow for centuries, it is also clear that the development of the Information Age has only accelerated the pace in recent years.

Today, there is a collision of the industrial-based organizations and information-based systems. Information-based technology systems are the catalysts for the rapid change that has led to the dissemination of information throughout the workplace. The world's leading nations are experiencing a shift to knowledge-based economies requiring knowledge workers. These knowledge workers must be highly educated and possess technology skills. As a result, technology is facilitating the globalization of the world economy.

Although it is still to be determined whether the Information Age is actually to become a revolution comparable to the agricultural and industrial revolutions, it remains a strong candidate. Indeed, service workers today complete knowledge transactions many times faster through intelligent software using photons over IP packet switching, compared with clerks using electrons over circuit-switching technology just a few decades ago.

In Table 9-1, we show that each of the major global transformations was a result of an underlying dynamic based on producing two or more orders of magnitude change for a fundamental measure of human productivity.[1]

Today, the service worker is beginning see the productivity gains in communicating knowledge transactions. Therefore the information revolution may be based on the falling cost of information-based transactions, which in turn fuel economic growth.

---

1. It is interesting to notice that these improvements can loosely be associated with the fundamental measures of the physical environment: space, energy, and time.

Table 9-1 Global Transformations

Global Transformation	Productivity Dynamic	Nature of the Improvement
Agricultural Revolution (8000 B.C. through A.D. 1700)	**SPACE:** 100 times improvement in the utilization of land	Farmer uses one acre to produce the equivalent food supply that a hunter-gather produces from 100 acres.
Industrial Revolution (1700 through 1950)	**ENERGY:** 100 times improvement in available power utilization	Factory worker's machine produces 100 times the horsepower of a farmer and his horse.
Information Revolution (1950—ongoing?)	**TIME:** Still to be determined; perhaps up to 100 times improvement in the speed of completing knowledge transactions	Still to be determined—service worker may complete knowledge transactions up to 100 times faster through intelligent software using photons over IP switching, compared to a clerk using manual interfaces and electrons over circuit-switching technology.

◆ How Does the Information Age Save Time?

The Information Age can be said to have begun in the 1950s, with the transistor, and it is now proceeding at an accelerated pace via the Internet; to date it has been estimated to have reached only a portion of its full potential. The major contribution of IT has been to reduce the number of worker hours required to produce a nation's output. The development and distribution of the remainder of this revolution is still unknown and uncertain.

What should be indisputable is that new technologies that evolved within the past half century have now begun to bring about changes in the way goods and services are produced and distributed. In particular, the Internet's rapid emergence has spawned an eruption of start-up firms, each seeking to find a unique niche. In spite of recent major disruptions in the e-business economy, the overall trend toward rapid growth of commercial ventures taking advantage of IT innovations is clear.

We can trace the emergence of the transistor as the initiation of a wave of innovative synergies, which ultimately brought the microprocessor, the computer, satellites, laser, and fiberoptic technologies. These, in turn, fostered an enormous new capacity to disseminate information.

Before this revolution in information technology, most twentieth-century business decisions were hampered by uncertainty about the timely knowledge of customers' needs, inventories, and materials. The remarkable surge in timely information has enabled business management to remove large swaths of inventory safety stocks and worker redundancies.

In 2001, Alan Greenspan, Chairman of the U.S. Federal Reserve, expressed the view that the dramatic decline in the lead times for the delivery of capital equipment has made a particularly significant contribution to the favorable economic environment of the past decade.[2] With reduced lead times, many of the redundancies built into capital equipment to ensure that it could meet all plausible alternatives could be sharply reduced. That meant fewer goods and worker hours are caught up in activities that were intended only as insurance to sustain output levels.

Design times and costs have fallen dramatically as computer modeling has eliminated the need for the large staff of architectural specification-drafters previously required for building projects. These developments emphasize the essence of IT— the expansion of knowledge and the reduction in uncertainty. As a result, IT raises output per hour in the total economy principally by reducing hours worked on activities needed to guard against the unanticipated. Narrowing the uncertainties reduces the number of hours required to maintain any given level of production readiness.

And yet, the process of distributing resources and markets globally is still in a superficial stage. The underlying truth is that the global economy is still restricted primarily to the capital markets. In most other areas, institutions remain intensely local. Trade, for example, is still predominantly regional. Relatively little trade flows beyond local regions: Asians trade mostly with Asians, and Latin Americans trade mostly with Latin Americans. Even in more developed regions, this practice holds true. Intra-European trade accounts for roughly 60 percent of all European trade.

Technology alone will not produce a global marketplace. The problem is developing trusting business relationships. People establish trust by dealing with one another on a reciprocal basis. It is extremely difficult to purvey that kind of information over a digital network.

In global digital commerce, people are now technically capable of carrying out a transaction, but they lack the value-added services that enable them to develop a

---

2. Alan Greenspan (CNNfn, July 11, 2000).

trust relationship. What globalization requires is not just network technology, but rather the creation of a whole new series of services that are able to convey the information needed for trust. Applications currently being developed as Web Services offer new opportunity for developing close, trusting business relationships on a global scale.

Global Economic Integration

Three fundamental factors have influenced the pace of global economic integration through human history: (1) human migration, (2) trade, and (3) movement of capital.

Extending back roughly seven thousand years, human migration originally represented the predominant mechanism of integration of societies. Today, economists focus on trade in goods and services as the key mechanism for integrating economic activities across countries. Over the past five decades, real-world gross domestic product (GDP) has risen at somewhat more than a four percent annual rate, with real GDP in developing countries growing in per capita terms at about the same pace as the industrial countries. The result has been that real living standards, as measured by real per capita GDP, have improved on average about threefold in just half a century. During this period, world trade has expanded at double the pace of real world GDP. As a result, the volume of world trade rose from barely one-tenth of the world GDP in 1950 to about one-third of the world GDP in 2000. By this measure, there has been a substantial increase in the degree of global economic integration through trade in goods and services during the past half century.[3]

The two fundamental factors that have driven global economic integration are continuing improvements in the technology of transportation and communication.

For transportation, the most dramatic improvements have been for air cargo, which, except for airmail, did not exist as a commercially important phenomenon 50 years ago. For some current products, international trade would not be feasible without comparatively cheap air cargo. Also, modern production management practices—just-in-time inventory techniques—rely on the use of air cargo. Ocean shipping costs have fallen substantially in the past half century, by a factor of four. Oil tankers of roughly 10,000 tons displacement have been replaced by supertankers

---

3. Estimated from www.imf.org/external/pubs/ft/weo/weo1098/, www.j-bradford-delong.net/TCEH/1998_Draft/World_GDP/Estimating_World_GDP.html, and www.bartleby.com/151/a61.html.

of up to 500,000 tons, with no increase in crew size. Integration with the domestic transportation networks of road and rail is speedy, efficient, and less prone to disruption. Land transportation costs are directly important for a good deal of international trade between contiguous countries and indirectly important for connecting international trade with domestic production and consumption. Land transportation costs have declined during the past half century, although less than for air cargo.

Communications costs—for voice, text, and data—have dropped enormously and are continuing to fall as a result of rapid improvements in information and communications technology. Probably the most important effect of improvements in communications has been felt on trade in services. For a variety of services, modern communications technology makes it possible and cost efficient to separate production and use in ways that were not previously feasible.

Looking forward, how might the fundamental factors of technological developments affecting natural barriers to trade influence the extent of global economic integration through international trade in goods and services? Most likely, technological improvements will continue to reduce the costs of transportation and communication.

For transportation, further absolute cost reductions cannot generally be as large as what has been achieved in the past century. In fact, during the past quarter century, although there have been continuing efficiency gains in transportation, the main technologies of land, sea, and air transport have not changed. Nevertheless, because the natural barriers to international trade for most goods arising from transportation costs are already quite low, technological limits on the likely pace of future cost reductions will probably not be very important, at least for the industrial countries. For developing countries, where the infrastructure of modern transportation is generally less well developed, opportunities for reductions in transportation costs are greater.

There is no doubt that advances in information and communications technology account for much of the rise in total productivity in recent years. As a result of these technological advances, the costs of processing and communicating all forms of information have been declining very rapidly. By its nature, much of the activity in the financial services industry has to do with the processing and communication of information. The costs of making stock exchange transactions for both retail and wholesale traders has dropped during the past 20 years, with the predictable result that there has been an explosion of the volume of transactions and a large increase in the number of retail investors.

In economic integration the focus is on integration through trade and movement of both labor and capital. There is, however, an important mechanism through the communication of economically relevant information and technology.

The prospect is that the process of global economic integration—which is being driven by essentially irresistible forces of technological advance—will take place through trade, through movements of people and capital, and through accessing information and taking advantage of new technologies.

The Impact of Information Technology Spending on Productivity

IT is a huge global marketplace valued at $1.8 trillion—one of the top industries worldwide. It has been growing at a rate substantially faster than the overall economy as measured by the GDP until 2001. More importantly, by making a substantial contribution to economic productivity, information and communication technology is helping countries and companies of all sizes reach their strategic goals. The "information economy" is a powerful economic force contributing 6 percent of aggregate global GDP to the world economy.

During the past years, computers, high-speed communications systems, and computer software have become more powerful and more useful to people at home and at work. With the higher productivity, efficiency, and innovation delivered every day by IT investments, countries see IT as critical to their long-term competitive advantage and so continue to invest.

The link between IT spending and the dramatic increase in the productivity of U.S. workers from 1995 through 2000 has been well documented, but economists want to know how much of a role IT played in achieving the productivity gain. As it turns out, it may be a lot.

One goal has been to discover the link between developments in computer hardware, software, and telecommunications equipment and the performance of the U.S. economy. The growth rate of nonfarm business labor productivity from 1991 to 1995 amounted to 1.5 percent per year. But it was outpaced in the second half of the decade when productivity rose 2.9 percent per year—nearly double its previous rate of growth.

The use of IT by businesses and efficiency gains in the production of computers and semiconductors combined to achieve this productivity surge. The total contribution of these two channels to the improvement in labor productivity was about three-quarters of a percentage point, meaning the two factors accounted for roughly 60 percent of the improvement in labor productivity growth.[4]

◆ Why Intelligent Wireless Devices Improve Productivity

By the mid-twentieth century, it was clear that information needed greater management. As the computer age began, information costs dropped. But the PC was different from other information tools. It did more than allow people to receive information. Now they could buy, sell, and even create information. Cheap, plentiful information became as powerful an economic dynamic as land and energy.

The falling cost in information since the 1950s can be understood by analogy to Moore's law, which says that each new chip contains roughly twice as much capacity as its predecessor, and each chip is released within 18 to 24 months of the previous chip. In other words, Moore's law means that the price-performance of microprocessors doubles about every 18 months. Starting in the 1950s, mainframes cost $10 million per million instructions processed per second (MIPS). By 1996 PCs cost $1 per MIPS (see Figure 9-1).

Although the computer has been contributing to information productivity since the 1950s and has experienced growth because of Moore's law, the resulting economic productivity gains were slow to be realized. Until the late 1990s, networks were rigid and closed, and changes in the telecommunication industry were measured in decades. Since then, the Internet has been called the grim reaper of information inefficiency. For the first time, ordinary people had real power over information production and dissemination. As the cost of information drops, the microprocessor in effect gives ordinary people control over information about consumer market production and distribution.

What makes the Internet such a catalyst for change is its ability to take advantage of the marginal cost of information both for business-to-consumer and business-to-business communication. Whereas traditional company clerks used electrons over the phone system circuit-switching technology, service workers can now process multiple orders acquired through automatic services, through intelligent software

---

4. According to Federal Reserve economists Daniel Sichel and Stephen Oliner, who wrote "The Resurgence of Growth in the Late 1990s: Is Information Technology the Story?" FEDS Papers, Finance and Economics Discussion Series, May 17, 2000.

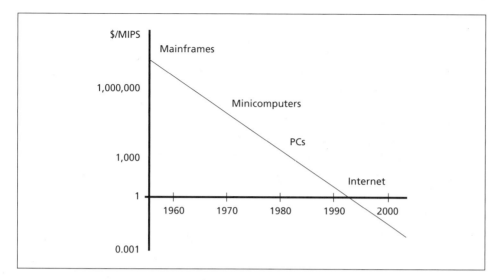

Figure 9-1   Moore's law

using photons over IP packet switching. Thus the Internet is the least expensive of all media and is a natural marketplace. What has been keeping the Internet from achieving its full potential has been limited bandwidth available directly to the consumer. Most telephone, wireless, and cable companies offer only limited access capabilities at relatively high prices. Eventually, cheap, fast Internet access will be available to every home and business, unleashing powerful effects. Eventually, the user interface will improve through the use of speech recognition. And eventually, software will deliver services that are credibly intelligent and helpful.

By applying the power of Moore's law, wireless chip technology will change from an upscale market luxury technology into a necessity for mobile devices. The new technologies will allow cellular carriers to build networks for less than $100 per customer, a cost reduction of tenfold compared with cable or phone companies. As wireless prices continue to fall, they will promote all of the four basic trends of the information revolution:

1. Decentralization
2. Reduced middle management
3. Automatic, knowledgeable customer service
4. Vertical and horizontal organization

Computers continue to evolve to smaller and smaller sizes, from mainframes to minicomputers to desktops to laptops to palmtops, and, by extension, to mobile devices. As their size has decreased, computers have become more portable, evolving from fixed-location devices to mobile devices. With mobility has come the need to replace hardwired network connections with wireless connections.

Within the next few years, the most prevalent computers may actually be small mobile wireless devices, such as cellphones, pagers, PDAs, pocket-sized PCs, and tablets. Their small size, relatively low cost, and wide availability from many manufacturers will ensure that many people will have one or more. The computing environment of small mobile wireless devices will be very different from today's predominant desktop computing environment.

At present, there are roughly 20 million Internet-enabled mobile devices in use around the world, but PDAs alone may account for 12 million wireless devices in 2003. Some estimates suggest there could be as many as 740 million wireless phone subscribers worldwide by 2003, along with 540 million hard-wired Internet consumers. Stamford, Connecticut–based Gartner Group predicts that investing in effective wireless technology will make mobile workers up to 30 percent more productive. International Data Corp. of Framingham, Massachusetts, believes that in the United States, the number of wireless Internet users will reach 61.5 million by 2003. In the United States, home Internet use is projected to grow to 101 million users in 2003. And there is no need to spend billions bringing copper wires to the billions of the world population currently unwired. Wireless will bring the necessary connections over all terrain.

Roughly half of today's $28 trillion world economy involves some related office work. This includes buying and selling transactions; banking applications; insurance, government, and education forms; and business-to-business transactions. This information processing is currently being done mostly by specialized humans and secondarily by machines. And the Internet is only beginning to scratch the surface of office work.

Banking, which typically involves straightforward, standardized transactions, could be one of the first major areas for widespread wireless access. Today, banks find themselves at a competitive crossroads. The ubiquitous mobile phone is the new contender in financial services, and it carries with it the potential for much broader access. Unlike earlier experiments with smartcards and the first PC banking services, mobile devices look like a natural channel for consumer financial services. Mobile operators have built networks and technology capable of cheap, reliable and secure, person-to-merchant and person-to-person payments. Wireless telecommunication actually can attack one of the bank's greatest strengths—control of the payment system. Wireless service providers now have the capability of challenging credit card associations, such as Visa, MasterCard, and American Express. Because mobile devices can provide the added value of real-time account information, they exert a competitive advantage over credit cards.

Although the first generation of online financial services was a disappointment, the next generation should be better. The growth in bandwidth and data processing capability is lowering the unit cost of using the technology. As speech recognition and 3G wireless technology develops, accomplishing such tasks as checking balances, paying bills, moving money between accounts, and performing other routine baking transactions will become easier. In other words, wireless delivers the interactivity to perform transactions on the spot, wherever and whenever that spot may be. Consequently, some think the best use for the Wireless Web is going to be in the business world.

Currently, there are differing revenue streams for wireless providers. Verizon Wireless, Nextel, and Sprint charge airtime for accessing the Web from a wireless phone, plus an additional cost for a Web-enabled phone. Alternatively, AT&T Wireless generates revenue by linking its subscribers with online retailers.

Devices using the Intelligent Wireless Web will offer both consumers and businesses access to products and services any time, anywhere. And by shifting even more power from producers to consumers, the falling cost of information provides a powerful feedback mechanism for the economic production cycle.

How much faster will intelligent applications over Wireless Web devices improve productivity in the next decade? No one knows. But the Intelligent Wireless Web holds a vision that may significantly contribute to an information revolution.

◆ Conclusion

In this chapter, we explored the driving forces behind the technological revolution that is transforming the world's economic system and may be producing significant demand for the Intelligent Wireless Web. We saw that the global transformation underway is a result of technology changes. We explored the implications of an Intelligent Wireless Web in accelerating productivity.

From this chapter, you may conclude that the Information Age is producing strong transforming global economic forces and the Intelligent Wireless Web may soon play a significant role through the introduction of

1. A growing number of mobile wireless devices for home and office providing broader access
2. Improving user interface to include speech recognition
3. "Nomadic" software from servers to our local devices as needed, including complete personal data and preferences through Web Services
4. Intelligent software that could improve information transactions and productivity

10

Progress in Developing the Intelligent Wireless Web

In this chapter, we take the components developed in earlier chapters and lay out a plausible framework for building the Intelligent Wireless Web, including our evaluation of the compatibility, integration, and synergy issues facing the five merging technology areas that will build it:

1. User interface: From click to speech
2. Personal Space: From tangled wires to multifunction wireless devices
3. Networks: From wired infrastructure to integrated wired/wireless
4. Protocols: From IP to Mobile IP
5. Web architecture: From dumb and static to intelligent and dynamic

Finally, we present strategic planning guidelines and the conclusions you could reach as a result of this book.

W e began this book by describing what we meant by the Intelligent Wireless Web and presenting an overview of the framework for plausibly constructing it. Our concept of an Intelligent Wireless Web wove together several important concepts related to intelligence (the ability to learn), wirelessness (mobility and convenience), and its advances in telecommunications and information technology that together promised to deliver increasingly capable information services to mobile users any time and anywhere.

We suggested putting these concepts together to form the Intelligent Wireless Web. We stated that it was certainly possible to develop intelligent applications for the Internet without media (audio/video) Web features or wireless capability. But, it was our suggestion that Web media such as audio could lead to improved user interfaces using speech and that small wireless devices widely distributed could lead to easier access for large portions of the world's population. The end result could be not just an intelligent Internet but a widely available, easily accessible, user-friendly, Intelligent Wireless Web.

Fundamentally, our vision for an Intelligent Wireless Web is very simple: it is a network that provides any time, anywhere access through efficient user interfaces to applications that learn. Notwithstanding the difficulty of defining intelligence (in humans or machines), we recognized that terms such as *artificial intelligence, intelligent agents, smart machines,* and the like refer to the performance of functions that mimic those associated with human intelligence.

The full range of information services is the next logical step, along with the introduction of a variety of different portable user devices (for example, pagers, PDAs, Web-enabled cell phones, small portable computers) that have wireless connectivity. The results will be wireless technology as an extension of the present evolutionary trend in information technology. In addition, artificial intelligence and intelligent software applications will make their way onto the Wireless Web. A performance index or measure may eventually be developed to evaluate the progress of Web intelligence.

In the following sections, we will bring together the components of the Intelligent Wireless Web and how it is being constructed. But building it will be a broad, far-reaching task involving more technology integration and synthesis than revolutionary inventions.

◆ Future Wireless Communication Processes

Ideally, the future wireless communication process should start with a user interface based on speech recognition by which we merely talk to a personal mobile device that recognizes our identity, words, and commands. The personal mobile device would connect seamlessly to embedded and fixed devices in the immediate environment. The message would be relayed to a server residing on a network with the necessary processing power and software to analyze the contents of the message. The server could then draw necessary supplemental knowledge and services from around the world through the Internet. Finally, the synthesized messages would be delivered to the appropriate parties in their own language on their own personal mobile device.

To build this ideal future wireless communication process we must connect the following technologies, along with their essential components:

▸ *Connecting people to devices—the user interface:* Currently, we rely on the mouse, keyboard, and video display; speech recognition and understanding deployed for mobile devices is a key component for the future.

▸ *Connecting devices to devices:* Currently, hard-wired connections between devices limit mobility and constrain the design of networks. In the future, the merging of wired and wireless communication infrastructure will require the establishment of wireless protocols and standards for the connection between devices; future smart applications require the development and improvement of intelligence services. Also needed is a method to measure the performance and intelligence of the Internet so that we can assess advancements.

▸ *Connecting devices to people:* To deliver useful information to the globally mobile user, future systems require advances in speech synthesis and language translation.

So let's start connecting the necessary technologies to fulfill the vision of an Intelligent Wireless Web.

The physical components and software necessary to construct and implement the Intelligent Wireless Web require compatibility, integration, and synergy of five merging technology areas:

1. *User interface:* To transition from the mouse click to speech as the primary method of communication between people and devices

2. *Personal Space:* To transition from connection of devices by tangled wires to multifunction wireless devices

3. *Networks:* To transition from a mostly wired infrastructure to an integrated wired/wireless system of interconnections

4. *Protocols:* Transition from the original IP to the new Mobile IP

5. *Web architecture:* To transition from dumb and static applications to new applications that are intelligent, dynamic, and constantly learning

A possible overall scheme of communications to implement the Intelligent Wireless Web is shown in Figure 10-1. In this representation, a speaker initiates both a

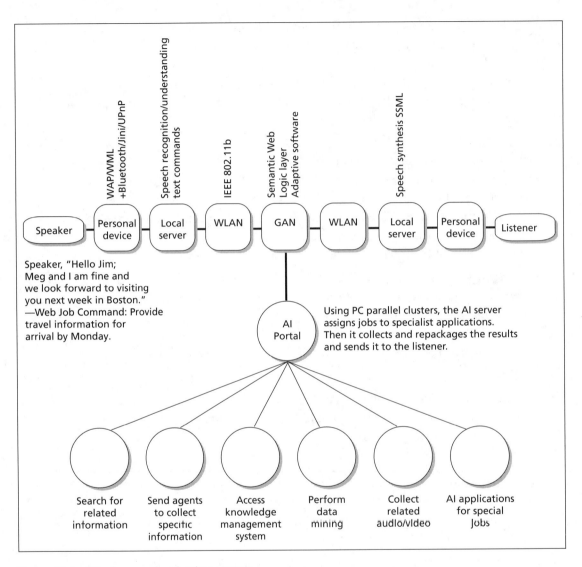

Speaker, "Hello Jim; Meg and I am fine and we look forward to visiting you next week in Boston."
—Web Job Command: Provide travel information for arrival by Monday.

Using PC parallel clusters, the AI server assigns jobs to specialist applications. Then it collects and repackages the results and sends it to the listener.

Figure 10-1 Wireless communication process

communication and a Web Service request by the following natural speech verbal request: "Hello Jim; Meg and I are fine and we look forward to visiting you next week in Boston." Web Job Command: Provide travel information for arrival by next Monday. The spoken message is received by a personal device within your Personal Space (see Chapter 3). It is wirelessly connected to a local server using an interface protocol (for example, Bluetooth, Jini, Universal Plug and Play, or Oxygen: see Chapter 3).

The local server recognizes the speaker's voice, interprets the spoken language message (see Chapters 2 and 8, including VoiceXML example on page 233), and transmits the first part of the message to "Jim," whose Internet address is obtained from the speaker's personal directory. The second part of the message is interpreted as a "Web Job Command" that requires action by either the Semantic Web or an AI Web Service. Both parts of the message are transmitted through the wireless local area network (WLAN), operating under standard IEEE 802.11b (as discussed in Chapter 4). The first part is then routed through the global area network (GAN) over the Web (see Chapter 7) and sent on its way to the destination identified by Jim's Internet address (see Chapter 5).

The Web Job Command, on the other hand, is assigned to an AI Web Service having the necessary capabilities to supervise solving this job assignment. The AI then tasks a series of specialized application servers to perform the necessary elements of the job in parallel. The component results are sent to the AI server, where they are integrated, and the overall result is then routed back to the speaker's Internet address. The integrated response is delivered to the final destination as a spoken message using speech synthesis technology (see Chapter 8). The response is, "There are three options for flights on your preferred airline arriving in Boston on Monday evening, as follows: One: at 5:00 P.M., Two: at 7:15 P.M., and Three: at 9:25 P.M. A reservation has been made for option One because that has been your preferred choice in the past. Please state your confirmation of option as "One," or, alternatively, state your preference for option "Two" or "Three," and reservations will be altered as necessary in your name" (see Figure 10-1).

In the next sections, we will highlight the innovative processes underway in each of these technological areas:

- ▶ *User interface:* From click to speech
- ▶ *Personal Space:* From wired to wireless
- ▶ *Networks:* From wired to integrated wired/wireless
- ▶ *Protocols:* From IP to mobile IP
- ▶ *Web architecture:* From dumb and static to intelligent and dynamic

◆ User Interface: From Click to Speech

We have evaluated communication between humans and their machines and found the problem of how to obtain speech recognition functionality in a hand-held or embedded device to be challenging; however, efforts currently underway look favorable for solutions in the relatively near term. Although we may expect speech interfaces to permeate society steadily, we anticipate that successful traditional interfaces such as the mouse and touch screen will continue to be in operation for a very long time, particularly for such high-power applications as selecting events on detailed graphical representations.

Certainly it is not a difficult problem for a handheld device (such as a cell phone) to perform limited speech recognition activities (such as voice-activated dialing). But because the demands for speech functionality increase with the greater complexity of the speech recognition tasks, it becomes increasingly more difficult to provide these capabilities on a small mobile wireless device with limited capabilities. Therefore the problem becomes one of distributing the capability for speech recognition and understanding between the local wireless device and remote processing resources to which it is connected.

This problem currently is being addressed in far-reaching research at several places, most notably at the MIT AI Laboratory and at Microsoft Research. The Microsoft effort is directed at technology projects supporting and leading to the vision of a fully speech-enabled computer. The Microsoft concept Dr. Who uses continuous speech recognition and spoken language understanding. Dr. Who is designed to power a voice-based pocket PC with Web browser, e-mail, and cellular telephone capabilities.

The highly promising initiative Project Oxygen is ongoing at MIT's AI Laboratory. This visionary effort is developing a comprehensive system to achieve the objective of any time, anywhere computing. In this concept, a user carries a wireless interface device that is continuously connected to a network of computing devices in a manner similar to the way cell phone communications maintain continuous connection to a communications network. The local device is speech enabled, and much of the speech recognition capability is embedded in the remote system of high-capability computers.

Systems for conversational interface are also being developed that are capable of communicating in several languages. These systems can answer queries in real time with a distributed architecture that can retrieve data from several different domains of knowledge to answer a query. Such systems have five main functions: speech recognition, language understanding, information retrieval, language generation, and speech synthesis.

Speech recognition may be an ideal interface for the handheld devices being developed as part of Project Oxygen, but Project Oxygen will need far more advanced speech recognition systems than are currently available to achieve its ultimate objective of enabling interactive conversation with full understanding. Figure 10-2 identifies the main requirements for an effective speech-based user interface and identifies the current status of each. To meet the needs of the Intelligent Wireless Web, the ultimate desired result is that speech recognition, understanding, translation, and synthesis become practical for routine use on handheld, wearable, and embedded devices.

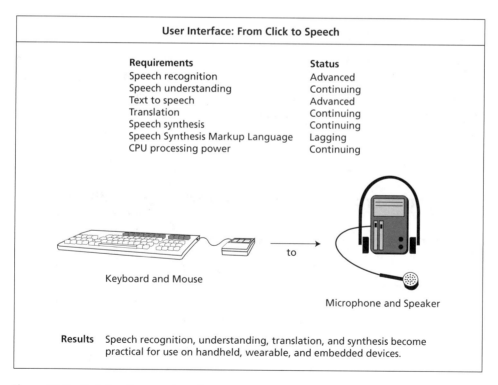

Figure 10-2   Building the user interface

◆ Personal Space: From Wired to Wireless

We imagined living our life within the confines of our own Personal Space—without wires, but with devices to "connect" us wherever we travel. Implementation of a WPAN, composed of the personal devices in our immediate environment, is one solution. In the office, devices improve work productivity by enabling access to data, text, and images relating to performing our jobs and by providing for analysis, access to software applications, and communications as needed. Creating a WPAN of our immediately available devices will enable a future in which a lifetime of knowledge may be accessed through gateways worn on the body or placed within the immediate environment (including our home, auto, office, school, and library).

WPANs also will allow devices to work together and share each other's information and services. For example, a Web page can be called up on a small screen and can then be wirelessly sent to a printer for full-size printing. A mobile WPAN can be created in a vehicle via interface devices such as wireless headsets, microphones, and speakers for communications.

As envisioned, WPANs will allow the user to customize communications capabilities, permitting everyday devices to become smart, tetherless devices that spontaneously communicate whenever they are in close proximity. Figure 10-3 summarizes the requirements and their status for this element of the Intelligent Wireless Web; the objective is to achieve the ability for handheld, wearable, and embedded devices to connect easily without wires and share software applications, as needed, producing office, home, and mobile WPANs.

◆ Networks: From Wired to Integrated Wired/Wireless

The process of network upgrades and integration seems endless. Even when new, advantageous technology becomes available, the existing legacy equipment retains value. Therefore, network integration is progressive and steady, but slow.

The earliest computers were stand-alone, unconnected machines. Corporate changes during the 1980s, resulted in the effort to consolidate company data for fast, seamless, integrated database communication capability. With this driving force, intranets and local networks increased in size and required ways to interface with each other. Over the past decade, enterprise models and architectures, as well as their corresponding implementation in actual business practices, have changed to take advantage of new technologies.

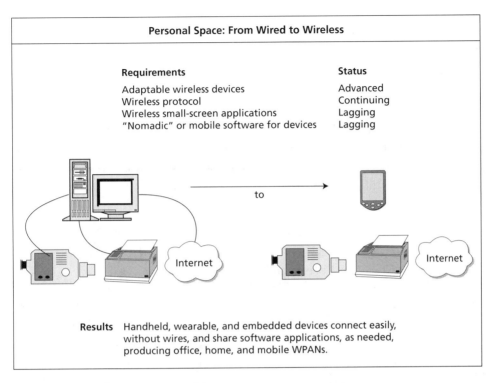

Figure 10-3   Building your Personal Space

The big lure to wireless is the potential for big money in implementing wireless architectures that can send information packets from people with small personal devices, such as cell phones, to a company's Web site and there conduct transactions. The number of wireless subscribers is expected to grow globally to more than 400 million by 2005.

The vast system of interconnecting wired and wireless networks that make up the Internet is composed of several different types of transmission media, dominated by wired media but including

1. Wired
   a. Fiberoptic
   b. Twisted pairs (copper)
   c. Coaxial cable

    2. Wireless

       a. Microwave

       b. Infrared

       c. Laser

Wireless LAN technology is rapidly becoming a vital component of data networks. IEEE Standard 802.11–compliant LANs produce applications based upon open systems. To optimize the operation of wireless systems, software options for interfacing wireless handheld appliances emulate various systems and directly connect to databases.

Radio frequency LANs (RFLANs) being installed today are fully integrated with their wired Ethernet counterparts as a fundamental requirement. RFLANs conforming to the IEEE 802.11 specification connect to an Ethernet TCP/IP backbone with a simple bridge, called an *access point,* are able to make the wireless network appear as just another network segment. Mobile devices associated with an 802.11 access point can communicate with nodes on the wired network just like any stationary workstation. This lets manufacturers and systems integrators bring to their wireless customers the benefits of technology bought and paid for by the much larger wired network market. Figure 10-4 shows the requirements and current status for elements of the Intelligent Wireless Web related to networking. The desired result is for networks to continue migration to optical fiber for long-haul stretches, with the last mile met by fiber, mobile wireless, and fixed wireless (local multichannel distribution system [LMDS] and multipoint multichannel distribution system [MMDS]) technologies.

◆ Protocols: From Internet Protocol to Mobile Internet Protocol

To achieve the mobility requirements of the Intelligent Wireless Web, the Wireless Appliance Protocol (WAP) provides a global standard for data-oriented services to mobile devices, thereby enabling any time, anywhere access. In so doing, access will be provided to far more end users than can be reached by the personal computer as a fixed end point. Figure 10-5 provides an overview of the changes needed to support the Intelligent Wireless Web. The anticipated result is to provide intelligent networking software for routing and tracking that leads to general changes in IP

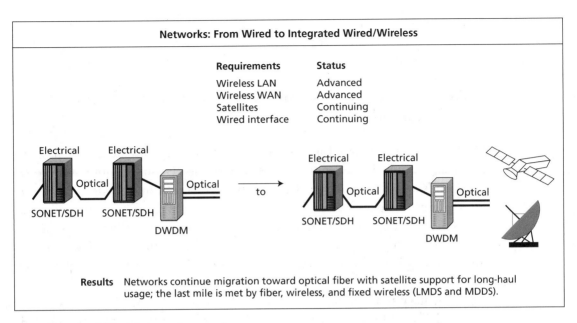

Figure 10-4   Building integrated networks

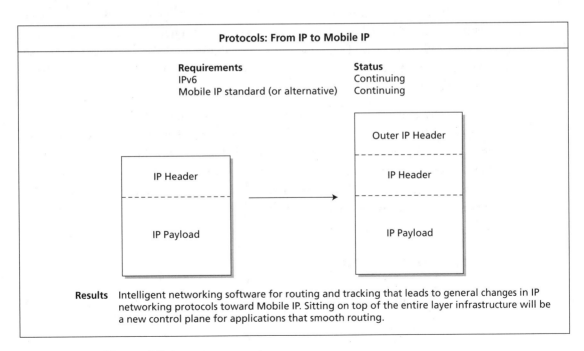

Figure 10-5   Building mobile Internet protocols

networking protocols toward mobile IP. Sitting on top of the entire layer infrastructure will be a new control-plane for applications that smooth routing.

◆ Web Architecture: Dumb and Static to Intelligent and Dynamic

Ideally, the wireless communication process should start with the user talking to a personal, or embedded, device that recognizes the person's identity, words, and commands. It will connect seamlessly to the correct transmission device, drawing on whatever resources are required from around the Web. In one case, only database search, sorting, and retrieval might be required. Or in another case, a specialized Web Service application program might be required. In any case, the information will be evaluated, and the content of the message will be augmented with the appropriate supporting data to fill in the "blanks." If there is appropriate supplementary audio or video, it will be included for reference. Finally, the results will be delivered to the appropriate parties in their own language through their own different and varied connection devices.

For the Web to learn how to conduct this type of intelligent processing, a mechanism is required for adapting and self-organizing on a hypertext network. In addition, it needs to develop Learning Algorithms that would allow it to autonomously change its structure and organize the knowledge it contains, by "learning" the ideas and preferences of its users.

The W3C suggests the use of better semantic information as part of Web documents and the use of next-generation Web languages. Figure 10-6 provides a summary of the Semantic Web architecture needed to support the Intelligent Wireless Web. Intelligent applications running directly over the Web, as well as AI Web Services served from AI service providers, will progressively increase the tasking performed with adaptive, dynamic, intelligent products.

◆ Strategic Planning Guidelines

Strategic planning leads to the determination of a course of action and allocation of resources necessary to achieve selected long-term goals. But charting strategic direction for wireless communications networks in a diverse and competitive landscape is complicated by an economy that has introduced dynamic rules for success.

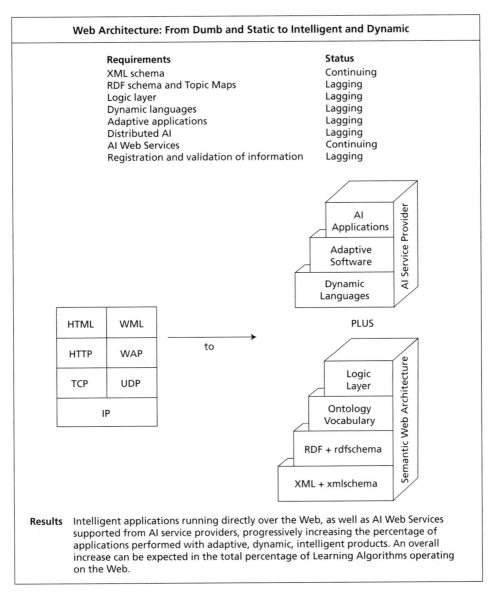

Figure 10-6   Building AI service providers with Semantic Web Architecture

Both the rate of technology change and the speed at which new technologies become available have increased. The shorter product life cycles resulting from this rapid diffusion of new technologies places a competitive premium on being able to quickly introduce new goods and services into the marketplace.

Therefore, to develop guidelines for strategic planning, we must consider two "discordant" requirements: first, to optimize the network's long-term investment while, second, optimizing the time to market for each new product. Finding the right balance is not easy. However, opportunities for wireless developers and service providers will exist when they can reach all mobile users by developing infrastructure to support

- Any wireless carrier
- Any wireless network (TDMA, CDMA, etc.)
- Any wireless device (pager, digital cell phone, PDA)
- Any wireless application
- Any Web format (WML, etc.)
- Any wireless technology (WAP, SMS, pager, etc.)
- Any medium (text, audio, TTS, speech recognition, or video)

Trying to accomplish such a grand goal as universal interoperability, however, demonstrates the fundamental importance of correctly balancing diverse technology areas. For example, the importance of integrating the needs of the five technological areas we have identified (user interface, Personal Space, networks, protocols, and Web architecture) could be critical. One way to approach balancing technological development could be by

1. Balancing innovations in software (for example, adaptive software, nomadic software) against innovations in hardware (for example, chip designs)
2. Balancing proprietary standards (motivating competition) against open standards (offering universal access)
3. Balancing local (centralized) Web innovations (for example, Web Services) against global (distributed) Web architectural evolution (for example, the Semantic Web)

We will consider each of these balancing acts in the next sections.

Balancing Hardware and Software Innovation

Strategic planning for changes in the user interface (while small wireless devices proliferate) could focus on balancing innovations in software against innovations in hardware. For example, speech recognition and speech synthesis offer attractive solutions to overcome the input and output limitations of small mobile devices, if they can overcome their own limitations in memory and processing power. Therefore user interface opportunities could exist if the right balance for the client-server relationship between the small device and nearby embedded resources is achieved. Such a balance could involve trading a small handheld device's chip size, memory, and power consumption against software applications' capability that downloads to meet user needs from a nearby server resource.

However, strategically, this will require integrating chip design engineering with specific software application engineering. It is no longer enough to build the fastest, most powerful chips possible and then let software engineers design their applications to fit the available capability. Integrated application performance teams are essential to planning applications such as speech synthesis and AI requirements and then setting specifications for the combination of the small device/embedded resource to properly achieve a balanced and efficient client-server, as well as peer-to-peer relationships.

Balancing Proprietary and Open Standards

Establishing standards is one of the crucial issues for the future of the communications industry. However, the convergence of technology and markets may dramatically change in the next decade. Therefore the strategic use of standardization to achieve a competitive advantage has become an important facet of business planning. Moreover, standardization provides a catalyst for creating a favorable environment for the deployment of new services and products in an orderly manner. There is recognition that a standard is never neutral, but reflects the industry's strengths and the technologies of those who elaborate it. Participation in the standards process benefits a company, not only in terms of new technology and industry dynamics but also in developing strategic tools to protect current investment in network and services.

It is no longer sufficient just to interconnect different networks through network standards; the end service aspects are even more important. The definition of standards for services is seen as a strategic marketing decision. There are also several less obvious advantages of developing standards. Participation in the prestandardization phase (which considers strategic issues, new architectures and interfaces, evolutionary scenarios, etc.) enables industry to identify major issues at an early stage. As a result, during this formative stage of standardization, a company can adopt appropriate internal positions and consider new product opportunities. Traditionally, there have been three ways for standards to evolve:

1. A vendor dominates a market and sets a de facto standard (for example, POTS telephony from AT&T or PC operating systems from Microsoft).

2. Standards organizations establish standards (for example HTML from W3C).

3. Vendor and market collaboration occurs but it is not clearly attributable to any one organization (for example, TCP/IP or VCR formats).

But communication technologies today are moving too fast for a single vendor to dominate, or for standards organizations to easily come to agreement. And there is no clear single dominating architecture or vendor. So, how will universal standards emerge? With the seemingly endless list of standards and protocols we have presented in nearly every chapter of this book, it should be apparent that the standards in several technology areas must be optimized simultaneously. This means integrating standards development teams. Teams could reflect multiple technology areas so that selections are made from the various technology options to achieve optimization based upon the collective goal of reaching globally interoperable standards.

Balancing Centralized and Distributed Web Architectures

Future wireless communication may be driven by decentralized network architecture integrating services that today span several network technologies. The most fundamental change to network intelligence could come from intelligence produced by decentralized Web architecture, such as by upgrading the IP. Or intelligence could come from a centralized process, such as Web Services, which provides a particular function or component from a central server to multiple users around the world. However, there will be a growing recognition that centralized components, globally distributed, and modifications to the underlying Web architecture, locally accessed, are two faces of one coin. Certainly, integrated and simultaneous development appear necessary.

Figure 10-7 presents a very rough timeline for technology development.[1] Of course, we fully acknowledge that this is conjecture and that the actual technology winners are yet to be determined.

---

1. Bogdanowicz, K. D. et al. "Scenarios for Ambient Intelligence in 2010," *ISTAG Report*. European Commission, February 2001.

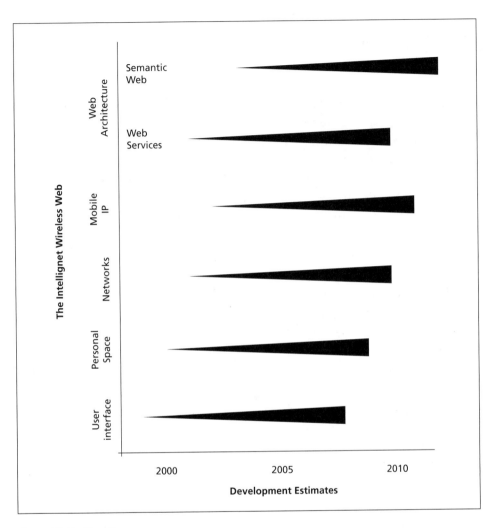

Figure 10-7 Timeline

◆ **Conclusion**

In this chapter, we presented the components developed in earlier chapters and outlined a feasible framework for building the Intelligent Wireless Web, including our evaluation of the compatibility, integration, and synergy issues facing the five merging technology areas: user interface, Personal Space, networks, protocols, and Web architecture.

Ten conclusions you could reach from this book about building the Intelligent Wireless Web include

User Interface

1. Speech recognition and speech synthesis offer attractive solutions to overcome the input and output limitations of small mobile devices, if they can overcome their own limitation of memory and processing power through the right balance for the client-server relationship between a small device and nearby embedded resources. The essential components for achieving this balance may be new chip designs coupled with open, adaptive nomadic software. The new chips may provide hardware for small devices that is small and lightweight, and that consumes little power while having the ability to perform applications by downloading adaptive software as needed.

Personal Space

2. Handheld, wearable, and embedded devices are enhancing many existing office, home, and mobile applications, making computing access more universal through WPANs.

3. Competition between the wireless networking standards Bluetooth and IEEE 802.11b, as well as general networking software, such as Jini and UPnP, will continue for several years as each finds strong points to exploit before a final winner emerges. MIT's Project Oxygen may introduce some innovative protocol alternatives within several years.

Networks

4. Wired and wireless networks will continue to merge and improve backbone performance to greater than the 10Tbps range, as well as produce improved interoperability.

5. Over time, there will be a migration of core networks to optical fiber simply because photons carry a lot more information more efficiently and at less expense than electrons. By 2003, ultra-long-haul (>4,000 km) high-bandwidth optical transport will be deployed in the United States. The last mile requirements will be met with a combination of fiber and wireless (replacing copper and coaxial cable). In dense metropolitan areas, free-space optical networks will provide 622Mbps of bandwidth to buildings without digging the streets. Second-generation LMDS and MDDS fixed wireless will be deployed to buildings requiring less bandwidth.

Internet Protocols

6. Intelligent networking software for routing and tracking will lead to general changes in IP networking protocols to include IPv6 and Mobile IP. Sitting on top of the entire layer infrastructure may be new control-plane software applications that may add intelligence to the network, for smooth integration of routing (layer 3) and possibly wavelength switching.

Web Architecture

7. Intelligent agents, intelligent software applications, and AI applications from AI service providers may make their way onto the Web in greater numbers as adaptive software, dynamic programming languages, and Learning Algorithms are introduced into Web Services (including both .NET and J2EE architectures).

8. The evolution of Web architecture may allow intelligent applications to run directly on the Web by introducing XML, RDF/Topic Maps, and a logic layer.

9. A Web performance index, or measure, may be developed to evaluate Internet progress in performing intelligent tasks using Learning Algorithms.

10. The Intelligent Wireless Web's significant potential for rapidly completing information transactions may make an important contribution to global worker productivity.

Finally, we ask again, "Wouldn't it be great to just tap your 'combadge' and be able to speak to anyone, any time, anywhere—the way they do on *Star Trek*? Or to say 'Computer,' followed by a perplexing question and receive an intelligent answer?"

The various technologies we have presented in this book may not be the actual path that evolves to produce the Intelligent Wireless Web. Hopefully, however, our vision of technology development and convergence may offer some perspective for the actual unfolding of the future of the Web. Needless to say, we fully acknowledge that there are competing visions for the development of various Web technologies and the actual winners are yet to be determined.

Appendix A

Standards Organizations

Throughout this book, we have referenced standards and specifications of national and international standards organizations. The following list names and describes some of the major standards bodies.

◆ American National Standards Institute (ANSI)

ANSI is a privately funded federation of leaders representing both public and private sectors. ANSI was organized in 1918 and is composed of professional and trade associations, academic institutions, government agencies, and consumer and labor organizations.

ANSI is the U.S. national organization defining coding standards and signaling. It functions as the U.S. representative to international organizations.

Contact information:
American National Standards Institute
11 West 42nd Street, 13th floor
New York, NY 10036
Phone: 212-642-4948
FAX: 212-398-0023

◆ Automatic Identification Manufacturers (AIM)

AIM is an industry association representing interests in automatic identification and data capture industry. The primary mission of AIM is to educate end users on integrated bar coding solutions.

Contact information:
Automatic Identification Manufacturers
634 Alpha Drive
Pittsburgh, PA 15238
Phone: 412-963-8009
FAX: 412-963-8753
Web: www.aim.org

◆ International Consultative Committee for Telegraph and Telephone (CCITT)

The CCITT is a committee of the United Nations organization, International Telecommunications Union (ITU).

Contact information:
U.S. Department of Commerce
National Technical Information Service
5285 Port Royal Road
Springfield, VA 22161
Phone: 703-487-4650
Web: www.itu.ch

◆ Infrared Data Association (IrDA)

The IrDA was established in 1993 to establish hardware and software standards for creating infrared communication links.

Contact information:
Infrared Data Association
P.O. Box 3883
Walnut Creek, CA 94598

Phone: 925-943-6546
FAX: 925-943-5600

◆ Institute of Electrical and Electronic Engineers (IEEE)

The IEEE is the U.S. standards organization for electrical and electronics industries. Networking standards are developed in IEEE 802 committees, including

802.1	Internetworking
802.2	Logic Link Control
802.3	CSMA/CD LANs
802.4	Token Ring LANs
802.5	Token Ring LANs
802.6	Metropolitan Area Networks
802.7	Broadband Technical Advisory Group
802.8	Fiber-Optical Technical Advisory Group
802.9	Integrated Voice and Data
802.10	Network Security
802.11	Wireless Networks
802.12	Demand Priority Access LANs

Contact information:
Institute of Electrical and Electronic Engineers
445 Hoes Lane
P.O. Box 1331
Piscataway, NJ 08855-1331
Phone: 908-981-1393
Web: www.ieee.org

◆ International Standards Organization (ISO)

The ISO has representatives from standards organizations from around the world.

Contact information:
International Standards Organization
1 Rue de Varembe'
Case pastale 56

CH-1211 Geneve 20
Switzerland
Phone: 41-22-479-0111
Web: www.iso.ch

◆ International Telecommunication Union (ITU)

The ITU is an intergovernmental organization. It adopts international regulations and treaties governing all terrestrial and space uses of the frequency spectrum.

Contact information:
International Telecommunication Union
Place des Nations
1211 Geneva 20
Switzerland
Phone: 41-22-730-6666
FAX: 41-22-730-5337

◆ International Engineering Task Force (IETF)

The IETF provides a forum for working groups to coordinate technical development of new protocols. The IETF started in 1986 as a forum for Defense Advanced Projects Agency (DARPA) contractors.

Contact information:
International Engineering Task Force
Web: www.ietf.cnri.reston.va.us/home.html

◆ Mobile and Portable Radio Research Group (MPRG)

The MPRG works to provide a national resource for research and education in wireless communications. Its mission is to provide design and analysis tools for manufacturers and government and consumer service providers.

Contact information:
Mobile and Portable Radio Research Group
Web: www.mprg.ee.vt.edu

◆ Mobile Management Task Force (MMTF)

The MMTF is an industrial group that promotes management standards addressing network administration.

Contact information:
Mobile Management Task Force
MMTF c/o Epilogue Technology Corporation
201 Moffet Park Drive
Sunnyvale, CA 94089

◆ Portable Computer and Communications Association (PCCA)

The PCCA was established in 1992 to advance portable computing.

Contact information:
Portable Computer and Communications Association
P.O. Box 2460
Boulder Creek, CA 95007
Phone: 831-338-0924

◆ The Semantic Web Community Portal: www.SemanticWeb.org

The site SemanticWeb.org is currently operated by three research groups:

1. The Onto-Agents and Scalable Knowledge Composition (SKC) Research Group at Stanford University
2. The Ontobroker Group at the University of Karlsruhe
3. The Protégé Research Group at Stanford University

SemanticWeb.org is designed to demonstrate ideas and concepts leading to the Semantic Web. The Web site focuses on the Semantic Web Research Community and demonstrates Semantic Web technology. Metadata is collected from the Web pages of the Semantic Web Research Community and used to present the Community to an interested audience. Goals of the SemanticWeb.org include

▷ Facilities to semiautomatically establish an explicit joint ontology. The ontology (a shared conceptualization) is necessary to distributed metadata and for the structure of the Web site. Ontologies are now created using explicit decisions from domain experts. SemanticWeb.org will provide an automated term creation protocol.

▷ Metadata creation tools

▷ Metadata repository: SemanticWeb.org requires a huge amount of data to be stored and created. An explicit, highly efficient metadata repository has to be built. The metadata repository facilitates a query language for semistructured data, which is particularly aiming at the querying of Resource Description Framework models.

▷ Web site creation and management facilities, enabling a declarative ontology-based description of the community portal and automated, efficient creation of XML-based pages.

Contact: Stepan Decker at steph@db.stanford.edu

◆ Wireless LAN Group

The University of Massachusetts, Amherst, Wireless LAN Group researches efficient wireless LAN architecture for quality of service requirements.

Contact information:
Wireless LAN Group
Web: www.ecs.umass.edu/ece/wireless

◆ Wireless LAN Interoperability Forum (WLIF)

The WLIF promotes wireless LAN through the delivery of interoperable products and services.

Contact information:
Wireless LAN Interoperability Forum
Web: www.wlif.com

◆ World Wide Web Consortium (W3C)

The W3C was founded in October, 1994 to lead the World Wide Web to developing common protocols that promote interoperability. An international industry consortium, jointly hosted by the Massachusetts Institute of Technology Laboratory for Computer Science (MIT/LCS) in the United States; the Institut National de Recherche en Informatique et en Automatique (INRIA) in Europe; and the Keio University Shonan Fujisawa Campus in Japan.

The W3C is led by Tim Berners-Lee, Director and creator of the World Wide Web, and Jean-François Abramatic, Chairman. W3C is funded by member organizations and is vendor neutral, working with the global community to produce specifications and reference software that is made freely available throughout the world.

    Contact information:
    Senior Contract Administrator
    Office of Sponsored Programs, E19-750
    Massachusetts Institute of Technology
    77 Massachusetts Avenue
    Cambridge, MA 02139
    Web: www.w3.org/Consortium

Appendix B

Wireless Standards

Although a wireless LAN could exist as a sole, general-purpose LAN, wireless LANs are more often seen as an extension to an existing LAN as a means to support mobile users. Standardization of wireless-LAN signaling and protocols are 802.11, formed by the Institute of Electrical and Electronic Engineers (IEEE). The IEEE 802.11 standard was finalized in June 1997. The standard defines three different physical implementations:

▸ Direct sequence spread spectrum (DSSS) radio

▸ Frequency hopping spread spectrum (FHSS) radio

▸ Infrared light

The two radio physical implementations operate in the 2.4GHz band and support 1Mb and 2Mbps data rates. The range is approximately 100 m indoors and 1,000 m outdoors. Further work by the IEEE 802.11 group is being done on use of the 5GHz band for 5.5Mbps and 11Mbps data rates. Within any 802.11 wireless LAN there are three possible elements:

▸ One or more wireless stations

▸ One or more wireless access points

▸ One portal

Wireless stations are typically portable and usually battery-powered. An access point is used to provide a central coordination function for wireless LANs. In the presence of an access point, the wireless stations no longer communicate with each other directly. All communication is transmitted through the access point. Therefore wireless stations no longer have to be within range of one another to communicate; they only have to be within range of an access point. The IEEE 802.11 standard doesn't define how access points communicate with each other or with a portal. A portal provides the services necessary to integrate a wireless LAN with a wired LAN.

Intel's recent decision to abandon the HomeRF platform in favor of IEEE 802.11B may be an important step toward standards convergence. Yet, as the industry leaders are finally coalescing around 802.11B, others are developing new standards, such as 802.11A. IEEE 802.11A employs Orthogonal Frequency Division Multiplexing (OFDM), a spread spectrum modulation technique that enables 200MHz of spectrum to be split into 52 subchannels, each carrying a separate stream of data. 802.11A will operate in the 5GHz UNII (unlicensed frequency band). Theoretically, 802.11A could increase transmission speed from 11Mbps to 54Mbps.

Appendix C

Graphs and the Web

The study of the Web as a graph yields valuable insight into Web algorithms for crawling, searching, and describing the characteristics of its evolution. Consider a directed graph whose nodes correspond to static pages on the Web, and whose arcs correspond to links between these pages. The key properties of the graphical form of the Web include its diameter, degree distributions, connected components, and macroscopic structure.

Much recent work has addressed the Web as a graph and applied algorithmic methods from graph theory in addressing search, retrieval, and mining problems on the Web. The graph theoretical analysis includes document content, as well as usage statistics, resulting in an understanding of domain structure and the role played by Web pages.

The power law in current Web crawls is a basic Web property. It has been found that most ordered pairs of pages cannot be bridged at all and there are significant numbers of pairs that can be bridged, but only using paths going through hundreds of intermediate pages.

> **The power law for in-degree:** The probability that a node has in-degree i is proportional to $1/i^x$, for some $x > 1$.

Thus the Web is not the ball of highly connected spaghetti that it has been thought to be; instead, the connectivity is strongly limited by a high-level global structure.

◆ Basic Graph Terminology

A directed graph consists of a set of nodes, denoted V, and a set of arcs, denoted E. Each arc is an ordered pair of nodes (u,v) representing a directed connection from *u* to *v*. The out-degree of a node *u* is the number of distinct arcs (the number of links from *u*), and the in-degree is the number of distinct arcs (the number of links to *u*). A path from node *u* to node *v* is a sequence of arcs. One can follow such a sequence of arcs to "walk" through the graph from *u* to *v*. If no path exists, the distance from *u* to *v* is defined to be infinity. If (*u*,*v*) is an arc, then the distance from *u* to *v* is 1.

Given a directed graph, a strongly connected component of the graph is a set of nodes such that for any pair of nodes *u* and *v*, there is a path from *u* to *v*. In general, a directed graph may have one or many strong components.

An undirected graph consists of a set of vertices and a set of edges, each of which is an unordered pair (*u*,*v*) of nodes. There is an edge between *u* and *v* if there is a link between *u* and *v*, without regard to whether the link points from *u* to *v* or the other way around. The degree of a node *u* is the number of edges incident to *u*. A path is defined as for directed graphs, except that the existence of a path from *u* to *v* implies a path from *v* to *u*. A component of an undirected graph is a set of nodes such that for any pair of nodes *u* and *v* in the set there is a path from *u* to *v*.

The interplay of strong and weak components on the (directed) Web graph turns out to reveal some unexpected properties of the Web's connectivity.

The diameter of a graph, directed or undirected, is the maximum over all ordered pairs (*u*,*v*) of the shortest path from *u* to *v*. The average connected distance is the expected length of the shortest path, where the expectation is over uniform choices from *P*.

◆ Characteristics of the Web

The pages and hyperlinks of the World Wide Web may be viewed as nodes and edges in a directed graph. This graph has about a billion nodes today and several billion links, and it appears to grow exponentially with time. The study of the Web as a graph is not only fascinating in its own right but also yields valuable insight into Web algorithms for crawling and searching that characterize its evolution. Experiments[1] on local and global properties of the Web graph on over 200 million

---

1. Broder, A. et al. "Graph structure in the Web," *IBM Report*, October 1999.

pages and 1.5 billion links indicated that the macroscopic structure of the Web is intricate and specific.

The analysis in these experiments revealed an interesting structure in the shape of a bow tie of the Web's macroscopic structure. Over 90 percent of the approximately 203 million nodes in the study formed a single connected component. This connected Web breaks naturally into four pieces. The first piece is a central core, all of whose pages can reach one another along directed links—this is the "core" of the Web. The second and third pieces are referred to as IN and OUT. IN consists of pages that can reach the core, but cannot be reached from it. OUT consists of pages that are accessible from the core, but do not link back to it, such as corporate Web sites that contain only internal links. Finally, the TENDRILS contain pages that cannot reach the core and cannot be reached from the core.

The core comprises about 56 million pages (out of the explored 203 million). Each of the other three sets contained about 44 million. For randomly chosen source and destination pages, the probability that any path exists from the source to the destination is only 24 percent.

Dynamic Languages

In this appendix, we present the Dylan Language. Additional information is available at

Functional Objects, Inc.
86 Chandler Street
Somerville, MA 02144-1912
www.functionalobjects.com

S tatic languages, such as C, require the programmer to make a lot of decisions about structure and the data. Dynamic languages such as Dylan (Dynamic Language) allow these decisions to be delayed and thus provide more responsive adaptive programming. Despite the potential of dynamic languages, they have, as yet, not experienced wide acceptance or success.

◆ Dylan

With the rapid development of the Internet, the Java programming language became very popular. In particular, it came with a virtual machine that could be embedded in Web browsers and a security model to control its activity. These days, however, Java has moved on, and developers are using the language for all sorts of applications. Java is perceived as a general-purpose programming language. The problem, however, is that Java may not be up to the job.

Linguistically, Java has several faults, such as code that is awkward and difficult to maintain. Some of these faults are the result of engineering compromises, and some are the results of efforts to reduce the complexity of the language. The problems include

- ▶ Single implementation inheritance
- ▶ Single argument method dispatch
- ▶ Primitive types distinct from objects
- ▶ Casting required
- ▶ No extensible syntax
- ▶ Poor iteration/collection integration

The solution may be to adopt a more advanced programming language, although not necessarily going back to C++. After all, Java's popularization of garbage collection and pointer-free programming has advanced software reliability.

Dylan is an alternative language with some of the required solutions to the problems inherent in static languages:

- ▶ Multiple implementation inheritance
- ▶ Multiple argument method dispatch
- ▶ Pure object types
- ▶ No casting required
- ▶ Extensible syntax
- ▶ Good iteration/collection integration

The Dylan programming language was originally developed at Apple Computer, in cooperation with researchers from Harlequin Group and Carnegie Mellon University. This language combined the efficiency of C++ with the simplicity of Smalltalk. The language combined native compilation and automatic memory management to enable a new generation of software development.

Apple shipped one version of Dylan IDE prototype in 1995. Apple abandoned their Dylan effort soon after 1995. Language development continued at Harlequin, which had begun work on a version for Windows. The first version of Harlequin Dylan was released in July 1998. In 1999, Harlequin abandoned their efforts also. Functional Objects, Inc. was then formed to continue Dylan development.

Dylan was designed to be a general-purpose, fully object-oriented language for use in systems, applications, and component programming. The language was designed to be simple, powerful, consistent, and rich in features. In particular, Dylan was designed with interaction in mind.

Dylan is a high-level language because it is easy to write, read, and extend. It also provides type safety and is object oriented. At the same time, Dylan can be considered a low-level language because it can access native platform APIs and can be used for the full range of programming tasks.

Dylan was specifically designed to allow programmers to create efficient abstractions. An efficient abstraction is efficiently designed and compiled. Dylan's ability to support efficient abstractions is its primary distinguishing feature from other languages.

Advantages of Dylan

Dylan is the "write anything, do everything" language, from scripting and prototyping to robust application and component development. Dylan can be customized to support targeted domains such as games and business-to-business Internet solutions. No other mainstream language has all of these capabilities:

▶ It uses a high-level syntax so that programs are easy to write, read, and maintain.

▶ It is fully compiled. Dylan programs run as fast as programs written in other compiled languages, such as C and C++.

▶ It progresses smoothly from functional to object-oriented style.

▶ The overhead of powerful features is incurred only upon use.

Interaction

▶ Dylan programs may be dynamically typed.

▶ Dylan was designed to interact with a "live" delivered application across a tether, allowing the development environment to interact with and modify an application while it is running.

Abstraction

▶ Dylan supports macros. The Dylan macro system allows creation of customized embedded languages while ensuring the integrity of the software.

▶ Instance variables in Dylan are accessed purely through generic functions, so that they can be readily replaced or even overridden with methods.

▶ Dylan greatly simplifies the implementation of most design patterns, by providing first-class types, functions, multimethods, and macros. Some design patterns (for example visitors, command, or facade patterns) are directly modeled in the language, saving designers or programmers the trouble and complication of coding them explicitly.

Power

Dylan is a high-level language providing powerful features that maximize programmer's ability to develop software quickly and naturally.

▶ Dylan supports advanced object-oriented features such as multiple inheritance and multimethods. These features allow structuring of programs to model the problem domain directly.

▶ Exceptions are object-based. Handlers can resume or abort the code that signaled the exception.

▶ Just as a function can accept multiple arguments when it is called, Dylan functions and other expressions can return multiple values.

▶ Dylan methods support optional keyword arguments.

▶ Methods can be used to create closures, which remember the environment in which they were created.

Appendix E

Wireless Security

As mobile commerce and wireless Internet access grow, security concerns about protecting data on wireless devices becomes an issue for businesses and consumers. In particular, transaction-based Internet access applications, such as checking stock quotes and banking via handheld devices, demonstrate the need for secure wireless connectivity.

The process of developing secure wireless networks is similar to the process of securing wired Internet transactions, but wireless security solutions must, in addition, consider bandwidth and memory limitations, battery life, and different network configurations, which aren't inherent to the Internet. The process of wireless security is not much different from that of wired security. Several components are required for any data networking security: authentication, secure transmission, and error checking.

One way to improve security is through the growing number of industry groups, standards committees, and vendor alliances vying to set standards for securing wireless transactions. These groups include the Wireless Application Protocol (WAP) Forum, Radicchio, the Bluetooth Special Interest Group, and the PKI Forum. They set the framework for how security features such as public key infrastructure (PKI) are implemented into WAP. Encryption ensures confidentiality by preventing eavesdropping, and WAP devices include their own security protocol, wireless transport layer security (WTLS). This is equivalent to secure sockets layer (SSL) but uses fewer resource intensive encryption algorithms, such as elliptic-curve cryptography (ECC).

WTLS is not currently compatible with SSL, the industry standard. This produces a security hole when the WAP gateway translates data from the WTLS protocol into a secure IP such as SSL. This gap in encryption presents a threat. However, the messages spend only a few milliseconds in the clear on a machine buried deep inside the carrier's facility.

◆ WTLS

WTLS functions similar to SSL, which is alternatively known as transport layer security (TLS). WTLS provides for client or server authentication and allows for encryption based on negotiated parameters between the handheld device and the WAP gateway. WTLS's key exchange protocol is uniquely suited for wireless applications. Vendors can implement any of three classes of authentication types.

The Class 1 (anonymous authentication) is for testing purposes. The client forms an encrypted connection with an unknown server. In Class 2 (server authentication), as with SSL, once clients are assured they are talking securely to the correct server, they can authenticate using user name/password. In Class 3 (server and client authentication), the server and the client authenticate each other's WTLS certificate.

WTLS specification does specify cryptographic algorithms that may be supported by WAP devices, but doesn't require any for basic functionality. One of the concerns with cryptography regards export of certain key lengths to other countries.

Unlike SSL, WTLS does not provide for end-to-end security. End-to-end security means the client and server have a secure session, and no other servers intervene. When a Web browser sets up an SSL session with a Web server, the browser and Web server are talking directly; when a credit-card number is sent over SSL, in effect, only the receiving Web server will be able to receive it.

Two options are becoming available for end-to-end WTLS security. The first is WTLS tunneling, which tunnels WTLS traffic through a service provider's network to a remote WAP gateway. WTLS proxy makes WTLS connections through the carrier's WAP gateway.

WTLS is about adding security to low CPU-powered wireless devices by making the cryptography efficient. Because personal digital assistant (PDA) and cell phone CPUs are typically slow, using SSL end to end can take anywhere from 30 seconds to several minutes, depending on the key size used to negotiate an SSL connection.

Emerging Security Tools

One emerging security tool is biometric devices that use unique physical identifiers such as voiceprints, fingerprints, or retinal images to positively identify the user. Even if someone should steal a mobile phone, the thief wouldn't be able to imitate the biometric security, such as voice or fingerprint.

Many of the obstacles confronting wireless security will disappear with the widespread adoption of third-generation wireless technology. The third-generation phones will be IP-based and sport more processing power, memory, and bandwidth.

By combining third-generation wireless with smart cards and biometrics, organizations may have a unified security system that works for both the wireless and wired worlds.

Visual Prolog

V isual Prolog is a programming environment for the Prolog programming language. It is capable of building commercial applications and includes a graphical development environment, compiler, linker, and debugger. Visual Prolog includes a large library with APIs, including Windows GUI, ODBC/OCI databases, and Internet (sockets, ftp, http, cgi, etc.). The development environment is written in Visual Prolog. Visual Prolog supports Windows, OS/2, Linux, and SCO UNIX. It is suited for applications such as expert systems, planning, and other AI-related problems.

Prolog was originally designed to be an AI language. Prolog's underlying semantics support frame- or rule-based systems, pattern-matching systems, and constraint-resolution systems. Visual Prolog has also been used to make administrative applications and database management, planning, and scheduling systems.

The traditional computer languages, such as C, BASIC, and Pascal, are procedural languages. In a procedural language, the programmer must provide step-by-step instructions. In other words, the programmer must know how to solve the problem before the computer can do it. The Prolog programmer, on the other hand, only needs to supply a description of the problem and the ground rules for solving it. From there, the Prolog system is left to determine how to find a solution.

◆ Prolog Uses Facts and Rules

A Prolog program consists of a list of logical statements, either in the form of facts, such as

father("Paul","Joanne")   "Paul is the father to Joanne"
father("Paul","Sally")   "Paul is the father to Sally"

father("Paul", "Sam")   "Paul is the father to Sam"
mother("Jeanette", "Joanne")   "Jeanette is the mother to Joanne"
mother("Joanne", "Tom")   "Joanne is the mother to Tom"

or in the form of rules, such as

sister(X,Y) :- father(Z,X), father(Z,Y).   "*X* and *Y* are sisters if they have the same father"

X, Y, Z are variables that are used to specify bindings between the different relations.

◆ Prolog Can Make Deductions

You can provide the Prolog program goals, for example, to conditions:

Goal father("Paul", "Joanne")   Prolog will answer *true* because the goal matches the stored facts.

If you use a variable in the goals, Prolog will find the value for the variable:

Goal father(X, "Joanne")   Prolog will answer *X* = "*Paul*" because it can look it up in the facts.

There is no difference between using facts and rules, for example, if the goal is

Goal sister(X, "Joanne")   Prolog will answer *X* = "*Sally*" because "*Sally*" can satisfy the rule for sister.

Similarly, Prolog can use its deductive ability to find all solutions to the problem

   Goal father("Paul", X)

Prolog will answer

   X = "Joanne"
   X = "Sally"
   X = "Sam"

The solutions are found through backtracking, in which all combinations are tried. This automatic backtracking mechanism combined with the built-in database (the facts) is one of Visual Prolog's most powerful tools.

In Prolog the number of program lines required to solve a given problem is typically only a fraction of that required by a procedural programming language such as C or Pascal. Clearly this can reduce development costs.

Prolog Development Center (PDC) was founded in 1984 with the development of a Prolog. Prolog support can be found at http://www.pdc.dk/viptechinfo/ pdcindex.htm and demos at http://www.pdc.dk/vipexamples/pdcindex.htm.

Appendix G

Knowledge Management: Case Study of Convera's RetrievalWare

Convera's RetrievalWare

Convera's RetrievalWare is an enterprise-wide knowledge retrieval system that allows flexibility and scalability across enterprise networks, intranets, and the World Wide Web. Convera RetrievalWare enables users to index and search a wide range of distributed information resources, including text files, SGML, XML, HTML, paper documents, relational database tables, over 200 proprietary document formats (such as word processors and publishing systems), and groupware repositories. Advanced search capabilities include concept and keyword searching, pattern searching, and query-by-example.

Convera Technologies
1921 Gallows Road
Vienna, VA 22182, USA
www.convera.com

◆ Introduction

Many businesses and organizations today are planning or deploying information portals to access the information within their organization and to provide their customers and partners with access to vital information.

These assets can include paper documents, text, images, e-mail, Web-based documents, relational databases, or videotape. The management of these assets, referred to as knowledge management, is the distribution, access, and retrieval of information between related individuals or workgroups.

Any organization that can index, search, and retrieve information assets quickly and easily via an enterprise information portal is managing knowledge.

At the center of all successful information portal strategies resides an application that enables the organization to capture, access, browse, search, retrieve, share, and use what is already known—knowledge retrieval.

The term *knowledge retrieval* describes the systems and tools that index, search, access, and browse an organization's information assets for repurposing and reuse. Once a knowledge-sharing process has been established, an intelligent process for filtering the glut of information into applicable data is required. Knowledge retrieval is a higher form of information retrieval because it has the ability to intelligently access and search any data type in any location through a unified Web interface to return more precise query results. It is important to note the differences between "data retrieval," "information retrieval," and "knowledge retrieval":

- ▶ *Data retrieval:* The low-end, Boolean search engines force users to wade through raw, frequently irrelevant bits of information.
- ▶ *Information retrieval:* Returns information in an organized manner, but lacks context and an understanding of the concepts underpinning the query (the difference between a financial "bank" and a river "bank," for instance), leaving knowledge workers with ambiguous results.
- ▶ *Knowledge retrieval:* High-end searches deliver information relevant to users' needs. To operate effectively, a knowledge retrieval system must be accurate, scalable, secure, extensible, open, and simple to use.

Knowledge retrieval bridges the gap between the user's desired concept (expressed in certain words) and the author's concept (possibly expressed in many different words). Concepts are then matched based on the semantics of the words used and applied against the query.

RetrievalWare as a Knowledge Retrieval Solution

Convera's RetrievalWare is a high-end knowledge retrieval solution providing a single point of access (information portal) into all of an organization's knowledge repositories; accurate, fault-tolerant, natural language search capability; and a scaleable, robust platform capable of supporting an enterprise-wide solution.

RetrievalWare divides searching into a pipeline of text-processing components. As the query words travel through the pipeline, they undergo several phases of analysis and processing, tuning the retrieval to be as accurate as possible. Figure G-1 presents a summary of the RetrievalWare text search process.

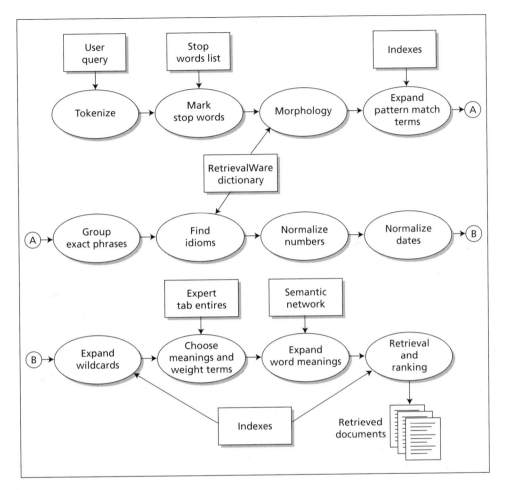

Figure G-1   RetrievalWare's text search process

Relevancy Ranking

During the final phases of the query process, documents are retrieved and relevancy ranked in two stages. In the first stage, RetrievalWare looks for the existence or absence of query words or related terms in the document. This process produces a user-controlled number of candidate documents meeting the criteria set in the query.

RetrievalWare then processes this retrieved set to determine an exact relevancy ranking. Relevancy ranking takes into account the following factors. Each factor adds a certain relative weight to the document score. Combined, these weights determine the document's overall relevance.

▶ *Completeness:* The greater the number of query words (either exactly or by reference), the higher the weight. A relevant document should contain at least one term or related term for each word in the original query. For example, if the document contains only three out of the four original terms in the query, then its maximum rank is 75 percent.

▶ *Contextual evidence:* The greater the number of related terms, the higher the weight. For example, the word "charge" near the words "credit," "debt," and "card" is more likely to mean "charge card" than to mean "ward," "battery energy," or "assign a task."

▶ *Semantic distance:* The more closely related the terms a document contains, the higher the weight. The semantic network contains information on how closely two terms are related (for example, words that are synonyms of each other are more closely related than words that are defined as antonyms of one another). This is used to compute the amount of contextual evidence that supports a word. The closer the terms in the document are in relationship to the query words, the more weight they are given.

▶ *Proximity:* The closer together the query words and related terms within the document, the greater the weight. A document is judged more relevant if it contains related terms that occur close together, preferably in the same sentence or paragraph. The system computes a factor for physical proximity, which is greatest for adjacent terms and decreases as terms become increasingly distant (physically) from each other.

▶ *Hit density:* The greater the ratio of query words and related terms to the total number of words in the document, the greater the weight. A document is judged more relevant if a large number of the total number of words in it are query words or related terms. Thus short documents with many hits are ranked higher than longer documents in which those same hits are present.

Search Technology

Convera RetrievalWare incorporates unique techniques to help find documents that would be impossible to find otherwise. Semantic or concept searching is used to find words that mean the same thing or enhance the meaning of a word.

This expansion has two purposes. The first is to paraphrase the user's query so that the author and the user do not need to use the exact same language to find each other.

For example, the user might ask for "international commerce," and this will still find documents that discuss "foreign trade." The ability to paraphrase the query frees the user from having to predict the words that an author might use when discussing a topic. The second purpose of semantic expansion is to enforce or enhance the meaning of a word chosen by the user. For example, the meaning of the word *tank* can be partly determined by the words around it. If the words military, vehicle, and army occur nearby, then the word *tank* is more likely to be the fighting vehicle and less likely to be a container for holding fuel.

Dictionaries

The RetrievalWare Semantic Network—a collection of about 500,000 words that expands to over 1.6 million semantic relationships and idioms—is the support behind concept searching. The Semantic Network is used during both indexing and querying. Users interact with the Semantic Network by setting the word expansion level for their query terms that determines which and how many related terms to include in the search. Users can also use the Semantic Network to choose specific meanings for their query terms. For example, when searching for banks, a user can easily instruct RetrievalWare to use only those meanings associated with financial institutions and not those dealing with the bank of a river.

The baseline Semantic Network provided with Convera RetrievalWare satisfies the vast majority of knowledge retrieval needs. However, RetrievalWare offers the flexibility to add multiple, domain-specific dictionaries either for query-only implementations or for querying and indexing. Specialized dictionaries can be used very effectively to index and retrieve highly technical documents or documents using an industry-specific vocabulary. Such dictionaries are easily created for Retrieval-Ware, or the existing Semantic Network can be edited to accommodate these changes.

Additional language support is provided by a series of language plug-in modules. These plug-ins make supporting new languages much easier by utilizing embedded language tags in both text and queries, allowing several languages to be combined in a single library, and providing for the implementation of multilingual querying in which search terms can be in multiple languages with multiple tags.

Pattern search (also known as adaptive pattern recognition processing [APRP]) is search technology pioneered by Convera Technologies. APRP is used to find words that are misspelled, whether they are errors made by an optical character recognition engine, errors made by the author, errors made when transcribing foreign names, or errors made by the searcher. For example, there are 39 different ways to spell Muhammad (it is the most popular first name in the world). Simply put, APRP is inherently fault-tolerant and allows RetrievalWare to find documents that would otherwise be lost.

Both pattern search and semantic expansion allow for user feedback, which is yet another way to improve search accuracy with RetrievalWare. With pattern search, the user can view the list of alternative spellings sorted with the most closely spelled words first. The user can then select the spelling variations that should be included in the query. When using concept searching, the user can view the word definitions and relationships in the semantic network and choose the specific meanings appropriate for the query. Both pattern search and semantic expansion can be easily combined in the same query so that users can choose, on a word-by-word basis, which words should be expanded with APRP and which ones should be expanded with the semantic network.

Experts Directory

In addition to retrieving and sharing explicit knowledge contained in various document repositories, it is the goal of a knowledge retrieval solution to facilitate the retrieval and sharing of knowledge that individuals possess based upon their own experience and learning. This is referred to as tacit knowledge and is not so easily captured, categorized, or shared because it is not written down. As a component to the overall knowledge map, RetrievalWare provides an Experts Directory that lists individuals with expertise in particular subjects. Any user may create an expert in the Experts Directory, and users can associate people from an Experts Directory with a category, thus combining the explicit and tacit knowledge in one accessible location.

The system administrator has the flexibility to control the information stored for each expert. Metadata can include practical information such as telephone number and e-mail address, as well as more category-specific information, including academic background, publications, and pertinent work experience. Each expert may be associated with one or more categories. Users browsing a category may view information about any of the experts associated with the category. Users browsing the Experts Directory are provided links to the categories associated with each expert. A key objective of knowledge management is to connect users with those people who are experts or who have valuable information in a specific category that is important to the organization. The Experts Directory enables organizations to catalog and navigate the human knowledge resources in combination with electronic documents.

Internet Spider

For most knowledge-consuming organizations, the Web is often viewed as an invaluable adjunct document repository. The vastness and lack of organization on the Web compound all the challenges of efficient knowledge retrieval. To address this potentially valuable repository, the Convera Internet Spider is a multimedia, high-performance Web spider/crawler for augmenting the knowledge retrieval capabilities of Convera for security purposes, Convera Internet Spider allows users to maintain a secure intranet while accessing and indexing Web sites outside a firewall. It can even enter password data automatically to retrieve access-controlled Web pages. The security system supports HTTP, secure sockets layer (SSL), HTTPS (HTTP over SSL), and proxy firewalls. Another feature of the Internet Spider is its ability to handle automatic redirection of URLs when hyperlink destinations change. Finally, it can automatically fill out CGI forms and handle HTTP cookies.

◆ Architected for Knowledge Retrieval

Scalability

Scalability is more than just fast searching. Rather, it is the ability to maintain search performance even when the demands on the system rise by orders of magnitude. An enterprise knowledge retrieval solution must scale to the worldwide scope of potential sources and users. Providers of online services in particular have unpredictable numbers of users searching heterogeneous document collections. The growth of multimedia repositories, such as video and image archives, simply ensures that the scale will grow ever larger. RetrievalWare provides proven, unfailing access to all data types across multiple platforms, even when the number of concurrent users and the size of the collections increase significantly.

Distributed Search and Merging Results

Most knowledge retrieval solutions are unable to perform an accurate merging of search results because they either depend on database statistics such as word frequency to generate relevancy scores or they have to broker their searches out to third-party repositories with different search engines. In many such systems, the same document, using the same query, can have widely varying relevancy scores because these scores depend on the repository containing the document. This prevents an accurate merging of search results because the ranked results are skewed by the specific repository being searched and normalization of relevancy scores across databases is very inaccurate. In contrast, a RetrievalWare query will consistently retrieve a document and compute the same relevancy score regardless of which repository holds the document. RetrievalWare enables distributed searching with accurate merging because the relevancy scores of documents retrieved are not based on repository-wide statistics. These relevancy scores have meaning and can be accurately compared across multiple libraries, search servers, or remote distributed search clusters.

Under RetrievalWare's unique architecture, the successful merging of search results can occur at any of three different levels:

1. Merging multiple libraries within each search server
2. Merging the results from multiple search servers in the client handler
3. Merging the results from multiple, distributed installations of RetrievalWare

The first level of merging results takes place on the search server itself. Each search server can search multiple libraries, merging the results as the query is being executed. Communication between the search server and the indexes is very fast. When executing a search, RetrievalWare will automatically return the best (most relevant) documents first. When a single search server is searching two libraries, the best documents from both libraries will be retrieved first, resulting in the most efficient and accurate search. The second level of merging search results takes place within a RetrievalWare search cluster. The results of multiple search servers (located on the same machine or distributed over multiple machines within a local area network) are merged by the client handler and made available to the client.

Finally, the third level of merging occurs on the client itself, which can merge the results of multiple remote RetrievalWare search clusters (possibly distributed across wide area networks) into a single result list that is then presented to the user.

◆ Conclusion

Today's low-end, Boolean-based search engines typically retrieve simply data. Knowledge retrieval has the ability to search all data formats and, in turn, use the information it finds to make each query as relevant as possible.

RetrievalWare retrieves knowledge in all formats, from paper to databases, from e-mail to document management libraries, and makes it valuable again. True knowledge retrieval affects the entire enterprise by answering questions in seconds that would previously have required hours and days of phone calls and e-mails to answer. Knowledge retrieval offers the efficiency and economy of saving the enterprise from relearning the same lessons from the same series of experiences and events.

As new and different data formats (voice, for example) increase an organization's knowledge assets, an even more sophisticated knowledge retrieval system is needed to seek and find those assets from a single point of access, using a single search engine.

Convera's Web site is at www.convera.com for more information.

Appendix H

List of Acronyms

A

AAL ATM adaptation layer

ABR asynchronous bit rate

ADM add/drop multiplexer

ADPCM adaptive differential pulse code modulation

ADSL asymmetrical digital subscriber line

AI artificial intelligence

AIM Automatic Identification Manufacturers

ALU Arithmetic Logic Unit

AMPS advanced mobile phone system

AMPS-D digital AMPS

AMR adaptive multirate coding

AN access node

ANS advanced network and services

ANN artificial neural network

ANSI American National Standards Institute

AON all-optical network

API application programming interface

APRP adaptive pattern recognition processing

ASF active streaming format

ASP application service provider

ASR automatic speech recognition

ASM

ASM adaptive stream management

ASSP application specific standard product

ATM asynchronous transfer mode

B

BER bit error rate

BSS broadcast satellite service, basic service set

C

CAD computer-aided design

CATV cable television or community antenna television

CBDS constant bit rate data service

CCITT Consultative Committee for Telegraph and Telephone

CDF channel definition format

CDMA code division multiple access

CDPD cellular digital packet data

CELP code excited linear prediction

CHTML cellular HTML

CL common Lisp

CLIPS C-Language Integrated Production System

CLOS Common Lisp Object System

CMISE common management information service elements

COM Component Object Model

CORBA Common Object Request Broker Architecture

CSMA/CD carrier sense multiple-access with collision detection

CT cordless telephone

CWPI Composition Web Performance Index

D

DAI distributed artificial intelligence

DARPA Defense Advanced Research Projects Agency

DBS direct broadcast satellite

DCC data communication channel

DISCOM2 Distance and Distributed Computing and Communication

DNS domain name service

DOOD Dylan Object-Oriented Database

DOM Document Object Model

DPCM differential pulse code modulation

DS digital service

DSL digital subscriber lines

DSP digital signal processor

DSSS digital sequence spread spectrum

DTD Document Type Declaration

DTP data transport protocol

DTW dynamic time warping

DWDM dense wave division multiplexing

E

ECC elliptic-curve cryptography

EDFA erbium-doped fiber amplifier

EDGE enhanced data rate for global evolution

EFR enhanced full-rate

EIP enterprise information portal

EJB Enterprise Java Beans

ENS electronic serial number

ESMR enhanced version of SMR

ESN electronic serial number

ETSI European Telecommunications Standards Institute

F

FCC Federal Communications Commission

FDDI fiber distributed data interface

FDM frequency division multiplexed

FDMA frequency division multiple access

FHSS frequency hopping spread spectrum

FM frequency modulation

FPLMTS future public land mobile telecommunication system

FTC Federal Trade Commission

FTP File Transfer Protocol

FFTC fiber to the curb

FTTH fiber to the home

G

GAN global area network

GDP gross domestic product

GEO geosynchronous earth orbit

GPS global positioning system

GPRS general packet radio service

GSL Nuance Grammar Specification Language

GSM global system for mobile service

H

HAVi home audio/visual interoperability

HDML Handheld Device Markup Language

HDSL high bit-rate digital subscriber line

HDTV high-definition television

HFC hybrid fiber coaxial

HSCSD high-speed circuit-switched data

HTML HyperText Markup Language

HTP HyperText Transfer Protocol

I

IDLC integrated digital loop carrier

IEEE Institute of Electrical and Electronic Engineers

IETF International Engineering Task Force

IGRP Interior Gateway Routing Protocol

IN intelligent networks

INM International Naming System

IP Internet Protocol

IPv6 IP version 6

IPX Internetwork Packet Exchange

IrDA Infrared Data Association

ISDN integrated services digital network

ISO International Standards Organization

ISP Internet service provider

IST intersymbol interference

IT information technology

ITTP Intelligent Terminal Transfer Protocol

ITU International Telecommunications Union

ITV interactive television

J

JPEG Joint Photographic Experts Group

JSGF Java Speech Grammar Format

JSP Java Server Pages

JVM Java Virtual Machine

K

kbps Kilobytes per second

L

LAN local area network

LED light-emitting diode

LEO low earth orbit

LLCL logical link control layer

LMDS local multipoint distribution service

LPC linear predictive coding

LPTV low-power television

LSP Lisp Server Pages

M

MAC media access control

MAE Metropolitan Area Exchange

MAN metropolitan area network

MDS multipoint distribution service

MEO medium earth orbit

MIDI musical instrument digital interface

MILAN Metacomputing in Large Asynchronous Networks

MIMD multi-instruction, multidata

MIME multipurpose Internet mail extensions

MIPS million instructions processed per second

MMDS multichannel multipoint distribution service

MML Mobile Markup Language

MMTF Mobile Management Task Force

MPEG Motion Picture Experts Group

MPP massively parallel processing

MPRG Mobile and Portable Radio Research Group

MSC mobile switching center

MSCS Microsoft Cluster Service

MSN mechanical serial number

MTSO mobile telephone switching office

N

NAP network access point

NASA National Aeronautics and Space Administration

NIC network interface card

NLP natural language processing

NMA network monitoring and analysis

O

OAA Open Agent Architecture

OADM optical add/drop multiplexer

OAM&P operations, administration, maintenance, and provisioning

OC optical carrier

O/E/O optical/electrical/optical

OFDM orthogonal frequency division multiplexing

OML Ontology Markup Language

OS operating system

OSI open systems interconnection

OSPF open shortest path first

OXC optical cross-connect

P

PAN personal area network

PC personal computer

PCCA Portable Computer Communications Association

PCM pulse code modulation

PCS Personal Communication System

PDA personal digital assistant

PDN packet data network

PHY physical layer protocol

PKI public key infrastructure

PLIP Parallel Line Internet Protocol

POP points of presence

POTS plain old telephone service

PTP point-to-point

PSMs problem-solving methods

PTM packet transfer mode

PVM Parallel Virtual Machine

Q

QoS quality of service

R

RBOCs Regional Bell Operating Companies

RDF Resource Development Framework

RFLAN radio frequency LAN

RIP Routing Information Protocol

RMA RealMedia Architecture

RMI Remote Method Invocation

RMFF RealMedia File Format

RPC remote procedure calls

RPE-LTP Residual Pulse Excitation—Long-Term Prediction

RSVP Real-time Reservation Protocol

RTP Real-time Protocol

RTSP Real-time Streaming Protocol

RTTP Real-time Transport Protocol

S

SAX Simple API for XML

SDH synchronous digital hierarchy

SGML Standard Generalized Markup Language

SGSN serving GPRS support node

SIMD single-instruction, multiple-data

SKC scalable knowledge composition

SLIP Serial Line Internet Protocol

SLP Service Location Protocol

SMATV single master antenna television

SMDS switched multimegabit data service

SMIL Synchronized Multimedia Integration Language

SMM symmetrical multiprocessing machine

SMP shared memory symmetric multiprocessing

SMR mobile radio

SMS short message service

SNMP Simple Network Management Protocol

SOAP Simple Object Access Protocol

SOM System Object Model

SONET Synchronous Optical Network

SOX Schema for Object-oriented XML Language

SQL Structured Query Language

SSL secure sockets layer

SSML Speech Synthesis Markup Language

STDM statistical time division multiplexing

SV speed verification

SWAP Shared Wireless Access Protocol

T

Tbps terabit per second, (1 trillion bits per second)

TCP Transmission Control Protocol

TDM time division multiplexing

TDMA time division multiple access

TLS transport layer security

TM Topic Maps

TTML Tagged Text Markup Language

TTS text-to-speech

U

UDDI Universal Description, Discovery, and Integration

UDP User Data Protocol

UML Unified Modeling Language

UMTS universal mobile telecommunications system

UPnP Universal Plug and Play

URL Uniform Resource Locator

UTP unshielded twisted pair

V

VDSL very-high-speed subscriber line

VOD video on demand

VoiceXML Voice Markup Language

VPN virtual private network

VSAT very small aperture terminal

VSELP Vector Sum Excited Linear Predictor

W

W3C World Wide Web Consortium

WADM wavelength add/drop multiplexer

WAG wireless accessing gateway

WAN wide area network

WAP Wireless Application Protocol

WASP Wireless Application Service Provider

WDM Windows Driver Model

WDP Wireless Datagram Protocol

WLIF wireless LAN interoperability forum

WLL wireless local loops

WML Wireless Markup Language

WPAN wireless personal area network

WSDL Web Services Descriptive Language

WTLS wireless transport layer security

X

XDR XML Data-Reduced

x-DSL x-digital subscriber line

XHTML Extensible Hypertext Markup Language

XLL Extensible Link Language

XML Extensible Markup Language

XSDL XML Schema Description Language

XSL Extensible Stylesheet Language

XSL-FO Extensible Style Language Format Objects

XSLT Extensible Stylesheet Language Transform

Appendix I

Glossary

Access Point (AP) An interface between the wireless network and a wired network.

Ad Hoc Network A wireless network composed only of stations—no access points.

Adaptive Noise Reduction Filter "Intelligent" noise filtering that analyzes each pixel and applies an appropriate filter to remove the noise.

Adaptive Routing A form of network routing whereby the path data packets travel from a source to a destination node depending on the current state of the network.

Address Resolution Protocol (ARP) A TCP/IP protocol that binds logical (IP) addresses to physical addresses.

Advanced Mobile Phone System (AMPS) The analog cellular phone system that is in the process of being replaced. The biggest problem with this system is the lack of capacity to handle the sheer number of users that demand voice service. The biggest problem for prospective data providers is the fact that the analog nature makes it difficult to support the data integrity necessary for digital data transmission.

Agent A piece of software that runs without direct human control or constant supervision to accomplish a goal provided by the user. Agents typically collect, filter, and process information found on the Web, sometimes in collaboration with other agents.

All-optical Network (AON) This term was first used to describe the first WDM network test bed, which was implemented at MIT's Lincoln Laboratory.

Analog Refers to an electronic device that uses a system of unlimited variables to measure or represent a flow of data. Radios use variable sound waves to carry data from transmitter to receiver.

Analog Cellular A telephone system that uses radio cells to provide connectivity among cellular phones.

Analog Signal An electrical signal having amplitude that varies continuously over time.

Applet A small software application or utility that is built to perform one task over the Web.

Appliance Runs applications using a visual interface between user and network.

Application Layer Establishes communications with other users and provides services by application layer of OSI reference model.

Asynchronous The ability to send or receive calls independently and in any order.

Asynchronous Transfer Mode (ATM) A cell-based connection-oriented data service for high-speed transfer that integrates circuit and packet switching.

Backbone The largest communications lines on the Internet, which connect cities and major telecommunication centers.

Bandwidth The carrying capacity or size of a communications channel; usually expressed in hertz (cycles per second) for analog circuits and in bits per second (bps) for digital circuits.

Basic Service Set (BSS) A set of 802.11-compliant stations that operates as a fully connected wireless network.

BFR (Big Fast Router) A generic term for the largest routers on the Internet, used by MAEs and NAPs.

Binding A concrete protocol and data format specification for a particular type of port.

Bit Error Rate (BER) This is the probability of data being received just as it is sent. The wireless environment introduces errors in the transmission of data. BER values of 10^{-2} (one error expected out of 100 data bits) are acceptable in voice transmissions, where human hearing will fill in the blanks, but values of 10^{-5} (one error out of 100,000 data bits) are necessary for efficient data communications.

Bit Rate The rate at which a presentation is streamed, usually expressed in kilobits per second (kbps).

Cascade Style Sheets (CSS) Code that ensures important style elements on a Web page appear consistently from page to page.

Cellular Digital Packet Data (CDPD) This is a data mode for AMPS analog cellular service. It sends data packets in the unused portions of the AMPS bandwidth, a technique that interleaves data traffic with voice. The major drawback is the upper limit on data transmission capability.

Circuit Switching A switching system that establishes a dedicated physical communications connection between end points, through the network, for the duration of the communications session; this is most often contrasted with packet switching in data communications transmissions.

Code Division Multiple Access (CDMA) This is a way of allocating bandwidth to support connections for PCS digital service. The call is spread over a series of frequencies based on a sequence of jumps that are semirandom in nature. The handset and the base station agree on the sequence ahead of time, which gives the base station the capability to minimize collisions within a cell. The spread spectrum approach minimizes signal loss within any particular frequency band, as well as providing security for the communications.

Component Object Model (COM) A group of conventions and specifications that lets you create interactions between software components in a structured, object-oriented way. COM is the foundation of ActiveX.

Connectivity Software A wireless system component that provides an interface between the user and the database or application found on the network.

Dark Fiber Fiberoptic cables that have been laid but have no illuminating signals in them.

Data Link Layer Transforms the packets of the network layer to a physical layer.

Data Mining Intelligently analyzing data to extract hidden trends, patterns, and information. Commonly used by statisticians, data analysts, and management information systems communities.

Data Rate The number of bytes per second used to represent a movie. Uncompressed VHS quality video is about 20Mbps. Single-speed CD-ROM quality is about 100kbps, and double-speed CD-ROM quality is about 200kbps.

Dense Wave Division Multiplexing (DWDM) An optical (analog) multiplexing technique used to increase the carrying capacity of a fiber network beyond what can currently be accomplished by time division multiplexing (TDM) techniques. Different wavelengths of light are used to transmit multiple streams of information along a single fiber with minimal interference. Dense WDM is a specific type of WDM wherein four or more wavelengths in the 15xx nanometer erbium-doped fiber amplifier (EDFA) gain region are used multiplexed on a fiber. Typical DWDM systems available today for long-distance transmission offer 16 to 40 wavelengths at 2.5Gbps (OC-48 SONET or STM-16 SDH) or 10Gbps (OC-192 SONET or STM-64 SDH) per wavelength. Systems up to 240 wavelengths have been announced. DWDM has been mainly deployed as a point-to-point, static overlay to the optical TDM network to create "virtual fiber." As such, DWDM is the precursor to optical networking. DWDM has drastically reduced the cost of transport by reducing the number of electrical regenerators required and sharing a single optical amplifier over multiple signals through the use of EDFAs.

Digital Using a predetermined numbering system to measure and represent the flow of data. Modern computers use digital 0s and 1s as binary representations of data.

Distributed Artificial Intelligence (DAI) Concerned with coordinated intelligent behavior: intelligent agents coordinating their knowledge, skills, and plans to act or solve problems, working toward a single goal or toward separate, individual goals that interact.

Download To copy a file from a server or network to your machine.

EFR Enhanced full-rate speech encoder and decoder defined by the European Telecommunications Standards Institute (ETSI) for the global system for mobile communications (GSM).

Enhanced Data Rate for GSM Evolution (EDGE) This enhancement to the GSM standard for a wireless data standard to bridge over to 3G technology. EDGE defines protocols that will carry data as fast as 384kbps.

Erbium-Doped Fiber Amplifier (EDFA) A key enabling technology of DWDM, EDFAs allow the simultaneous amplification of multiple signals in the 15xx nanometer region (for example, multiple 2.5Gbps channels) in the optical domain. EDFAs drastically increase the spacing required between regenerators, which are costly network elements because they (1) require optical/electrical/optical conversion of a signal and (2) operate on a single digital signal (for example, a single SONET or SDH optical signal). DWDM systems using EDFAs can increase regenerator spacing of transmissions to 500 to 800 km at 2.5Gbps. EDFAs are far less expensive than regenerators and can typically be spaced 80 to 120 km apart at 2.5Gps, depending on the quality of the fiber plant and the design goals of the DWDM system.

Expert System A computer program that has a deep understanding of a topic and can simulate a human expert, asking and answering questions and making decisions.

Extensible Markup Language (XML) Separates content from format, thus letting the browser decide how and where content gets displayed. XML is not a language; it is a system for defining other languages so that they understand their vocabulary.

Fast Start A feature of QuickTime that allows movies to be viewed inline in Quick-Time-compatible browsers before the whole movie has been fully downloaded.

Fiber The structure that guides light in a fiberoptic system.

Fiberoptics The use of light to transmit data, video, and voice. Fiberoptic cable has a better bandwidth and carriers a signal longer than cable wire.

Frame A data packet that consist of a header that identifies it according to network protocols, an address of the recipient's network, a data field, an error-checking field, and an identification trailer.

Frequency Division Multiple Access (FDMA) This method of allocating bandwidth to PCS service is based on the division of the available bandwidth into a series of channels, each of which is assigned to a call with a cell. It is the basis for the AMPS system, and also is used to some extent in GSM.

Frequency Hopping (FH) This practice is used in several communications systems to avoid interference that is restricted to particular frequencies. Both the transmitter and the receiver send the signal at a series of consecutive frequencies that are tracked.

General Packet Radio Service (GPRS) This is an intermediate service before the dissemination of 3G technology.

Global Positioning System (GPS) A worldwide satellite-based radio navigation system providing three-dimensional position, velocity, and time to anywhere on the earth.

Global System for Mobile Communications (GSM) This is the dominant PCS system in Europe. It is based on a combination of TDMA and FDMA techniques.

Grammar A speech grammar specifies a set of utterances that a user may speak to perform an action or supply information and provides a corresponding string value to describe the information or action.

Header A chunk of data, delivered from a source to a rendering plug-in when first connecting to a stream, usually used to initialize the stream.

HTTP playback A reasonable method for sending short clips from a Web server using the HTTP protocol. HTTP streaming does not support all the datatypes of and is not as robust as real-time streaming protocol (RTSP), however.

Hub A point where communications lines are brought together to exchange data.

Hyperlink Elements such as text, graphics, and other objects embedded in a Web page's HTML code that establishes connections to related Web pages or elements.

HyperText Markup Language (HTML) The programming language the World Wide Web uses to display pages, links to other pages, and so on.

Hypernavigation Occurs when a rendering plug-in directs the client to display a URL at a specified time in a stream. When the plug-in issues a hypernavigation request, the default Web browser opens.

International Standards Organization (ISO) A nontreaty standards organization active in development of open systems interconnections.

Intersymbol Interference (ISI) This describes the tendency of PCS data to smear across multiple bits of data within a transmission. It is a major problem of radio communications, when components of a signal do not arrive as the same time at the receiver.

Internet Protocol (IP) The set of rules that governs the transmission of data from one computer to another over the Internet.

Internet Protocol Address (IP Address) The numeric address used to locate computers on a TCP/IP network. The numbers include four groups, each separated by a period.

Internet Service Provider (ISP) A company that lets users dial into its computers, which are connected to the Internet.

InterNIC Created by several organizations to handle domain name registry.

Key Frame In temporal compression, an image that is the basis for determining which changes in sequential difference frames need to be stored.

kHz Kilohertz, the audio sample rate; a measure of how accurately (frequently) sound is sampled. Higher sample rates yield better sound quality, with better high-end response but larger files.

Knowledge Discovery The process of complex extraction of implicit, previously unknown, and potentially useful knowledge from large datasets. Coined in 1989 by artificial intelligence and machine learning researchers.

Knowledge Management The process of creating, capturing, and organizing knowledge objects. A knowledge object might be a research report, a budget for the development of a new product, or a video presentation. Knowledge management programs seek to capture objects in a repository that is searchable and accessible in electronic form.

Learning The process of automatically finding relations between inputs and outputs given examples of that relation.

Light-emitting Diode (LED) An optoelectronics device used to produce modes of light beamed into an optical fiber in a wide range of wavelengths.

Lightpath Analogous to virtual circuits in the asynchronous transfer mode (ATM) world, a lightpath is a virtual circuit in the optical domain that could consist of multiple spans, each using a different physical wavelength for transmission of information across an optical network.

Local Area Network (LAN) A network that connects computers within a geographically small region, often within just one building.

Logical Link Control Layer (LLCL) The highest layer of IEEE 802 reference model providing functions of a data link control.

Mean Filter Replaces a pixel with the average value of its surroundings. Applying a uniform mean filter blurs the image.

Median Filter Replaces a pixel with the "most typical" value of its surroundings while ignoring extreme values. Applying a uniform median filter tends to remove small details.

Message Authentication Code A number computed from the contents of a text message that is used to authenticate the message. A MAC is like a digital signature.

Metropolitan Area Exchange (MAE) The largest hubs on the Internet, where major telecommunication operators connect their networks.

Multimode fiber One of two forms of optical fiber that has a larger core than single-mode fibers. They propagate, or spread, many modes of light through the core simultaneously.

Nanometer A unit of measurement used to measure a wavelength (one-billionth of a meter).

Network Access Point (NAP) A hub for exchanging information between telecommunication carriers.

Network Services Services that provide cross-platform methods for managing network communications. Any server-side or client-side RealSystem component can use network services to create TCP or UDP connections for reading and writing data. Network services also provide interfaces that let components resolve DNS host names and listen for TCP connections on specified ports.

Object A unique instance of a data structure defined according to the template provided by its class. Each object has its own values for the variables belonging to its class and can respond to the methods defined by its class.

Ontologies Collection of statements written in a language such as Resource Development Framework (RDF) that defines relationships between concepts and specific logic rules. Semantic data on the Web will be understandable by following the links to specific ontologies.

Opaque Optical Networks The current vision of the optical network whereby conversions from the optical to the electrical and back to the optical domain are required periodically. Such O/E/O conversions are required in order to retime the signal in the digital domain, clean up signal impairments, allow fault isolation, and provide performance monitoring (particularly of signal bit error rate).

Operation An abstract description of an action supported by the service.

Optical Add/Drop Multiplexer (OADM) Also termed a Wavelength Add/Drop Multiplexer (WADM), an optical network element that lets specific channels of a multichannel optical transmission system be dropped and/or added without affecting the through signals (the signals that are to be transported through the network node). OADMs, like their electrical ADM counterparts, can simplify networks and lower the cost of network nodes by eliminating unnecessary demultiplexing of through signals.

Optical Amplifier A device that increases the optical signal strength without an O/E/O conversion process.

Optical Carrier (OC) Optical carrier; a designation used as a prefix denoting the optical carrier level of SONET data standards. OC-1/STS-1, OC-3/STS-3, OC-12, OC-48, and OC-192 denote transmission standards for fiberoptic data transmission in SONET frames at data rates of 51.84Mbps, 155.52Mbps, 622.08Mbps, 2.48832Gbps, and 9.95Gbps, respectively.

Optical Network The optical network will provide all basic network requirements in the optical layer; namely capacity, scalability, reliability, survivability, and manageability. Today, the wavelength is the fundamental object of the optical network. Currently, basic network requirements can be met through a combination of the optical transport layer (DWDM today), which provides scalability and capacity beyond 10Gbps, and the SONET/SDH transport layer, which provides the reliability, survivability, and manageability needed for public networks. The long-term vision of an "all-optical network" is of a transparent optical network where signals are never converted to the electrical domain between network ingress and egress. The more practical implementation for the near term will be of an opaque optical network, that is, one that works to minimize but still includes O/E/O conversion. Optical network elements will include terminals, dynamic add/drop multiplexers, and dynamic OXCs.

Optical Network Management Products An emerging category of optical networking software products that operate at the granularity of a lightpath and that provide provisioning and management of lightpaths in the network at a minimum. These products will be developed both by equipment vendors, as offerings integrated with transport and switching products, and by third-party network management software vendors. This product class will include network and element management systems and will generally be required by service providers to stand alone, as well as integrate with existing operations support systems.

Optical Switching Products An emerging category of optical networking products that operate at the granularity of a lightpath and provide the following functionality at a minimum: performance monitoring and management; restoration and rerouting enabled by interswitch signaling; wavelength translation; the establishment of end-to-end lightpaths; and delivery of customer services. Optical cross-connects (OXCs) are included in this category.

Pattern Recognition The operation and design of systems that recognize patterns in data.

Personal Communications Service (PCS) This is a general term for services that include digital cellular voice service, paging services, data transmission, and other services provided by the digital cellular infrastructure.

Plain Old Telephone Service (POTS) This acronym is used within the telecom industry.

Port A single end point defined as a combination of a binding and a network address.

Port Type An abstract set of operations supported by one or more end points.

Public Encryption Key An asymmetric scheme that uses two keys for encryption.

Regression Prediction The operation and design of systems that develop models of data useful for the description of the data and for prediction.

Resource Development Framework (RDF) Schema for defining information on the Web. RDF provides the technology for expressing the meaning of terms and concepts in a form that computers can process. RDF can use XML for its syntax and URIs to specify entities, concepts, properties, and relationships.

Router A hardware device that receives and transmits data packets from one LAN (or WAN) to another. A router reads the address in a packet and determines the best path for the packet to travel to its destination.

Semantic Web Communication protocols and standards that would include descriptions of the item on the Web such as people, documents, events, products, and organizations, as well as relationships between documents and relationships between people.

Server A computer that other computers connect to for the purpose of retrieving information. In this book, generally used to mean the computer that hosts your Web page.

Service Discovery The process of locating an agent or automatic Web-based service that will perform a required function.

Short Message Entity (SME) Class of devices that can send and receive short messages using SMS.

Short Message Service (SMS) A protocol for sending alphanumeric messages using cell phones and pagers.

Simple Object Access Protocol (SOAP) A protocol for the exchange of information in a distributed environment. SOAP is an XML-based protocol consisting of three parts: an envelope (a framework for describing what is in a message and how to process it), a set of encoding rules (for expressing instances of application-defined datatypes), and a convention for representing remote procedure calls and responses.

Site An object that receives rendered data for display. The client core supplies a site, and the rendering plug-in registers as a site user. The plug-in can then send data without providing platform-specific commands for data display.

Signal-to-Noise Ratio (SNR) An engineering measure of the amount of information that can be extracted from a transmitted signal. This is important given that there is a limited amount of bandwidth available for wireless communications.

Splitter A device that creates multiple optical signals from a single optical signal.

Standard Generalized Markup Language (SGML) A language that lets developers create other markup languages.

Synchronous Digital Hierarchy (SDH) The international standard for transmitting digital information over optical networks. Term used by ITU to refer to SONET.

Synchronous Optical Network (SONET) Standards for transmitting digital information over optical networks. Fiberoptic transmission rates range from 51.84Mbps to 9.95Gbps. It defines a physical interface, optical line rates known as OC signals, frame formats, and an operations, administration, maintenance, and provisioning (OAM&P) protocol. The base rate is known as OC-1 and runs at 51.84Mbps. Higher rates are a multiple of this such that OC-12 is equal to 622Mbps (12 times 51.84Mbps).

Tbps Terabit per second (1 trillion bits per second); an information carrying capacity measure used for high-speed optical data systems.

Time Division Multiple Access (TDMA) The TDMA access scheme divides each frequency band into a series of time slots. Users are assigned a set of time slots during which they are allowed to broadcast. This technique is better at handling heavy traffic than others, because there is a hard upper limit on the amount of bandwidth that a particular user will utilize, but this also has weaknesses.

Time Division Multiplexing (TDM) An electrical (digital) multiplexing technique used to allow multiple streams of information to share the same transmission media. For transmission at 155Mbps or above, the electrical TDM signal is typically converted to an optical signal for transport. SONET and SDH standards in North America and the rest of the world, respectively, set the bit rates, frame formats, and other physical and operational characteristics for these optical signals.

Topic Maps (TM) TMs provide a standardized notation for interchangeably representing information about the structure of information resources used to define topics and the relationships between topics. The structural information conveyed by TMs includes (1) groupings of addressable information objects around topics (occurrences) and (2) relationships between topics (associations). A TM defines a multidimensional topic space.

Transmission Control Protocol (TCP) HTTP uses TCP as the protocol for reliable document transfer. If packets are delayed or damaged, TCP will effectively stop traffic until either the original packets or backup packets arrive.

Transmission Control Protocol/Internet Protocol (TCP/IP) Two protocols used together to govern communication between Internet computers. TCP breaks data traveling on the Internet into small packets. As the packets travel, TCP checks for errors and reassembles the packets in the proper sequence upon arrival.

Transparent Optical Networks The original vision of the "all-optical network" as a network in which a signal is transported from source to destination entirely in the optical domain. After ingress into the network, the signal is never converted to the electrical domain for analog operations such as amplification and filtering or any other purpose. Signals are amplified, shaped, demultiplexed, remultiplexed, and switched in the optical domain with regardless of the digital content of the signal, for example, bit rate, modulation scheme, or protocol. Digital transparency implies transparency to digital characteristics such as bit rate, format, and protocol. "Digital transparency" is misleading because analog signal characteristics such as optical power budget are extremely dependent on a digital signal's bit rate and format. Similarly, though modulation transparency implies transparency to whether a signal's modulation is baseband or broadband, amplitude, phase, or frequency, in truth optical power budget will depend strongly on the modulation scheme used. Transparent optical networks are limited in two ways: (1) by analog signal defects (for example, gain tilt, noise, chromatic dispersion, and cross-talk) that accumulate over distance, and (2) by the difficulty of monitoring performance and isolating faults as a signal traverses a network.

Types A container for data type definitions using some type system (such as XML Schema Descriptive Language [XSDL]).

Universal Description, Discovery, and Integration (UDDI) A specification of Web Services' information registries. In this distributed registry, businesses and services are described in common XML format.

Universal Resource Identifier (URI) A URI defines an entity. URLs are a type of URI.

Universal Resource Locator (URL) The familiar codes (such as http://www.sciam.com) that are used as hyperlinks to Web sites.

User Control Point (UCP) A proprietary messaging protocol owned by Cisco.

Virtual Reality Markup Language (VRML) A language used to put 3D images on the Web. Developers use it to provide description of a three-dimensional world complete with lighting and navigation.

Voice Markup Language (VoiceXML) This standard attempts to marry automated telephone service with the power of Web technology. VoiceXML allows developers to create grammar for both spoken input and grammars for input through touch-tone key process.

Wavelength A measure of the color of the light for which the performance of the fiber has been optimized. It is a length stated in nanometers (nm) or in micrometers (um).

Wavelength Division Multiplexer A passive device that combines light signals with different wavelengths on different fibers onto a single fiber. The wavelength division demultiplexer performs the reverse function.

Wavelength Translation A function of some OADMs and OXCs whereby a signal entering the network element (NE) on one physical wavelength leaves the network element on a different physical wavelength. This signal could be part of a single lightpath. NEs available today can do fixed wavelength translation, meaning two physical wavelengths are predetermined and cannot typically be changed without human intervention at the NE. Emerging optical network elements will provide dynamic wavelength translation, which will allow the outgoing physical optical path to be changed to suit protection and restoration needs, customer service expectations, or other scenarios.

Web-Ready A term used to refer to movies that are optimized for distribution on the World Wide Web. Movies must be flattened for cross-platform playback and fast start, and must not contain unsupported data types. Web-ready movies should also have a low enough data rate that most target users can watch them without unreasonable waiting.

Web Services A new model for creating dynamic distributed applications with common interfaces for efficient communication across the Internet. They are built around ubiquitous, open standards such as TCP/IP, HTTP, Java, HTML, and XML, as well as newer standard technologies, such as SOAP, WSDL, and UDDI.

Web Services Descriptive Language (WSDL) Specification on how abstract information about Web services is represented in XML and which extensible mechanisms enable the binding of abstract specifications to concrete implementations.

Wide Area Network (WAN) A data communications facility involving two or more computers situated at different sites.

Wireless Application Protocol (WAP) This protocol defines the specification that lets users access information from the Internet with wireless devices, such as cell phones.

Wireless Markup Language (WML) A markup language used to annotate documents for display on handheld devices.

Wireless Metropolitan Area Network (WMAN) Provides communication links between buildings within a city environment, avoiding installation costs of cabling.

World Wide Web (WWW) The graphical subset of the Internet.

XML XML stands for Extensible Markup Language. The key feature of XML in comparison with HTML is that it provides the ability to define tags and attributes, which is not allowed under HTML. XML is a subset of the SGML designed for use on the Internet. It supports all the features of SGML, and valid XML documents are therefore valid SGML documents.

XML Schema Description Languages (XSDL) The W3C recommendation that goes beyond DTD with the addition of XML datatypes, namespace support, and inheritance mechanisms.

Bibliography

Abdoullaev, A. *Artificial Superintelligence.* F.I.S. Intelligent Systems, 1999.

Alesso, H. P. "On the Relationship of Digraph Matrix Analysis to Petri Net Theory and Fault Trees." *Reliability Engineering*, 10:93–103, 1985.

Alesso, H. P. *e-Video: Producing Internet Video as Broadband Technology Converges.* Addison-Wesley, 2000.

Ash, D., and Dabija, V. *Planning for Real-Time Event Response Management.* Prentice Hall, 2000.

Berners-Lee, T., Hendler, J., and Ora, L. "The Semantic Web." *Scientific American*, pp. 35–43, May 2001.

Bogdanowicz, K. D., et al. "Scenarios for Ambient Intelligence in 2010." *ISTAG Report*, European Commission, Feb. 2001.

Bollen, J., and Heylighen F. "Algorithms for the Self-Organization of Distributed, Multi-user Networks." In Trappl, R. (ed.). *Proceedings of the 13th European Meeting on Cybernetics and Systems Research.* Austrian Society for Cybernetic Studies, Vienna, pp. 911–917.

Broder, A., et al. "Graph Structure in the Web." *IBM Report*, Oct. 1999.

Brusilovsky, P. "Methods and Techniques of Adaptive Hypermedia." In *User Modeling and User-Adapted Interaction.* Vol. 6; pp. 87–129. Kluwer Academic, 1996.

Carteret, B.A., et al. Needs Assessment for Remote Systems Technology at the Chernobyl Unit 4 Shelter. UCRL-ID-128425; PNNL-11692. Sept. 1997.

Cawsey, A. *The Essence of Artificial Intelligence.* Prentice Hall, 1998.

Cowell, R. G. (ed), Dawad, P. A., and Laurtizen, S. L. *Probabilistic Networks and Expert Systems (Statistics for Engineering and Information Science)*. Springer Verlag, 1999.

De Bra, P., and Calvi, L. "A Generic Adaptive Hypermedia System." *Proceedings of the 2nd Workshop on Adaptive Hypertext and Hypermedia*. Pittsburgh, June 20–24, 1998.

Debenham, J. *Knowledge Engineering: Unifying Knowledge Base and Data Base Design*. Springer Verlag, 1998.

Dertouzos, M. L. *The Unfinished Revolution*. HarperCollins, 2001.

Dertouzos, M. L. "The Future of Computing." *Scientific American,* July 1999.

Efremovych, A. G., et al. Declaration Patent for the Invention of a Cable Handling Device for Robotic Systems. Ukraine Patent Number (11) 36478 A. April 16, 2001.

Geier, J. *Wireless LANs: Implementing Interoperable Networks*. MacMillan Technical Publications, 1999.

Gershenfeld, N. *When Things Start to Think*. Owl Books, 2000.

Goldberg, R. *A Practical Handbook of Speech Codes*. CRC Press, 2000.

Guttag, J. V. "Communications Chameleons: Multipurpose Communications Systems Will Be the Links of Tomorrow's Wireless Computer Networks." *Scientific American,* July 1999.

Hearst, M. A., and Hirsh, H. "AI's Greatest Trends and Controversies." *Trends & Controversies*, Editors Report, University of California, Berkeley, 2001.

Hertz, S. R., Younes, R. J., and Hoskins, S. R. "Space, Speed, Quality, and Flexibility: Advantages of Rule-Based Speech Synthesis." *Conference Proceedings, AVIOS 2000,* May 22–24, 2000, San Jose, CA, pp. 217–227 (2000).

Highsmith, J. A. III. *Adaptive Software Development: A Collaborative Approach to Managing Complex Systems*. Dorset House, 2000.

Hobbs, M., Migrating to a Mobile Architecture. www.webtechniques.com/archives/2000/00/hobbs (Accessed August 2001).

Jain, L. C. *Knowledge-Based Intelligent Techniques in Industry*. CRC Press, 1998.

Lesser, V., et al. "BIG: A Resource-Bounded Information Gathering Agent," *Proceedings of the Fifteenth National Conference on Artificial Intelligence* (AAAI-98). Madison, WI, 1998.

Lindsay, R. K., et al. *Applications of Artificial Intelligence for Chemical Inference: The DENDRAL Project.* McGraw-Hill, 1980.

McGrath, S. *XML by Example: Building E-Commerce Applications.* Prentice Hall, 1998.

McInerney, F., and White, S. *FutureWealth.* Truman Talley Books, 2000.

MIT. AI Labs. http://oxygen.lcs.mit.edu/ (Accessed August 2001).

Ogbuji, U. "An Introduction to RDF: Exploring the Standard for Web-based Metadata." IBM Web site, www.ibm.com (Accessed December 2000).

Pearl, J. *Probabilistic Reasoning in Intelligent Systems: Networks of Plausible Inference.* Morgan Kaufmann, 1997.

Pfeifer, R., and Scheier, C. *Understanding Intelligence.* MIT Press, 1999.

Rabiner, L., and Juang, B. *Fundamentals of Speech Recognition.* Prentice Hall, 1993.

Remmell, E. "Mobile IP for the Masses: Specifications and Challenges." Web site, www.embedded-control-europe.com (Accessed 2001).

Riva, A., and Ramoni, M. "LispWeb: A Specialized HTTP Server for Distributed AI Applications." *Computer Networks and ISDN Systems.* 28(7–11):953, 1999.

Tamura, T., Oguchi, M., and Kitsuregawa, M. "Parallel Database Processing on a 100 Node PC Cluster: Cases for Decision Support Query Processing and Data Mining." In *Proceedings of SC97: High Performance Networking and Computing,* 1997.

Toffler, A. *The Third Wave.* Bantam Books, 1980.

Weiss, G. (ed). *Multiagent Systems: A Modern Approach to Distributed Artificial Intelligence.* MIT Press, 1999.

Zue, V. "Talking with Your Computer." *Scientific American,* July 1999.

Index

1394 standard. *See* IEEE, standards
802.11 standard. *See* IEEE, standards

A

ActiveSky, 148
Adaptive differential pulse code
    modulation, 38
Adaptive software, 180–182
  basics, 215–218
  protocol development, 25–27
  Web Architecture, 224, 265
Address Resolution Protocol, 153
ADPCM (adaptive differential pulse code
    modulation), speech coding, 38
Aether (WASP), 124
Agents, AI, 183–184
  intelligence, definition, 4
AI. *See also* DAI
  applications, 171
  attributes, 170
  basics, 170–171
  communication process, 256
  computational complexity theory
    classifications, 172
  current research, 258
  history, 27, 169
  intelligence, definition, 4
  learning, 178–179
  learning, adaptive software, 180–182
  learning, agents, 183–184

learning, data mining, 182–183
learning, neural networks, 179–180
methods, 173
methods, expert system architecture,
    178
methods, expert system tools, 177
methods, inference, 176–177
methods, knowledge representation,
    176–177
methods, searches, 174–175
methods, searches, computer chess
    example, 175–176, 200–202
Semantic Web Architecture, 23–24
server architecture, 186
versus human intelligence, 171
Web Architecture, 224
AI Laboratory, MIT
  Oxygen, basics, 15–16
  Oxygen, current status, 258–259
  Oxygen, N21s, 79–85, 132–133
AIM (Automatic Identification
    Manufacturers), 274
Air2Web WAG service, 123
Algorithms
  genetic algorithms, 218–219
  Learning Algorithms, 205–207
alphaWorks, 234
Alter Ego WAG service, 123
ALUs (Arithmetic Logic Units), computer
    chips, 82

American National Standards Institute, 273

AMPS-D (digital advanced mobile phone service), 120

Analog signals, 98
  multiplexors, 100

ANNs (artificial neural networks), 180

ANSI (American National Standards Institute), 273

Application Specific Standard Product, 83

Arithmetic Logic Units, computer chips, 82

ARP (Address Resolution Protocol), 153

Artificial intelligence. *See* AI

Artificial neural networks, 180

Askey Piccolo PC010 pocket PCs, 61

Association rules, data mining, 183

ASSP (Application Specific Standard Product), StrongARM processors, 83

ATM (asynchronous transfer mode)
  basics, 99
  versus IP packet switching, 18, 92, 105

Automatic Identification Manufacturers, 274

B

Babelfish Translation Service, 234

Backbones, 102

Bandwidth
  balancing network elements, 18
  connectivity issues, 94
  wired and wireless networks, 130–131
  wired network constraint, 91

BeVocal voice-activation product, 47

Biometric devices, security, 293

BizTalk XML, 194

Bluetooth wireless connection standard, 15
  basics, 72–74
  PAN standards for home, 67, 69
  security improvement, 291

Bridges, wireless LANs, 115

Broadband technology
  basics, 128–129
  comparisons, 128

Brute force AI search technique, 174

Butler-in-a-Box, Mastervoice, 40

C

C-Language Integrated Production System, 177

Canadian National Research Council, direct voice input, 40

Carrier Sense Multiple Access with Collision Direction
  characteristics, 139
  MAC, 114

CAT 5 Ethernet, PAN standards for homes, 67

CCITT (International Consultative Committee for Telegraph and Telephone), 274

CDMA (code division multiple access), 19, 138
  2G technologies, 141–142
  accessibility to WAP, 158
  basics, 143–144
  characteristics, 139
  migration to 3G technologies, 120, 147
  versus TDMA, 148

CEBus standard (EIA-600), 65–67

Cell-switched networks, 105

Cellular transmission
  basics, 138–140
  WANs, 119–120

CELP (code excited linear prediction), 36–37

Chemical Markup Language, 194

cHTML (compact HTML), 162

Circuit-switched networks, 103–104

Classification/clustering, data mining, 183

Client-server network model, 91
  WAP, 160
CLIPS (C-Language Integrated
    Production System), 177
CLOS (Common Lisp Object System),
    25–26
  Common Lisp, CL-HTTP system,
    187
Clustering, 100
  data mining, 183
CML (Chemical Markup Language), 194
Coaxial cable, data transmission, 18, 20,
    90, 92–93, 98, 261
  Ethernet, 117
  PAN standards for homes, 67
Code division multiple access. *See* CDMA
Code excited linear prediction, 36–37
Commerce-One, 193
Common Lisp Object System. *See*
    CLOS
Common Object Request Broker
    Architecture. *See* CORBA
Compact HTML, 162
Compaq pocket PCs, 61
Component Object Model, 195
Computational complexity theory
    classifications, 172
Computer chess (IBM's Deep Blue), AI
    search method, 175–176, 200–202
Computer chips
  RAW, 80–82
  StrongARM, 83
  Transmets, 81–82
Conita PVA voice-messaging services, 47
Convigo (WASP), 124
Copper wire data transmission, 18, 20, 90,
    92–93, 117, 261
CORBA (Common Object Request Broker
    Architecture), 76
  Web Services, 195, 198
Cordless telephone technology, FPLMTS
    and UMTS, 122

CSMA/CD (Carrier Sense Multiple Access
    with Collision Direction)
  characteristics, 139
  MAC, 114
Cyc (enCYClopedia), 192

D
DAI (distributed artificial intelligence).
    See also AI
  basics, 184–187
  distributed computing, 220–223
  Web Architecture, 224, 265
DARPA (Defense Advanced Research
    Projects Agency) projects
  Oxygen, 15
  SPEAKeasy, 72
  SpectrumWare, 72
Data mining, AI, 182–183
Data transmission media, 18, 20. *See also*
    specific types
  types, 90, 92–93
  wireless networks, 107–108
Database management
  basics, 204–205
  Learning Algorithms, 205–207
DBS (direct broadcast satellite), 18, 20
DCOM (Distributed Component Object
    Model), 196
DECIPHER product, 42
Deep Blue supercomputer, computer
    chess, 175–176, 200–202
Defense Advanced Research Projects
    Agency project
  Oxygen, 15
  SPEAKeasy, 72
  SpectrumWare, 72
Dense wavelength division multiplexing,
    93, 102–103
Differential pulse code modulation, 37–38
Digital advanced mobile phone service,
    120
Digital Audio/Video home networks, 63

Digital signals, 98
  backbones, 102
  multiplexors, 100
Direct broadcast satellite. *See* DBS
Directory Services Markup Language, 194
DisCom2 (Distance and Distributed
    Computing and Communication),
    185
Distributed artificial intelligence. *See* DAI
Distributed Component Object Model,
    196
Document Type Declarations, 192
DPCM (differential pulse code
    modulation), speech coding, 37–38
Dr. Who product, 42
DSML (Directory Services Markup
    Language), 194
DSSS radio, IEEE 802.11 standard, 281
DTDs (Document Type Declarations),
    192
DWDM (dense wavelength division
    multiplexing), 93, 102–103
Dylan (Dynamic Language), 25, 287–290

E
E-mail, Internet services, 5
E. Ink, electronic ink, 62
ebXML (Electronic Business XML), 196
EDGE (enhanced data rates for global
    evolution), 144, 147
EDI (Electronic Data Interchange), 194
EIA-600 standard (CEBus), 65–67
EIP (Enterprise Information Portals), 89
    basics, 190–192
    Web Services architecture, 198
Elan text-to-speech (TTS), 41
Electronic and mechanical serial numbers,
    telephones, 139
Electronic Business XML, 196
Electronic Data Interchange, 194
Electronic ink technology, 60, 62
Enhanced data rates for global evolution,
    144, 147

Enhanced mobile radio, 122
Enterprise Information Portals. *See* EIPs
Enviro 21 (E21) Project Oxygen, 80–85
ESMR (enhanced mobile radio), 122
Ethernet
    advantages, 95, 98
    ATM, 99, 105
    basics, 100–101
    CAT 5, 67
    home networks, 63
    wireless LANs, 117
Expert systems, AI methods, 177–178
EXPTIME problems, 172
Extensible Markup Language. *See* XML
Extensible Stylesheet Language, 193–194
Extensible Stylesheet Language
    Transform, 193–194

F
Fast Ethernet, 95, 98
Fast Fourier Transform algorithm, 36
FDDI (fiber distributed data interface), 95
    ATM, 99
FDM (frequency division multiplexed),
    100–101
FDMA (frequency division multiple
    access), 120
    2G technologies, 141
    characteristics, 139
FHSS radio, IEEE 802.11 standard, 281
Fiber distributed data interface, 95, 99
Fiberoptic data transmission, 90, 92–94,
    98, 261
    DWDM, 102–103
    Ethernet, 117
File Transfer Protocol. *See* FTP
Firewire standard (IEEE), 63
FPLMTS (future public land mobile
    telecommunications system),
    cordless telephone technology,
    122
Frame-relay networks, 98
FreeSpeech 2000 product, 42

FreeTranslation.com, 235
Frequency division multiple access. *See* FDMA
Frequency division multiplexed, 100–101
FTP
    Internet services, 5
    TCP/IP model, 153
Future public land mobile telecommunications system, 122

G
Galaxy architecture, 49–50
GANs (global area networks)
    AI server architecture, 186
    communication process, 256
    connectivity issues, 95
General packet radio service, 144–147
Genetic algorithms, 218–219
GEO satellites, 122–123
Geosynchronous earth orbit satellites, 122–123
GGSN GPRS support nodes, 145
Gigabit Ethernet, 95, 98
    basics, 100–101
Global area networks. *see* GANs
Global positioning systems, 122
Global system for mobile communications. *See* GSM
Go Translate, 234
GPRS (general packet radio service), 144–147
GPS technology, 122
Graphs and Web
    characteristics, 284–285
    terminology, 284
GSM (global system for mobile communications), 138
    accessibility to WAP, 158
    basics, 120–121
    HDML, 19
    ITTP, 19
    mobile communications, 142–143

H
Handheld Device Markup Language. *See* WML
Handy 21 (H21) Project Oxygen, 80–85
HAVi protocol, 67–68
HDML, 19
HDR, migration to 3G technologies, 147
Heuristic AI search technique, 174
High-speed circuit-switched data. *See* HSCSD
Hitachi HPW handheld PCs, 61
Home Audio/Video interoperability. *See* HAVi protocol
Home Phone Network Alliance. *See* HomePNA
HomeAPI networks, 67–68
HomeConnex networks, 67
HomePNA networks, 67–68
HomePNA standards, 67–68
HomeRF networks, basics, 66–67
HSCSD (high-speed circuit-switched data), 144
    migration to 3G technologies, 147
HTML (HyperText Markup Language), 5
    cHTML, 162
    DAI applications, 187
    Semantic Web Architecture, 265
HTTP (HyperText Transfer Protocol), 5
    DAI applications, 187
    Semantic Web Architecture, 265
    TCP/IP model, 153–154
HVAC Comfort Network, 63, 68
HyperText Markup Language. *See* HTML
HyperText Transfer Protocol. *See* HTTP

I
IBM
    Deep Blue supercomputer, computer chess, 175–176, 200–202
    EIP, 191
    Pervasive Computing, 79
IConverse (WASP), 124

IEEE Institute of Electrical and Electronic Engineers)
  basics, 275
  standards, 1394, 63, 66–67
  standards, 1394, home networks, 63, 66–67
  standards, 802.11, 281–282
  standards, 802.11, history, 73
  standards, 802.11, origin, 56
  standards, 802.11, RFLANs, 107
  standards, 802.11, wireless LANs, 108, 116–118
  wireless LAN standards, 281–282
IETF (International Engineering Task Force), 276
  Mobile IP Working Group, 21–22
IGRP (Interior Gateway Routing Protocol) protocol, 99
IIOP, 196
IN (Intelligent Networking), 18
  advanced data transmission services, 92
IN CUBE voice command, 40
Industrial, Scientific, and Medical bands, 115
Inference engines, 215
Information Age. *See also* Intelligent Wireless Web
  effect on workers' output, 243–245
  global economic integration, 245–247
  historical perspective, 239–243
  IT spending effect on productivity, 247–248
Infrared (IR), 93, 107
  home networks, 63
  IEEE 802.11 standard, 281
  LANs, 113, 115
Infrared Data Association. *See* IrDA
Institute of Electrical and Electronic Engineers. *See* IEEE
Intelligence
  agents (*See* Agents, AI)
  AI, testing, 170–171
  computational complexity theory classifications, 172

definition, 4–5
  human *versus* AI, 171
  IQ (intelligence quotient), 4
Intelligent Networking. *See* IN
Intelligent Terminal Transfer Protocol, 19
Intelligent Wireless Web. *See also* Information Age
  centralized and distributed architectures, 268–269
  communication process outlook, 254–257
  communications cycle, 12
  definition, intelligence, 4–5
  definition, Web, 5–6
  definition, wireless, 5
  hardware and software innovations, 266–267
  mobility considerations, 130–132
  networks, 9, 16–20, 255, 260
  networks, capable of learning, 181–182
  Personal Space, 9, 14–17, 255
  planning guidelines, 264–265
  proprietary and open standards, 267–268
  protocols, 9, 19–22, 255, 262–264
  user interfaces, 9–13, 255
  vision for future, 6–7
  Web Architecture, 9, 22–24, 255, 264–265
  wireless devices, effect on productivity, 248–251
Interactive television 119
Interactive Voice Assistant (IVA), 43
Interior Gateway Routing Protocol, 99
International Consultative Committee for Telegraph and Telephone, 274
International Engineering Task Force. *See* IETF
International Standards Organization. *See* ISO
International Telecommunication Union, 276

Internet. *See also* Wireless Internet
basics, 151–152
definition, 5
history, 152
mobile protocols, basics, 154–155
mobile protocols, Mobile IP, 155–156
transfer protocols, 152–154
Internet Inter-ORB Protocol. *See* IIOP
IP (Internet Protocol), 5
transition to Mobile IP, 262–264
IP packet switching
basics, 104–105
versus ATM, 18, 92, 105
IPv4 and IPv6
Mobile IP, 21–22
Mobile IP, transition from IP, 263
mobile protocols, 154, 156
IQ, 4
IrDA (Infrared Data Association), 262
basics, 274
PAN standards, 68–69
ISM (Industrial, Scientific, and Medical)
bands, 115
ISO (International Standards
Organization)
basics, 275–276
ISO/IEC 13250 standard, 212
ISO/OSI seven-layer model, 152–153
iTranslator, 234
Itronix handheld PCs, 61
ITTP (Intelligent Terminal Transfer
Protocol), 19
ITU (International Telecommunication
Union), 276
ITV (interactive television), 119
IVA (Interactive Voice Assistant), 43

J

J2EE (Java 2, Enterprise Edition)
basics, 196–197
progression toward Semantic Web
Architecture, 23
versus .NET, 197–200
J2ME (Java 2, Micro Edition), 197

J2SE (Java 2, Standard Edition), 197
Java Object Serialization, 76
Java Remote Method Protocol, 76
Java Speech Markup Language, 232
Java Virtual Machine, 76
Jini wireless connection standard, 15
AI adaptive software, 182
basics, 74–78
history, 74
PAN standards for home, 67, 69
Jornada pocket PCs, 61
JRMP (Java Remote Method Protocol),
76
JSML (Java Speech Markup Language),
232
JVM (Java Virtual Machine), 76

K

Knowledge
definition, 177
representation and inference in AI,
176–177
Knowledge discovery, 205–207

L

Language Force translation software,
234
LANs
Ethernet, 101
networks, integration, 126
networks, merging from wired to
wireless, 94–97
networks, migration, 126–128
networks, types, 56
Laser data transmission, 93, 107, 262
Learning Algorithms, 205–207
Learning, AI, 178–179
adaptive software, 180–182
agents, 183–184
data mining, 182–183
neural networks, 179–180
LEO satellites, 122–123
Linear predictive coding. *See* LPC
Lisp Server Pages, 187

LMDS (local multipoint distribution service), 262
    network integration, 20, 125–126
    wireless WANs, 118–119
Local area networks. *See* LANs
Local multipoint distribution service. *See* LMDS
Logic layer, Semantic Web, 214–215, 265
LonTalk protocol, 67–68
LonWorks networks, 66–67
Low earth orbit satellites, 122–123
Low-power television, 119
LPC
    basics, 36–37, 230
    speech coding, 38
LPTV (Low-power television), 119
LSP (Lisp Server Pages), 187

M
MACs (media access controls)
    LANs, 114
    network layer, 73
MAE (metropolitan area exchange), 124
Mainstream handheld PCs, 61
Man-machine communications, 32
MANs
    connectivity issues, 95
    Ethernet networks, 100–101
    types of networks, 56
Massachusetts Institute of Technology. *See* MIT
Mastervoice Butler-in-a-Box, 40
Math ML (Math Markup Language), 194
MCF (Metacontent Framework), 194
Mechanical and electronic serial numbers, telephones, 139
Media access controls. *See* MACs
Medium earth orbit satellites, 122–123
MEO satellites, 122–123
Metacomputing in Large Asynchronous Networks, 185
Metacomputing platforms, 185
Metacontent Framework, 194
Metropolitan area exchange, 124

Metropolitan area networks. *see* MANs
Microwave transmission, 92, 107, 262
    basics, 111–112
    LANs, 113
MILAN (Metacomputing in Large Asynchronous Networks), 185
MIT (Massachusetts Institute of Technology)
    AI Laboratory, 15, 79
    Dylan, 25
    Oxygen, basics, 15–16
    Oxygen, current status, 258–259
    Oxygen, N21s, 79–85, 132–133
MMDS (multipoint microwave distribution system)
    wired/wireless networks, integration, 20, 262
    wireless networks, 107
    wireless WANs, 118–119
MML (Mobile Markup Language), 162
MMTF (Mobile Management Task Force), 277
Mobile and Portable Radio Research Group, 276
Mobile IP
    basics, 155–156
    transition from IP, 262–264
    Working Group of IETF, 21–22, 155–156
Mobile Management Task Force, 277
Mobile Markup Language, 162
Mobile radio, 122
Mobile software
    Bluetooth, basics, 15, 72–74
    Bluetooth, security improvement, 291
    Jini, 15
    Jini, AI adaptive software, 182
    Jini, basics, 74–78
    Jini, history, 74
    PAN standards for home, 67, 69
    Personal Space, 70–72
    UPnP, basics, 78
    UPnP, AI adaptive software, 182
Mobile switching center, 140–141

Mobile telephone switching office, 119
Mobile wireless technologies
    2G, basics, 141–142
    2G, CDMA, 138–139, 141–144
    2G, GSM, 142–143
    2G, TDMA, 138–139, 141–143
    2G, *versus* 3G, 146
MPRG (Mobile and Portable Radio
    Research Group), 276
MSC (mobile switching center), 140–141
MShift (WASP), 124
MTSO (Mobile telephone switching
    office), 119
Multiplexors, 101–102
    DWDM, 102–103
Multipoint microwave distribution
    system. *See* MMDS

N
N21s (Project Oxygen), 132–133
NAPs (network access points), 124
Narrowband modulation, 115
NAS Systems Division power grid, 185
Naturally Speaking product, 41
.NET Web Services
    basics, 196
    versus J2EE, 197–200
Network 21 (N21) Project Oxygen,
    80–85
Network access points, 124
Networks. *See also* LANs; MANs; PANs;
    WANs; wired networks; wireless
    networks; wireless LANs; wireless
    WANs
    elements needing balancing, 9, 18–19
    emerging technology areas, 9, 16–18,
        20, 255, 259
    integrating, basics, 124–125
    integrating, LMDS, 125–126
    integrating, schools, 130
Neural networks (AI), 179–180
NP problems, 172
    AI examples, 172–173
NTS Dreamwriter handheld PCs, 61

O
Object Management Group, 76, 195
Object-oriented dynamic languages *versus*
    static languages, 25
Olympus's Eye-Trek (small display), 62
Open Shortest Path First protocol, 99
OpenDoc, 195
Optical fiber, data transmission, 18, 20
OSGi, service gateway networks, 67–68
OSI (Open Systems Interconnection)
    seven-lay model with ISO, 152–153
OSPF (Open Shortest Path First) protocol, 99

P
P problems, 172
Packet switching (IP)
    basics, 104–105
    versus ATM, 18, 92, 105
Palm OS, 149–150, 163
Palm PDAs, 62, 150
PANs (personal area networks), 14
    connectivity issues, 94
    home applications, 63–64
    home applications, automation
        systems, 63–66
    home applications, basics, 62–65
    home applications, integrating with
        WPANs, 63
    home applications, network types, 63
    home applications, technologies and
        standards, 66–70
    standards, 802.11, origin, 56
    standards, related to wireless LANs, 75
Parallel databases, 222
Parallel Line Internet Protocol, 153
Parallel Virtual Machine, 222–223
PCCA (Portable Computer and
    Communications Association), 277
PCM, speech coding (pulse code
    modulation), 37–38
Personal area networks. *See* PANs
Personal Space
    basics, 55–57
    current status, 255, 260

Personal Space, *continued*
   emerging technologies, 9, 14–17
   home applications, 63–64
   home applications, automation
     systems, 63–66
   home applications, basics, 62–65
   home applications, integrating with
     WPANs, 63
   home applications, network types, 63
   home applications, PAN technologies
     and standards, 66–70
   mobile software, 70–72
   mobile software, Bluetooth, 72–74
   mobile software, Jini, 74–78
   mobile software, UPnP, 78
   personal device proliferation, 57–62
   relationship to WPANs, 59–60
   research projects, Oxygen, 79–85
Pervasive Computing research projects,
   79
PhoneLine network, homes, 63, 68
Physical network layer, 73
PKI (public-key infrastructure) Forum,
   security improvement, 291
PLIP (Parallel Line Internet Protocol),
   153
Pocket PC technology, 149–150, 163
   examples, 61–62
PocketVideo, 148
Point-to-Point Protocol, 116, 153
Portable Computer and Communications
   Association, 277
Portable Distributed Objects, 195
Power Translator, 234
Powerline Network, homes, 63, 66–68
PPP (Point-to-Point Protocol), 116, 153
Princeton University, WorldNet, 206
PROgramming in LOGic. *See* Prolog
Programming languages, types,
   216–217
Programming software
   adaptive programming, 25
   Dylan, basics, 287–290

   guidelines toward automation,
     26–27
   static languages *versus* object-oriented
     dynamic languages, 25
   Visual Prolog, 295–296
Project Oxygen, 15–16
   basics, 15–16
   current status, 258–259
   N21s, 132–133
   technology trends, 49–50
Prolog, 200
   Prolog (Visual) programming
     environment, 295–296
PROMT, 234
Prosodic modeling, 231
Protocols, Intelligent Wireless Web
   emerging technologies, 9–10, 19–22,
     255, 262–264. *See also* specific
     protocols
PSPACE problems, 172
PSTN (Public Switch Telephone
   Network), 140–141
Public Utility Computing research
   projects, 79
Public-key infrastructure (PKI) Forum,
   security improvement, 291
Pulse code modulation, 37–38
PVM (Parallel Virtual Machine), 222–223

R
Radicchio, security improvement, 291
Radio frequency LANs, 107, 262
Radio wave transmission
   home networks, 63
Radio wave transmission, 18, 20, 90,
   92–94
   basics, 107–108
   LANs, 114
   LANs, ISM bands, 115
   LANs, local bridges, 115
   LANs, MAC, 114
   LANs, narrowband modulation, 115
   LANs, spread spectrum modulation, 115

SMR and ESMR, 122
WANs, 118
RAW (Reconfigured Architecture Workstation) computer chips, 80–82
RDF (Resource Development Framework)
basics, 210–211
converging with Topic Maps, 212
progression toward Semantic Web Architecture, 23–24, 265
Semantic Web, basic model, 213
Semantic Web, logic layer, 214–215
Web Architecture, 224, 265
RealPlayer streaming media, 147
Reconfigured Architecture Workstation, 80–82
Recording technologies, 36–38
Remote logins, Internet services, 5
Remote Method Invocation, 76
Residual pulse excited long-term predictor, 38
Resource Development Framework. *See* RDF
RetrievalWare, 191
RFLANs (radio frequency LANs), 107, 262
RIM Blackberry 957 PDAs, 62
RIP (Routing Information Protocol), 99
RMI (Remote Method Invocation), 76
Routers
basics, 96, 98–99
routing protocols, 99
RPE-LTP (residual pulse excited long-term predictor), speech coding, 38

S
SANDi PVA voice-messaging services, 47
SANs (storage area networks), connectivity issues, 95
Satellite data transmission, 18, 20, 90, 97
broadband applications, 122–123
microwaves, 111–112
transition from wired networks, 263
Scalable Vector Graphics, 194

SDH (Synchronous digital hierarchy), 100–101
DWDM, 103
SDLWebflow, 235
Search for Extraterrestrial Intelligence, 221
Security Network, homes, 63, 68
Security, wireless networks
biometric devices, 293
organizations/protocols, 291–292
Self-organizing software, 25–27
basics, 215–218
vision for Intelligent Wireless Web, 181–182
Semantic Web. *See also* Web Architecture
database management, 207
element of Intelligent Wireless Web, 213
emerging technology areas, 9–10
goals, 22–23
inference engines, 215
logic layer, 214–215
progressing from static Web architecture, 24
RDF, 210–211
RDF, converging with Topic Maps, 212
Semantic Web Community Portal, 193, 277–278
Topic Maps, 211–212
transition in Web Architecture, 264–265
Web learning process, 202–203
XML, 207–210
Sequence analysis, data mining, 183
Serial Line Internet Protocol, 153
Service Location Protocol, 77–78
SETI (Search for Extraterrestrial Intelligence), 221
SGML (Standard Generalized Markup Language), 23–24, 192
SGSN GPRS support nodes, 145
Shared Wireless Access Protocol, 66–67
Sharewave Digital Wireless, 66–67
Short Message Protocol, 100
Simple Mail Transfer Protocol, 153

Simple Network Management Protocol. *See* SNMP

Simple Object Access Protocol. *See* SOAP

Single master antenna television, 119

SLIP (Serial Line Internet Protocol), 153

SLP (Service Location Protocol), 77–78

SMATV (single master antenna television), 119

SMDS (Switched Multimegabit Data Service), ATM, 99

SMP (Short Message Protocol), 100

SMR (mobile radio), 122

SMTP (Simple Network Management Protocol), TCP/IP model, 153

SNMP (Simple Network Management Protocol)
    TCP/IP model, 153
    wireless LANs, 113

SOAP (Simple Object Access Protocol), 194
    .NET strategy, 196, 198
    Web Services, 195

Software (mobile)
    Bluetooth, basics, 15, 72–74
    Bluetooth, security improvement, 291
    Jini, 15
    Jini, AI adaptive software, 182
    Jini, basics, 74–78
    Jini, history, 74
    PAN standards for home, 67, 69
    Personal Space, 70–72
    UPnP, basics, 78
    UPnP, AI adaptive software, 182

System Object Model, 195

SONETs (synchronous optical networks)
    DWDM, 103
    versus Ethernet, 101

SOX Schema for Object-Oriented XML, 192–193

SPEAKeasy project, 72

SpectrumWare project, 72

Speech coding, 37-38

Speech Interface Framework working group, 12

SpeechPower product, 41

Speech recognition/understanding, 11, 259
    basics, 43–46
    cellular phone manufacturers, 62
    clicking mouse to speech, 36
    current/planned applications, 39–43
    languages, 34–36
    man-machine communications, 32
    process, 35
    recording, compression and analysis technologies, 36–38
    stages, 46–47
    technology trends, 48–50
    voice recording and analysis, 32–34
    voice recording technology, history, 33
    voice activation, 47
    WAP, 158

Speech Server/VoiceXML Interpreter, 40

Speech synthesis, 259
    language translations, 233, 236
    language translations, tools, 234–235
    prosodic modeling, 231
    TTS systems, 227–230
    user interfaces, 11–12

Speech Synthesis Markup Language, 12, 230–233, 259

SpeechMagic product, 42

Spread-spectrum technology, 66–67, 73
    LANs, 113, 115

SRI Speech Technology and Research Laboratory, DECIPHER, 42

SSML (Speech Synthesis Markup Language), 12, 230–233, 259

Standard Generalized Markup Language, 23–24, 192

Stanford University, Cyc (enCYClopedia), 192

Storage area networks, 95

Streaming video technologies, 147–148

StrongARM processors, 83

SVG (Scalable Vector Graphics), 194

SWAP (Shared Wireless Access Protocol), 66–67

Switched Ethernet, 95
Switched Multimegabit Data Service,
 ATM, 99
Switches
 basics, 96, 98–99
 types of switching, 103–106
Symbol PPT pocket PCs, 61
Synchronous digital hierarchy. *See* SDH
Synchronous optical networks. *See*
 SONETs
System Object Model (SOM), 195
Systran, SystranPro and Systran
 Enterprise, 235

T
Tagged Text Markup Language, 19
TCP, 5
 basics, 154
 Mobile IP, 22
 Semantic Web Architecture, 265
TCP/IP, 5
 ATM, 99
 ISO/OSI seven-layer model, 69,
  152–153
 PAN standards for homes, 69
TDM (time division multiplexed),
 100–101
TDMA (time division multiple access),
 120, 138
 2G technologies, 141
 accessibility to WAP, 158
 basics, 143
 characteristics, 139
 versus CDMA, 148
Tellme voice-activation product, 47
TELNET
 Internet services, 5
 TCP/IP model, 153
TEMIC speech processing, 40–41
Terminal node controllers, 108
Text-to-speech. *See* TTS
ThinAirApps (WASP), 124
Time division multiple access. *See* TDMA
Time division multiplexed, 100–101

TNCs (terminal node controllers), 108
Token-ring networks, 95
Topic Maps, 211–212
 converging with RDF, 212
 Semantic Web Architecture, 23–24
Transcend, 235
Transmets computer chips, 81–82
Transmission Control Protocol. *See* TCP
Transmission Control Protocol/Internet
 Protocol. *See* TCP/IP
TransSphere, 234
TTML (Tagged Text Markup Language),
 19
TTS (text-to-speech) systems
 basics, 227–230
 current status, 259
 Speech Synthesis Markup Language,
  230–233
 VoiceXML, 232–233
2Road (WASP), 124

U
UDDI (Universal Discovery, Description,
 and Integration), Web Services, 195
UDP (User Datagram Protocol), 153–154
 Semantic Web Architecture, 265
UMTS (universal mobile
 telecommunications system), 122
Uniform Resource Locators, 5
Universal Discovery, Description, and
 Integration, 195
Universal Plug and Play. *See* UPnP
Universal remote controls, 63
Universal Translator, 234
Universal mobile telecommunications
 system. *See* UMTS
UPnP (Universal Plug and Play) wireless
 connection standard, 15
 AI adaptive software, 182
 basics, 78
 PAN standards for homes, 67, 69
URLs (Uniform Resource Locators), 5
USB home networks, 63
User Datagram Protocol. *See* UDP

User interfaces
    Intelligent Wireless Web component,
        9–13, 255
    Intelligent Wireless Web component,
        current status, 255, 258–259

V

Vector Sum excited linear predictor, 38
Visual Prolog, 295–296
Vocoder, 36
Voice Action product, 42
Voice Logistics Suite, 42
Voice Power product, 41
Voice recording and analysis, 32–34
Voice recording technology, history, 33
Voice Wave product, 41
Voice Xpress product, 41
Voice Activation technologies, 47
VoiceActivation product, 42
VoicePlus/VoicePro, 41
VoiceXML, 232–233
VoiceXML Forum, 12
VSELP (Vector Sum excited linear
    predictor), speech coding, 38

W

W3C (World Wide Web Consortium)
    basics, 279
    progression toward Semantic Web
        Architecture, 23
    Semantic Web, 202–203
    Speech Interface Framework working
        group, 12
    WSDL, 163
    XML Schema Language, 192
    XSL, 193
WAG services, 123
WANs. *See also* wireless WANs
    Ethernet networks, 100–101
    merging from wired to wireless
        networks, 95–97
    network integration, 126
    network migration, 126–128
    types of networks, 56

WAP (Wireless Application Protocol), 20,
    262
    basics, 157–159
    client-server architecture, 159–160
    PAN standards for homes, 69
    security improvement, 291
    Semantic Web Architecture, 265
    speech recognition, 158
    WDP, 160
    Web applications, 193
WASP (Wireless Application Service
    Providers), 123–124
    WAG services, 123
WDP (Wireless Datagram Protocol), 160
Web
    database management, 5–6, 204–207
    definition, 5–6
    graphs, terminology, 283
    graphs, Web characteristics, 284–285
    intelligence, example, 200–202
    intelligence, local or global existence,
        229
    learning process, 202–204
Web applications. *See also* Web Services
    Cyc, 192
    EIP, 190–192
    RetrievalWare, 191
    XML standards, frameworks, and
        schema, 192–195
Web Architecture. *See also* Semantic Web
    emerging technology areas, 9–10
    goals, 22–23
    progression from static Web
        architecture, 24
    transition to Semantic Web
        Architecture, 264–265
Web Interface Definition Language, 194
Web IQ, 4–5
Web Services. *See also* Web applications
    basics, 196–197
    distributed objects, various names,
        195
    EIP architecture, 198
    Microsoft .NET, basics, 196

.NET *versus* J2EE, 197–200
progression toward Semantic Web Architecture, 23
Web Architecture, 224, 265
Web Services Description Language. *See* WSDL
WebDAV (Web-based Distributed Authoring and Versioning), 194, 198
WhisperID and WhisperLM products, 42
Wide area networks. *See* WANs
WIDL (Web Interface Definition Language), 194
Windows CE. *See* Pocket PC technology
Windows Media Player, 147
Wired networks
  bandwidth constraints, 91
  client/server model, 91–92
  components, 91
  connectivity issues, 93–94
  data transmission media, 90, 92–93
  data transmission media, backbones, 102
  Ethernet, 95, 98
  FDDI, 95
  merging with wired networks, 110
  multiplexors, 101–102
  multiplexors, DWDM, 102–103
  network types, 94–95
  routers, 96, 98–99
  switches, 96, 98–99
  switches, types of switching, 103–106
Wireless access gateway services, 123
Wireless Application Protocol. *See* WAP
Wireless Application Service Providers. *See* WASP
Wireless Datagram Protocol, 160
Wireless Internet. *See also* Internet
  basics, 158–159
  client-server architecture, 159–160
  protocols, 157
  speech recognition, 158
  WDP, 160
  Web services, comparison, 162–164
  WML, 157

WML, alternatives, 161–162
WML, basics, 160–161
WML, W3C standard, 157
Wireless LAN Interoperability Forum, 278
Wireless LANs, 19–20, 112–113
  communication process, 256
  IEEE 802.11 standard, 116–118
  infrared (IR) data transmission, basics, 115
  network integration, 126
  network migration, 126–128
  point-to-point, 116
  radio-based transmission, basics, 114
  radio-based transmission, ISM bands, 115
  radio-based transmission, local bridges, 115
  radio-based transmission, MAC, 114
  radio-based transmission, narrowband modulation, 115
  radio-based transmission, spread spectrum modulation, 115
  standards, basics, 281–282
  standards, related to PANs, 75
  transition from wired networks, 263
  Wireless LAN Group, 278
Wireless Markup Language. *See* WML
Wireless mobile technologies
  2G, basics, 141–142
  2G, CDMA, 138–139, 141–144
  2G, GSM, 142–143
  2G, TDMA, 138–139, 141–143
  2G, *versus* 3G, 146
  3G, basics, 144–145
  3G, GRPS, 144, 145–147
  3G, migration from earlier technologies, 147
  basics, 137–138
  cellular, 138–140
  handheld devices, 149–151
  MSC, 140–141
  projections, 148
  PSTN, 140–141
  standards, 139

Wireless mobile technologies, *continued*
  streaming video, 147–148
  Web services, 149–150, 163
Wireless networks. *See also* Wireless LANs;
    Wireless WANs
  basics, 106–107
  benefits, 108–109
  concerns, 109
  crowded airways, 109, 111
  data transmission media, 90, 92–93
  merging with wired networks, 110
  microwave transmission, 111–113
Wireless personal area networks. *See*
    WPANs
Wireless transport layer security, 291–292
Wireless WANs, 19–20
  basics, 119–120
  current status, 122–123
  ITV, 119
  LMDS, 118–119
  LPTV, 119
  MMDS, 118–119
  network integration, 126
  network migration, 126–128
  SMATV, 119
  transition from wired networks, 263
  WASP, 123–124
Wireless, definition, 5
WLIF (Wireless LAN Interoperability
    Forum), 278
WML (Wireless Markup Language), 19,
    21, 157
  alternatives, 161–162
  basics, 160–161
  Semantic Web Architecture, 265
  WAP, 162
  XML standards, 193–194, 198
World Translator, 235

World Wide Web. *See* Web
World Wide Web Consortium. *See* W3C
WorldNet, 206
WPANs (wireless personal area networks)
  IEEE Working Group, 56
  integrating PANs into, 63
  new network infrastructure, 56
  relationship with Personal Space,
    59–60, 259
WSDL (Web Services Description
    Language)
  .NET strategy, 196
  basics, 163
  XML standards, 194
WTLS (wireless transport layer security),
    291–292
WWW (World Wide Web). *See* Web

X

X-10 control devices, 67–68
XDR (XML Data-Reduced), 193
XML (Extensible Markup Language)
  basics, 207–210
  progression toward Semantic Web
    Architecture, 23–24, 265
  SSML, speech synthesis, 12
  standards, frameworks, and schema,
    192–195
  Web architecture, 224
  WML, 158–159
XML Data-Reduced (XDR), 193
XML Schema Language, 192
XPath (XML Path Language), 194
XPointer XML, 194
XSL (Extensible Stylesheet Language),
    193–194
XSLT (Extensible Stylesheet Language
    Transform), 193–194

Date Due

AUG 12 2005			

BRODART, CO.   Cat. No. 23-233-003   Printed in U.S.A.